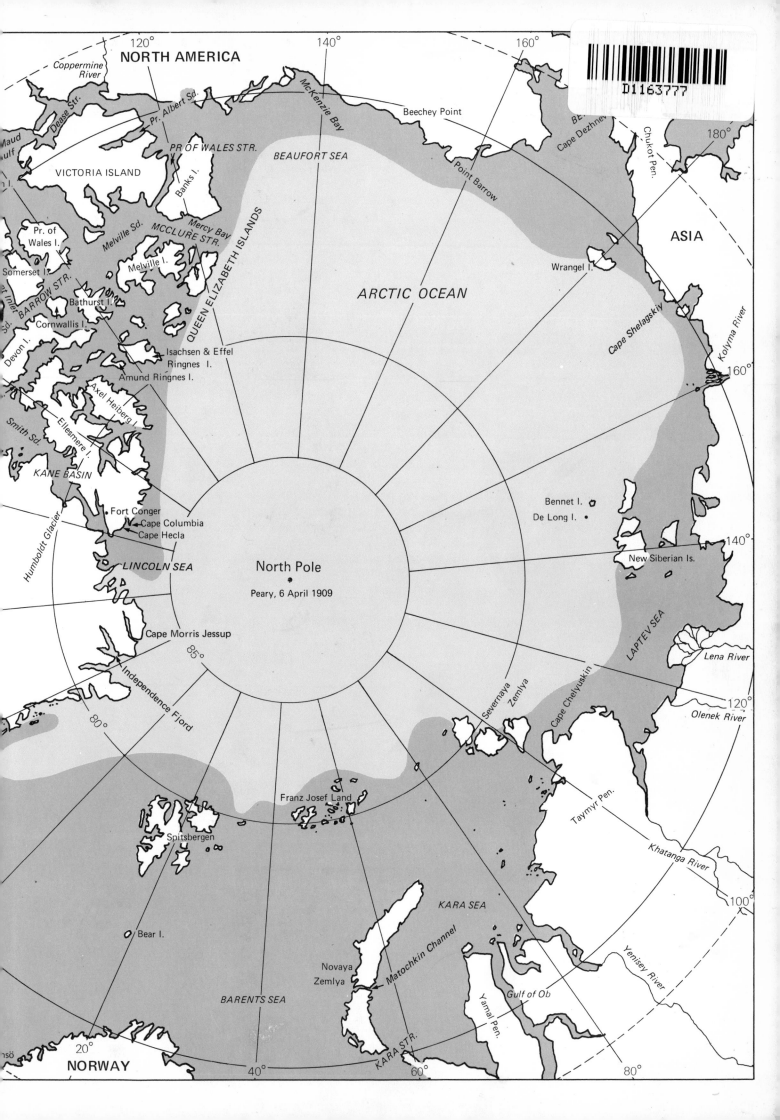

A HISTORY OF
POLAR
EXPLORATION
David Mountfield

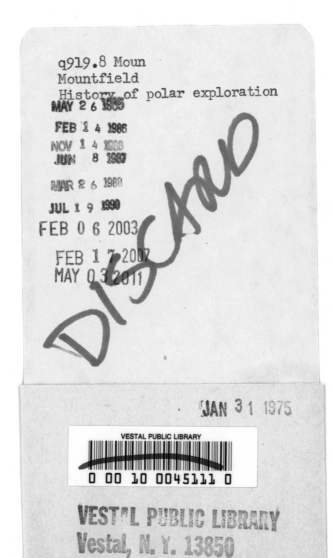

A HISTORY OF
POLAR
EXPLORATION
David Mountfield

The Dial Press

New York 1974

Nowhere has knowledge been purchased at greater cost of privation and suffering.
Fridtjof Nansen

title page
A grotto in the Antarctic ice, formed by the bridging-over of a crevasse. The ship in the background is Captain Scott's *Terra Nova*. Photograph by Herbert G. Ponting.

Copyright © 1974 by
The Hamlyn Publishing Group Limited

Originally published in Great Britain by
The Hamlyn Publishing Group Limited
Feltham, Middlesex

Library of Congress Catalogue Card Number:
73-17943

Manufactured in Great Britain

ISBN Number: 0-8037-3738-6

First Dial edition 1974

Color Plates

Contents

Introduction

'Because it's there', said Mallory when some bold and curious person inquired why he wanted to climb Mount Everest. Whether one thinks his answer exquisitely apposite or evasively glib perhaps depends on individual temperament, but it has a certain chilly, all-encompassing inevitability, like Gertrude Stein's comment on a rose. Having reached the top of the mountain, there is nothing much to do except plant the flag and retire.

Exploration in general has had more complex and wider causes. Personal ambition can never be discounted, but the history of geographical discovery by Europeans is part of the history of European society (including nations of European origin in other continents). In different times, different motives operated. The Turks controlled the eastern trade routes, and Europeans sought a sea passage to the Far East, probing the Arctic ice for a way. In the 19th century, imperial ambitions opened up new regions, sometimes imposing political authority on countries still unexplored, while in our own day it is hard to reject the belief that the basic purpose of the greatest feats of exploration has been military – or, as governments prefer to say, 'defence'.

Religious, commercial, political, military – all these and other motives played their part in polar exploration. Yet the story is pre-eminently a story of individuals. Towards the end of the 19th century the approach to the South Pole in particular took on the characteristics of an international competition, but although chauvinism was not absent, the relations between the great Antarctic explorers remained on the whole surprisingly good-natured. Not every character was amiable, and there were a few villains, but even a row on the scale of the Peary-Cook controversy fades into insignificance when compared with the astonishing deeds of heroism, the inspiring examples of the nobility of man under severe stress, that mark the history of polar exploration.

'It is,' wrote Nansen, 'the *man* that matters', and this book is about the men who explored the polar regions – the illiterate fishermen, ambitious merchants, professional sailors, eager individualists: the curious, the determined, the inspired, the avaricious – the men who for whatever reason went to find out. Through their experience and their writings a broader picture may emerge, for it was no less an authority than Sir Clements Markham, polar historian and patron of Captain Scott, who said that 'biography is the best vehicle for the conveyance and retention of geographical knowledge'.

In a short book only a brief account of even the greatest explorers is possible and many interesting and accomplished people must be consigned to a paragraph, a sentence, or even a subordinate clause. There is no space for more than a short sketch of the physical conditions of the polar regions; there is only an occasional indication of technological change, the briefest discussion of social background. There is almost nothing about scientific research or flora and fauna, and even the fashionable subject of conservation crops up only in the form of a passing criticism of the brave but stupid whalers and sealers of the 19th century or a grimace in the direction of the Soviet Union and Japan, the two nations that still insist on extracting their legal pound of blubber from the polar seas.

In his provocatively titled book *The Friendly Arctic*, Vilhjalmur Stefansson divided polar exploration into four historical phases. In the first phase, from the Middle Ages to the late 18th century, the polar regions were generally regarded with dread. For a long time men had believed that extreme climates were fatal: in the frozen Arctic or the torrid equator Europeans could not survive, and if they ventured into those regions they would freeze or fry. The whole southern hemisphere seemed to be inaccessible because of the barrier of the equator.

This notion was gradually demolished by the voyages of the early explorers: fishermen sailed to Iceland and beyond; Bartolemeu Diaz crossed the equator without mishap. But the far north was still an area to which men travelled with foreboding and only when impelled thither by necessity; they went cautiously and in the summer months only; polar exploration was conducted almost entirely by ships. As late as 1777, Captain Cook, a man of keen foresight, thought it unlikely that anyone would go farther south

than he had gone and saw no advantage in doing so.

In the second phase, initiated by Parry and completed by McClintock, the polar winter was still feared but no longer regarded as unbearable. Earlier, those who had wintered in polar regions had done so by accident (and comparatively few had survived), but Parry demonstrated that men could live through the Arctic winter without serious discomfort. Explorers began to leave their ships and travel overland. The Antarctic interior, however, remained untrodden.

The third phase–in the Arctic the age of Peary–marks a great step forward in technique. European man had been incredibly slow to recognize what seems obvious–that the Eskimos, who live there all year round, had evolved ways of living in the Arctic regions that were well worth imitating. Peary also put an end to the fear of the Arctic winter. As he demonstrated, travel was easier in the hard winter freeze than in the treacherous summer thaw. In the Antarctic, similar advances in techniques led to the conquest of the South Pole, although the argument

for winter travel did not (one could say almost literally) 'hold water' there.

Stefansson's fourth phase–the explorer's demonstration of his ability to live off the land even in parts avoided by the Eskimos–was postulated (one cannot help thinking) chiefly to provide a category into which Stefansson could fit himself. Now, over fifty years later, it seems reasonable to place Stefansson with Peary, Scott, Amundsen, Shackleton and the other great leaders of the 'third phase', which might be regarded as the last, romantic age of polar exploration. 'Romantic' in the popular sense for (with no disrespect to such outstanding men as Admiral Byrd), subsequent polar exploration became more a matter of technology and teamwork than individual enterprise, and 'last' because in one sense the history of polar exploration culminated in the conquest of the poles.

Much, of course, remained to be explored, and there were still lands unmapped, seas uncharted. But although the last chapter of this book attempts to provide a brief survey of events up to and after the International Geophysical Year, it

would be impossible to cover all or even most of the scientific expeditions to the polar regions that have taken place in this century.

Several writers and explorers as recently as thirty or forty years ago remarked on the extraordinary ignorance of polar conditions which they encountered among their readers or lecture audiences. Many people seemed to know only that the poles were to be found at the ends of the earth and that they were extremely cold. Beyond that, a tissue of misconceptions, half-truths and sheer fantasy prevailed. That is not so today. The recent developments in mass communications have made people much better informed about the world they live in, and television in particular has been quick to exploit the potential of the Arctic (and to a less degree the Antarctic) as sources of entertainment, instruction and delight. Everyone now knows that polar bears live in the Arctic and penguins in the Antarctic. Nobody now supposes that the polar winter drives men mad or that the Arctic Ocean is a

motionless sheet of ice. What follows is merely an indication of some of the major obstacles that the polar explorers had to overcome (more will appear as the story proceeds) and a reminder that the Arctic and the Antarctic are at opposite ends of the earth: they have much in common but are by no means alike.

The similarities between the two regions are obvious enough. Both are very cold, with much ice and snow. Both have long dark winters in which the sun does not appear for days on end, depending on distance from the pole (in theory, the darkness should last for six months at the pole, but refraction of sunlight shortens this period and makes the polar darkness less black) and both have perpetual daylight in midsummer. But the similarities are superficial compared with the differences.

The Arctic consists of an ocean surrounded by large land masses; the Antarctic consists of a land mass surrounded by ocean. From this fundamental opposition, quite different characteristics develop. Above all, the Antarctic is very much colder than the Arctic. As everyone knows, what is called a continental climate is subject to greater extremes than a maritime climate in the same latitude, which is warmed in winter and cooled in summer by the ocean. Water holds heat longer than earth: an ocean is more temperate than a continent. Antarctica, though small by comparison with Asia or North America, is a true continent with an area of over five million square miles. Not only that, it is a particularly lofty continent, its average elevation being higher than any other.

Almost all the mainland of Antarctica is covered with a permanent ice-cap, which in some places is more than a mile deep (and depresses the land in parts as much as 200 feet). This ice-cap, pushing ever outwards and down, extends beyond the land to form the great ice shelves that border the sometimes invisible coastline of the continent along nearly half its total length. The vast Antarctic ice-cap is not reflected in the far north, where the only comparable feature is the ice-cap of Greenland. There is no permanent ice in the Arctic Ocean. In that ocean, and beyond the ice shelf in Antarctica, is floating pack ice, consisting of floes anything from a few yards to many miles across. The floes may jam up and form a solid surface covering thousands of square miles, with ridges up to fifty feet high where the ice has buckled and been forced up, but sooner or later they break up again. It is impossible to reach the North Pole over the ice in a continuous, undeviating march; diversions or delays are always caused by breaks, called leads, in the ice.

The limit of the pack ice varies with the seasons and also from year to year. It is not therefore a very satisfactory indicator of the polar frontiers. Nor, however, are the polar circles, for Antarctica extends beyond the circle in many places, and an Antarctic environment is encountered as far north as the tip of South America.

opposite
The icebreakers *Edisto*, of the United States Navy and the *Northwind*, of the United States Coast Guard, cut a path for the British research ship *John Biscoe* through the Antarctic ice pack which, from the air, looks like some exotic marble, intricately veined. The *John Biscoe* was carrying supplies and personnel to British bases when she became trapped in the ice in 1959.

below
Early sailors in Antarctic waters were amazed by the vast flat tablelands of ice, quite unlike the icebergs of the far north, that glided slowly past them in the currents. Until the phenomenon had been actually witnessed the origin of these great islands, sometimes a mile or more across, was not known for certain. The Antarctic ice-cap is for ever pushing steadily outwards, projecting miles into the sea beyond the limit of the land in floating ice shelves. Now and then a huge chunk breaks off, and another 'ice island' floats slowly away on its long journey to extinction. Photographed by Herbert G. Ponting.

Fortunately, it is not necessary in a book of this kind to use the terms 'Arctic' and 'Antarctic' as precisely as a geographer would require. Very roughly, the Antarctic can be said to begin in the neighbourhood of 50° South (approximately the region where the cold Antarctic currents are submerged beneath the warm currents from the tropics). Arctic conditions are even more variable in latitude because the Arctic is surrounded by land rather than ocean, and it is impossible to draw a reasonably constant line round the earth; but in most places the limit lies somewhere between 60° North and the Arctic Circle.

In the above sense, then, the Antarctic is much 'larger' than the Arctic – because it is much colder and thus spreads its influence farther. Antarctica affects the temperature as far away as Sydney, and a world map – or better, a globe – shows other striking illustrations of this influence: the distance between the North Pole and the city of Edinburgh is less than the distance between the South Pole and the island of South Georgia, an icy treeless place where the temperature occasionally climbs only to the height of 42 °F – in midsummer.

There is no doubt about it – the Antarctic is extremely cold; the periodically occupied Soviet research station of Vostok, where temperatures approaching −130 °F have been recorded, is probably the coldest known place on earth.

Vostok is on the high Antarctic plateau, less than 800 miles from the pole. In the Arctic the coldest place is to be found much farther from the pole, in one of those Siberian settlements where the milkman delivers the milk in convenient chunks. Places in Montana and the Dakotas regularly record lower temperatures than the North Pole. Not that the Arctic in winter is a warm place. Of course it is not, but it is not uniquely cold as is the Antarctic.

The Arctic has nearly a thousand species of wild flowers; mainland Antarctica has two, both rare, and found only in Graham Land. Summer in the Arctic, although it lasts only a few weeks, can be extremely hot. Stefansson spent the summer of 1910 in Canada well north of the Arctic Circle where 'for six weeks the temperature rose to the vicinity of 90° in the shade nearly every day'. The summer heat, he insists, was far more trying that the winter cold. His discomfort was much increased by that well-known Arctic menace, the mosquito, which bit his dogs so severely that their eyes swelled up until they could not see. People are still sometimes surprised to hear of swarms of mosquitoes in the

A pressure ridge – the bane of the polar explorer. Vast pressures build up in the ocean ice until, at points of stress, the surface buckles and jagged ridges, occasionally as high as fifty feet, are formed. Manœuvring a sledge across one of these ridges may be impossible, causing long and tedious detours to find a way past. Photograph by Herbert G. Ponting.

Arctic, but explorers have been complaining about them bitterly since the 16th century. Antarctic travellers are not troubled by the attentions of this immensely dislikeable insect.

Mosquitoes, though unpleasant, are not usually dangerous. Other hindrances to travel are. Nearly all the explorers of the great age of discovery found their ships enshrouded in 'stinking fogges' in the North Atlantic. In an uncharted sea, with only the most primitive aids to navigation, fog was a double menace, for it usually meant calm, and in a calm the ships were immobile. At any moment a huge 'mountain of ice' might loom upon them, crushing their vessel and hurling them into the deadly sea. Not until the days of radar and observation networks was the danger ended; the fate of the *Titanic* is a reminder of the power of the iceberg.

The southern latitudes are fairly free of fog though not of icebergs, but Antarctica has certain hazards of its own to throw in the way of the explorer. Like the seas around it (the Roaring Forties are well named) it is a region of very high winds, which have been measured at speeds over 100 miles per hour. Sir Douglas Mawson wrote amusingly of how his men learned to walk into the wind inclined at an angle that in normal conditions would have toppled them on their

faces. No one would lightly venture out in an Arctic storm, but the ferocity of an Antarctic blizzard is blinding, immobilizing, paralysing.

Blizzards are formed not by falling snow but by the wind lifting snow from the ground, and snowfall in the polar regions is not as heavy or frequent as is commonly supposed. On the contrary, much of the land in the Arctic is free from snow during the summer: the tourists who go to Point Barrow, Alaska, on their twenty-four-hour round trips take their obligatory husky ride in a sledge mounted not on skis but on wheels. Even in the winter, Arctic snowfall is not particularly heavy, while on the high Antarctic plateau, one of the driest regions in the world, annual precipitation is only about two inches. There is no rain here (unlike the Arctic), and the snow that does fall bears little resemblance to the big soft flakes that most people are accustomed to. It falls in fine grains, softer than salt but sharper than flour. As it almost never thaws in that region, this comparatively slight snowfall is sufficient to maintain the mighty glaciers, which are formed of compressed snow rather than frozen rain-water.

Wherever there are glaciers (and the Antarctic ice-cap is simply a large glacier) the traveller must be on the look-out for a sudden rift in the surface, descending sheer-sided for perhaps hundreds of feet. Such a rift, called a crevasse, occurs where a considerable strain is imposed on the ice, typically by some change in the underlying topography, which eventually makes it split. The peculiar danger of the crevasse is that later falls of snow camouflage it, making it virtually invisible. A man or even a loaded sledge may pass over a snow-bridged crevasse without danger, perhaps without knowing it is there, only for its presence to be disastrously revealed by a following vehicle. One of the advantages of dog travel is that a good dog will usually sense the presence of a crevasse and give adequate warning.

Everyone who has travelled near the magnetic poles has seen the phenomenon of the aurora (Northern Lights in the Arctic, Southern Lights

The Arctic pack, an autumn mixture of old ice and new, makes a scene of messy desolation, as on some alien planet. The great difficulty of travelling in the Arctic Ocean is that much of it is neither solid ice nor open water – equally unsuitable for sledges or boats, as in this photograph.

A British Snocat in a tricky predicament during the Trans-Antarctic expedition, 1957–58. The vehicle was extracted after much labour with the aid of steel beams thrust under the tracks. In spite of electronic warning devices, a concealed crevasse is probably still the greatest hazard in crossing a glacier.

in the Antarctic), that amazing display of super-terrestrial fireworks described by the Maoris as the 'burning of the sky'. The object of much superstitious awe in ancient times, the aurora is caused by solar radiation and at times when the sun is particularly active may be seen from places far outside the polar circles. The aurora is one of the bonuses of polar travel which, it is universally agreed, cannot be reproduced in words or even photographs. The same can be said for other optical phenomena some of which, however, are not so harmless. In the dry, clear air of the Antarctic it is possible to see a great distance in fine weather, and this may result in distances being seriously underestimated. Similar miscalculations occur in the hot, desert areas of the world (deserts are not by definition hot, and Antarctica is as true a desert as the world contains). Refraction of light produces mirages as striking as those seen in hot deserts as well as extraordinary and beautiful images in the icy air.

It is not necessary to travel in the polar regions to suffer from snow-blindness (or any of various other ill effects caused by living in a snowy, icy environment). Alpine mountaineers use protective glasses as well as polar explorers. Snow-blindness tends to affect the old hand sooner than the tyro; having suffered from it once, the eyes are more easily affected next time. Like most of the other hazards of polar travel there is, in theory anyway, no reason why anyone should be troubled by snow-blindness now as long as the correct precautions are taken. It is of course a temporary condition, seldom lasting more than a day or two, but it is not only incapacitating, it is exceedingly painful—worse, some say, than the fiercest toothache.

Perhaps more dangerous is the condition aptly known as white-out, which occurs most often in windy, drifting weather or in fog, but may attack tired eyes even when visibility is comparatively good if the sun is obscured by cloud. In a white-out, everything appears to merge: the lack of shadow and contrast makes the world appear flat and featureless, the sense of distance and direction is lost, and it is all too easy to walk into a crevasse.

In the second half of the 20th century, the Arctic has almost ceased to be frightening. Exploration, scientific research and commercial exploitation have drawn its teeth (and threaten to destroy its delicately balanced ecology). Antarctica, a fiercer region, can still seem threatening, and although its defences have been breached in many places it remains an alien environment, more friendly than the Moon but still the least hospitable on earth. No doubt the ingenuity of creatures that have contrived to lay an oil pipeline across Alaska will ultimately find a way to tap the Antarctic mineral deposits buried under a mile of ice, but at present Antarctica remains largely unexploited.

If the polar regions no longer seem immensely dangerous and terrifying places, it is because the polar explorers over the past 300 or 400 years have drawn aside the veils of mystery and ignorance and revealed their true character. Fear resides in ignorance; what we understand does not frighten us. The first man to get up on his hind legs and walk probably felt very scared; no doubt he stepped forward cautiously, stumbled frequently and often fell before he got the knack of it. To 16th-century sailors, the Denmark Strait was a terrifying place; the creak and crunch of the Greenland ice filled them with strange fears.

The process of learning has been slow and fraught with disaster. In some ways, indeed, the slowness of the process is surprising. Centuries passed before men began to dress themselves in an appropriate manner for living in a cold climate: Franklin and his men strode into the Arctic wearing top hats. Often, too, important discoveries were ignored, forgotten or simply disbelieved. The experiences of the Norsemen in Greenland were unknown to Davis and Hudson. Baffin's discoveries disappeared from maps soon after his death and did not reappear until they were confirmed by Ross and Parry in the 19th century. Shortly before the First World War Stefansson, in conversation with the eminent oceanographer Sir John Murray, happened to remark on how ice formed from salt water loses its salinity; and was astonished to observe that this (to him) well-known fact was greeted with the stony silence of disbelief.

The lesson that the Arctic was, as Stefansson insisted, a 'friendly' place was not learned easily. But no one now, unless very careless or unlucky, suffers from frostbite. The scourge of all mariners for centuries—scurvy—now seems as distant as witchcraft and bear-baiting. But the hazards of polar travel were overcome in the only possible way, by experiment and experience. How that experience was gained is the story of polar exploration.

The First Arctic Explorers

All books about polar exploration begin with Pytheas of Massalia, and this one is no exception. As he was the first man to travel in far northern Europe and to report what he had seen, Pytheas cannot be ignored. But he is a problem.

In brief, Pytheas is said to have sailed along the north-west coast of Europe; round Britain; and to the semi-legendary land of Thule, land of the midnight sun, the farthest north of inhabited lands. Unfortunately, nearly everything that is said about Pytheas depends on scholarly guesswork. He wrote a book, perhaps two books, about his travels, but they are lost. His account comes second-hand, through the quotations (how accurate no one can say) of later classical writers many of whom were antagonistic to him. Polybius, a well-travelled man himself who was possibly motivated to belittle the achievements of earlier rivals, poured scorn on many of Pytheas' statements. The learned geographer Strabo, a contemporary of Jesus of Nazareth, took his cue from Polybius and exerted great effort to show that Pytheas was a liar.

In modern times the reputation of Pytheas has been restored, or rather it has risen higher than it ever was, for Pytheas was doubted even by his contemporaries. In fact the pendulum has probably swung too far: some recent accounts are inclined to stretch the evidence to make more of Pytheas' famous voyage.

Pytheas was a native of the prosperous Greek city of Massalia, which stood where Marseilles stands now. Although the reason for his voyage was commercial—and therefore Pytheas is often assumed to have been a professional pilot hired by mercantile interests in the city—it seems more

A glimmering midnight on the coast of northern Norway, land of the midnight sun. The northern seas were full of wonders for a Mediterranean seaman and Pytheas, wherever precisely he did go, certainly ventured into regions of which he could have known nothing previously beyond vague rumour.

likely that he was a man of some standing who could afford to indulge his interest in astronomy and geography. Even the date of Pytheas' voyage is uncertain; but as he was mentioned by a pupil of Aristotle—though not by Aristotle himself—it probably took place in the 320s BC or soon afterwards.

There was very little contact between the Mediterranean world and northern Europe in the 4th century BC but there was some fairly regular trade, of which the most significant item was tin. It seems to have been Pytheas' purpose to break the lock that the Carthaginians maintained on the Straits of Gibraltar and issue forth in search of the origins of this useful mineral. They were not so very far away—in Brittany and Cornwall in fact—and as Pytheas sailed so much farther, he clearly had other objectives in view. He was, as even his opponents concede, a skilled astronomer in his time. He discovered that the Pole Star did not mark the pole exactly, as had been assumed, and he invented an instrument something like a sundial with which he was able to calculate the latitude of Massalia quite accurately, though only at solstice or equinox. He did not use it on his travels and had, of course, no maps or instruments; he navigated by the stars.

His ship was perfectly capable of making a long ocean voyage. She probably resembled the later Mediterranean galley quite closely, relying largely on oars but with a single, square sail.

Passing Gibraltar, Pytheas sailed forth into the Atlantic; he hugged the coast of Spain and south-west France rather than risk the short cut across the Bay of Biscay, and investigated the phenomenon of the tides, always a source of fascination to Mediterranean seamen. He crossed to the British coast, the limit of the known world at that time, and reported in detail on the methods of the Cornish tin-miners. The natives were 'unusually hospitable and . . . gentle in their manner'. Pytheas appears to have completed the circumnavigation of Britain via Land's End, Kent and the Orkneys. He never said in so many words (so far as we know) that he had sailed all round the island, but this is the clear implication of his description of Britain. He is not known to have visited Ireland, which could hardly be overlooked on a voyage down the west coast of Britain, but Ireland is related fairly accurately to Britain in the maps of the 3rd century BC geographer Eratosthenes and the assumption is that the information came from Pytheas.

The voyage seems to have been conducted in a leisurely manner with frequent stops to survey the countryside and meet the inhabitants, so much so that, as Polybius sneeringly remarks, Pytheas gave the impression that he had 'walked all over Britain'. He also vastly over-estimated the size of Britain, but such an error was not unnatural in the circumstances and the evidence in favour of Pytheas' circumnavigation comfortably outweighs the few points that cast doubt on it.

The voyage to Thule is more controversial. In the first place it is possible to interpret what Pytheas is reported to have said about it not as personal experience but as an account given to him by people he met. In the second place, it seems odd that Pytheas, in the middle of his circumnavigation of Britain, should have suddenly shot off to the north in search of Thule and, having found it, returned to his starting point and placidly renewed his round-Britain cruise. This objection may be overcome by supposing—and this is not unlikely—that Pytheas made more than one voyage to the north.

But what did Pytheas have to say about Thule?

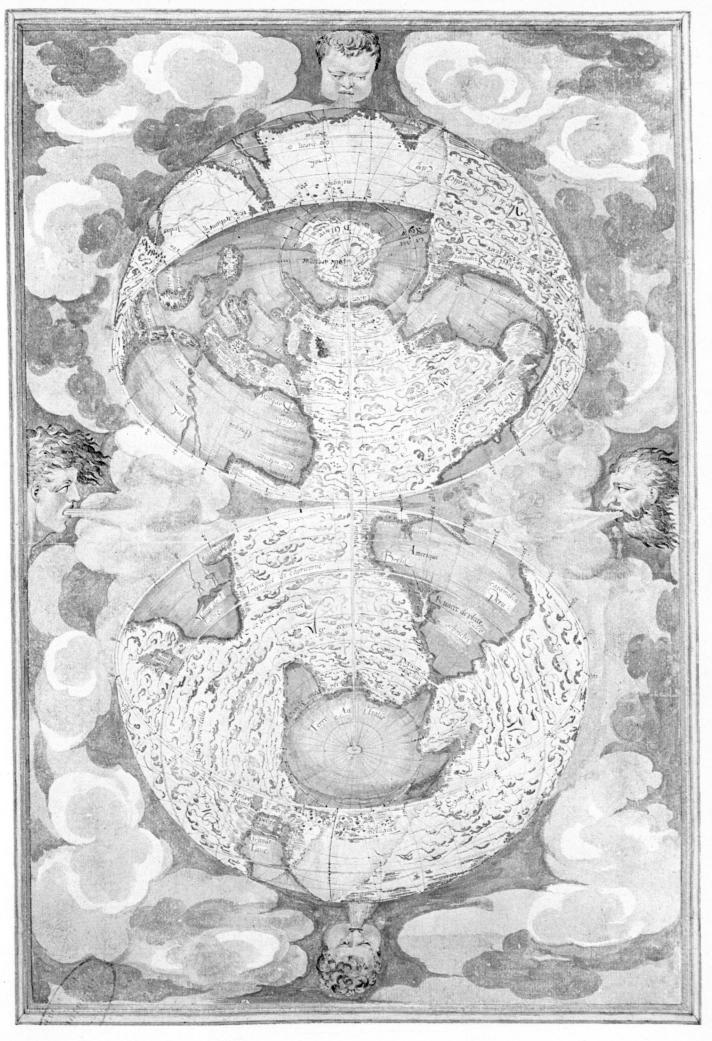

Lancaster Sound. A remarkable iceberg, shaped like a
whale's tooth.

It is, he said, the farthest north of the British Isles, six days' sail from the mainland. The term 'British Isles' was used loosely by Pytheas and by his successors; anything farther north than Britain was naturally called British, and the argument that Thule is nothing more exciting than the Shetland Isles does not hold water. Thule is only one day's sail, Pytheas reported, from the frozen sea and in summer the night is only two or three hours long. The people there eat wild berries and millet (oats?), as the climate is too cold for cattle and most crops. They do, however, get honey from bees, and they make a kind of mead from the honey.

Where is this curious place? It would be pleasant to think that the bold Greek, who extended man's knowledge of the world so far, had actually reached Iceland, and Iceland has often been identified as Pytheas' land of Thule. But it seems unlikely. Although no measurement could be more elastic than 'a day's sail' (probably about as reliable as the African custom of describing distance in terms of the number of cigarettes that might be smoked on the journey), Iceland is more than six days' sail from Scotland, and as winds and currents are contrary, it is unlikely that Pytheas could have made the journey even if he knew exactly where he was going. Moreover, Iceland was probably uninhabited at that time; and it has never had any bees.

If Thule was anywhere, the likeliest place seems to be Norway. The distance fits; Norway, although it extends into the Arctic Circle, does have bees in milder parts. The people may have supported themselves in the way that Pytheas describes.

There remains one further matter concerning Thule that was related by Pytheas: the curious phenomenon he called the 'sea lung'. As Polybius quoted him, he said 'there is neither sea nor air, but a mixture like sea lung, in which earth and air are suspended; the sea lung binds everything together'. Much dotty ingenuity has been devoted to explaining this weird statement. A common suggestion is that sea lung means jelly fish, but that does not help to explain the environmental conditions that Pytheas was trying to indicate. Nansen thought he meant the 'ice sludge' in the sea that is found around drift ice, but had to admit that it was unlikely that Pytheas sailed far enough from land to encounter drift-ice (if, however, Thule was Iceland, he would not have had to travel so far). A recent historian of the Arctic supports Nansen's view, seeing in Pytheas' sea lung 'a word picture, perhaps, of the gentle and rhythmical undulation of the ice rising and falling with the movement of the sea, linked possibly with some suggestion of the exhalations of the sea-mist which so often hangs, cold and dank, above the ice edge in the Arctic'.

After that is a relief to turn back to the critical Polybius, whose reaction to Pytheas' 'word pic-

The walrus provided meat and fuel for early travellers and has always been very important to the peoples of the far north. With no fear of man, little in the way of natural weaponry, and an inoffensive disposition the large and clumsy beasts were slaughtered in comparative safety and ease. Cases have been reported, by Nansen for instance, of a walrus sinking a canoe and a herd will usually combine against a common enemy. From an engraving by Theodore de Bry.

ture' can be imagined. His sarcasm is withering. Still, we cannot tell whether Polybius quoted Pytheas with perfect accuracy in the first place, and while future attempts to account for the 'sea lung' will be enthusiastically welcomed by students of the curious it probably must remain, like other details of Pytheas' voyage, an insoluble puzzle.

But unless, following Polybius, the account of Pytheas' discoveries is interpreted as nothing more than a traveller's tall story, Pytheas must be acknowledged as one of the greatest of all explorers. His voyage was not surpassed for over a thousand years; indeed there is little to record of Arctic exploration between Pytheas and the age of the Vikings.

Yet some curious voyages took place in the North Atlantic in the meantime, none more curious than those of certain Irish monks, whose urge for solitude was so strong that they ventured forth in curraghs, small boats of hide stretched on a wooden frame. Driven from the Western Isles by the Norsemen, they made their way to Iceland, but had hardly established themselves when the pagan Norse arrived there too.

A quiet life, it seems, was no easier to find in the 9th century than at any other time.

The explosion of the Vikings in northern Europe in the 9th century has never been fully explained. Population pressure could have accounted for the expansion in Norway, but it seems unlikely that Denmark, with its far greater agricultural potential, could have been similarly cramped. Possibly the Danes were reacting to Frankish pressure. The ferocious raids of the Scandinavians are well known and although they began as hit-and-run affairs with plunder as their object, the Norsemen soon started to settle beyond Scandinavia. They had colonized north-western Scotland many years before and in the second half of the 9th century they settled in Iceland.

The existence of Iceland had been known in Norway for some time since ships bound for the Faroes had come upon it after being blown off their course. A large number of people (one estimate says 30,000) settled in Iceland in the late 9th and early 10th centuries so that virtually all the inhabitable land was occupied.

The ships that carried the Scandinavian

colonists across the North Atlantic were not the warfaring longships that struck terror into the people of Britain but taller, broader vessels with a deck and a large square sail (longships relied mainly on oars). They were certainly seaworthy, and probably not much inferior to the ships of Columbus 500 years later. But voyages in those waters were always extremely hazardous: in one Norse fleet, caught by a storm, only 14 out of twenty-five ships reached their destination.

From parts of Iceland the tops of the Greenland mountains can be seen a on a clear day, and the Norsemen must have soon become aware of the proximity of Greenland. Two Icelanders led a small party across the Denmark Strait in 980 and spent the winter on Greenland's east coast. No doubt this exploit came to the ears of Eric Thorvaldsson, better known as Eric the Red.

Eric's father had been outlawed from Norway for murder (a common offence among the Norsemen) and had settled in the north-west corner of Iceland–the part nearest Greenland. Eric himself, who was probably born in Iceland, was forced to leave it in 982 for the same reason that had caused his father's banishment from Nor-

way, and he spent the three years' exile to which he was sentenced in exploring the land to the west.

Crossing the Denmark Strait, he found his way barred by the coastal ice that was to frustrate the 16th-century English explorers. He rounded Cape Farewell and sailed up the west coast as far as the region where Godthaab is now. There he spent the winter, and the following summer resumed his voyage northward. He spent his second winter near the extreme south, and in his last summer of exile explored still farther north, returning when winter approached to the fjord named after him, near Julianehaab.

Eric was immensely pleased with his discoveries. He had found the answer, he thought, to Iceland's population problem and when he returned home in 985 he embarked upon a highly effective publicity campaign for the colonization of the country he calculatingly named Greenland. The name was worthy of Madison Avenue. 'Greenland' sounded a lot more homely than 'Iceland' and, like all good PR men, Eric could not be faulted in strict accuracy. Parts of south-western Greenland were no less habitable than

A fishing boat threads its way through a Greenland fjord. In the time of Eric the Red, the climate in southern Greenland may have been a little milder than it is today.

21

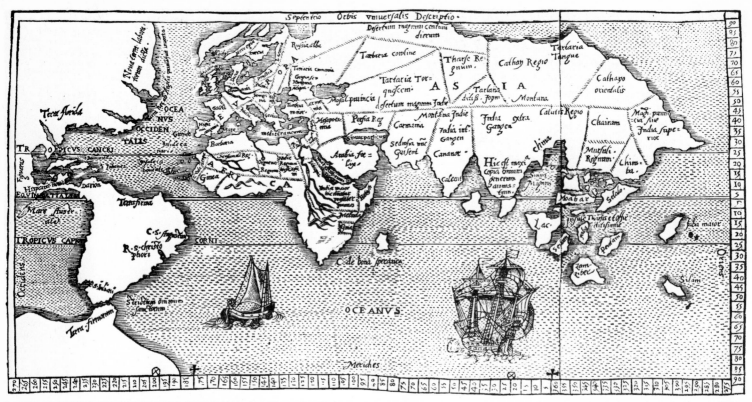

Iceland and were indeed green. There was plenty of grass for grazing, and the Icelanders who eventually settled there kept large herds of cattle. In the 10th century it seems that the Gulf Stream flowed nearer Greenland than it does now and the climate was appreciably milder.

Led by Eric in what has been called the largest polar expedition before Admiral Byrd, the Icelanders founded two main settlements in Greenland; the larger, or Eastern, settlement around Julianehaab and the Western settlement around Godthaab. For many years they lived in fair comfort, grazing their cows in the green valleys, catching fish in the glittering fjords, hunting reindeer on land, and seals, walrus and whales at sea. Eric's son Leif brought Christianity to the Icelanders and voyaged to North America. Other intrepid sailors like Bjarni Jerjulfsson and Thorfinn Karlsefni sailed to the North American mainland and raised a host of much-argued questions for posterity. Their deeds are recorded in the great Icelandic *sagas*, but the *sagas* were not written down for many years and were never records of hard historical fact. On

such tricky questions as the location of 'Vinland' a conservative opinion is safest: it is not really likely that the Scandinavians travelled to Florida, as has been suggested, nor even to Virginia. The only indisputable evidence of a Norse settlement in North America is in northern Newfoundland. However, no one would deny that Leif Ericsson 'discovered' America before Christopher Columbus.

The Icelandic settlements in Greenland eventually dwindled away and disappeared altogether in the 15th century. Worsening climate has sometimes been blamed and Hans Egede, the missionary who arrived in 1721 to help the Greenland Christians and found none left to help, suspected the Eskimos of genocide. The true explanation is probably that the two people had interbred and Norse culture gradually absorbed.

Like Pytheas the Greek, Eric the Viking would probably stand even higher among Arctic explorers if his activities were known in greater detail. He certainly explored more of Greenland than any man until modern times. He knew Davis Strait long before the Elizabethan captain after whom it is named. He knew Baffin Bay before Baffin, and he or his followers probably explored Baffin Island, known to them as Helluland – land of flat stones.

The Norsemen sailed to the east as well as the west. At about the time that Iceland was being settled, a man named Ottar (or Othere), a chieftain from northern Norway, rounded the Kola Peninsula and sailed into the White Sea. He encountered savage tribes in north Russia and killed large numbers of walrus as well as several whales, thereby supplementing his already large fortune.

The story of Ottar comes from a rather highly placed source, none other than King Alfred of Wessex, that splendid scholar-king who is the only English monarch to earn the cognomen 'Great'. As part of his self-appointed task of educating his people as well as defending them from the Danes, Alfred had translated from the Latin a 5th-century history of the world by the Spaniard Orosius. Never afraid of improving a good story, the King incorporated what Ottar had told him over the fire in some great Anglo-Saxon hall in his translation of Orosius. To what extent Alfred also elaborated on Ottar's tale is a question that must remain unanswered.

Like Eric's, the exploits of Ottar – and of all the Vikings – were lost to later ages. When Richard Chancellor sailed into the White Sea he did not know that a Norwegian chief had been there nearly 700 years before; Greenland had to be rediscovered during the Renaissance. Some accounts survived – the 11th-century monk Adam of Bremen repeated the story of Eric the Red – and perhaps the Viking legend lingered on among the fishermen of north-west Europe. But for the scholars and map-makers of the 15th century, it was as if the great Norse voyages had never been.

The Quest for Trade Routes: the 16th Century

Like so much else, the modern age of discovery begins with the Renaissance. The outstanding dates are well known: Columbus' landfall in the West Indies, 1492; Vasco da Gama's voyage to India, 1497–98; the first circumnavigation of the globe by Magellan (or, since Magellan died *en route*, by Sebastian del Cano) in 1519–21. Englishmen also remember the discovery of North America by the shadowy figure of John Cabot in 1497 and Drake's repetition of Magellan's feat in 1577–80.

Discovery was not of course the main object of the Renaissance voyages. A spirit of pure curiosity, though not to be discounted in the 15th century any more than in the 20th, has seldom been the primary motive of geographical exploration. More mundane desires–money, fame–as well as possibly more exalted ones–missionary fervour–have always played a lesser or greater part. In the Renaissance, most voyagers were not looking for new lands and they were sometimes far from pleased when they unexpectedly stumbled upon them. To his dying day, it is said, Columbus refused to believe that he had done anything so inconvenient as to discover America. The results of John Cabot's voyages to North America were so disappointing that no one troubled to record their final outcome. On returning from his second voyage–if, indeed, he did return–Cabot promptly disappeared into obscurity, and except for occasional forays among the Newfoundland cod, the English made few serious efforts to follow the trail that he had blazed for three generations afterwards.

The little ships that set out upon uncharted seas to carry European culture into undiscovered lands were driven by those mighty engines of political expansion, trade and religion. The *conquistadores*, as one of them said with uncommon candour, went to the West Indies 'to serve God and His Majesty, to give light to those who were in darkness, and to grow rich'. Unfortunately, before the soul of Aztec or Inca could be saved it was often necessary to assert the superiority of Christianity by sword and gunpowder, a method of proceeding that to us makes the whole exercise seem highly undesirable, although it had the advantage of making the attainment of the last of the *conquistadores'* aims much simpler.

However, plundering the inhabitants was not the way that most explorers set out to make their fortunes; it was a bonus. Columbus and his successors were seeking honest trade; in particular, a route to the Far East and the Pacific islands, source of Europe's most desired luxury goods. This trade had been going on for centuries, but the overland route was slow and unpredictable at the best of times, and the rise of the Ottoman Turks had made it increasingly hazardous. Since it was eventually repulsed the threat of Islam to western Europe in the 15th and 16th centuries is often forgotten. Spain was only reclaimed for Christianity after a long hard struggle in the late 15th century and the Turks, who overran eastern Europe, approached within sight of the walls of Vienna and dominated the eastern Mediterranean in the 16th century, appeared at least as menacing as, say, Russia after the Second World War. The expansion of Europe westward in the 16th century was to some extent a response to this pressure from the East.

Faced with the necessity for going west, it was fortunate that the Europeans were actually able to do so. Given favourable winds and currents, there appears to be almost no limit to the voyages that can be accomplished even in the frailest of vessels, as Thor Heyerdahl has so triumphantly demonstrated; yet it is unlikely that the European voyages of exploration could have been made with existing knowledge, equipment and technique at any time earlier than the 15th century.

All the same, in the year that Columbus set out theoretical knowledge was, to say the least, hazy.

Not only was information sparse, such as did exist was not widely available. The writings of the medieval Arab travellers like Masudi and Ibn Batuta, who reached Siberia in 1332, were known only indirectly, if at all, in the 15th century. Moreover, no distinction was made between fact and fiction. People were eager for tales of travel (as people always are: any organizer of Women's Institute lectures will testify that foreign travel is the most popular lecture subject); but the accurate observations of a Marco Polo and the wholly imaginary tales of a 'Sir John Mandeville' were lapped up indiscriminately. A late 16th-century engraving of South American Indians gives a generally accurate impression of them with the striking exception of one gentleman who, headless, bears his face on his chest. No one thought this especially odd; no odder, at any rate, than the alligator which also featured.

People of the 15th century assumed, often correctly, that the learned men of antiquity were wiser and better informed than they. They were inclined to believe the statements of classical authors even when they were contradicted by experience, and contrary evidence had to be very solid before classical assumptions were abandoned. Aristotle's elegant theory of the universe was knocked on the head by that strange and brilliant man, the monk Copernicus; yet Tycho Brahe, born after Copernicus' death, could not bring himself to accept that the earth moved round the sun. Educated men knew, of course, that the earth was round. Columbus would hardly have set out west to find the East if he had thought otherwise. But it is likely that the humbler members of the crew thought they were on a fool's errand and might have said of their master, like the character in Shaw's *Saint Joan* when informed of a sage who held that the earth is round and that it moves round the sun: 'What an utter fool! Couldn't he use his eyes?'

Advances in geography in the 15th century began with the rediscovery of the works of the 2nd-century Alexandrian, Ptolemy. Although Ptolemy was known to the Arabs, and parts of his writings had percolated into Europe through the work of Arab geographers, it was not until a Byzantine manuscript was translated into Latin in the first decade of the 15th century that the Ptolemaic system became generally known.

Ptolemy's astronomy was based on Aristotle and therefore of dubious value. His *Geography*, however, did represent an advance and provided the basis for map-making for well over a hundred years.

Ptolemy's maps (or maps based on his data) contain some remarkable items, one of the most famous being the indication of the sources of the Nile in East Africa. But although Ptolemy represented an improvement on the conception of the world prevailing in medieval Europe, it must be said that his version of the oceans and continents, apart from the small area that was already well known, bears only the most distant relationship to the world as we know it. Generally speaking, Ptolemy had far too much land and not enough water. He underestimated the size of the earth by 25 per cent, extended the land mass of Asia too far to the east, and placed a huge mass of *terra incognita* in the extreme south. These misconceptions were to prove both influential and persistent. Columbus struck land approximately where, according to Ptolemy, he

would have come upon the eastern fringes of Asia–hence his reluctance to believe it was anything else.

The legend of the southern continent, *terra australis*, lived even longer and continued to haunt the imagination of explorers long after evidence against its existence had been produced. (According to Ptolemy the southern land was not a separate continent but a conjunction of Africa and China that turned the Indian Ocean into an inland lake.) It is possible that Magellan's ship, which sailed south through the Moluccas and along the coast of Timor, may have come within sight of the northern coasts of Australia, and it is more than possible that subsequent Portuguese voyages in that region approached, perhaps even touched on, Australian coasts. Such observations, if they occurred, would have encouraged the myth of *terra australis*. It is worth pointing out also that, after all, there *is* a southern continent–Antarctica–even though it is on nothing like the scale shown in Renaissance maps.

If men's knowledge of the world beyond western Europe was crude, it was at least less inaccurate at the end of the 15th century than it was at the beginning.

Similarly, the actual ships that made the first transoceanic voyages, though not ideal for the task, were more suitable than the ships of a hundred years earlier. They were not specially designed for exploration (there was often little fundamental difference between warships and merchant ships in the 15th century), and the ships in which the discoverers sailed were sometimes, as a result of paltry funds from sceptical governments, old or in bad shape. Magellan's ship was condemned as unsafe by one critical observer; yet she sailed round the world.

The 14th-century merchant ship of northern Europe was a rather tubby vessel, strongly built but hard to manœuvre and slow, with a single mast and square sail. It looked much less graceful than the sleek Mediterranean lateen-rigged vessel with two or three masts. The main improvements of the 15th century resulted from a marriage of the two types, producing offspring which, with many variations, provided the pattern for ships in all parts of Europe for a long time to come. The flagships of the early explorers were usually something between the mighty carrack, a ship of 600 tons or more, powerful and capacious but unwieldy, and the little caravel, a ship of under 100 tons, light and strong but uncomfortable—many having no full deck and not much in the way of cabin accommodation. Columbus' ships are usually called caravels, but the *Santa Maria* was more substantial than that name suggests.

Navigation was a neglected art before the late 15th century and navigational aids were rudimentary. Most important was the compass, long in use in the Mediterranean. Compasses of the 15th century were accurate to within about five degrees. Seamen could measure the depth, as they still do in many places, with a lead and line. Latitude could be ascertained with quadrant or astrolabe, although the movement of the ship made these instruments extremely difficult to use at sea, and they were soon replaced by the cross-staff, another invention of the Arabs.

Latitude could be determined with reasonable accuracy by a capable navigator. Not so longitude—and this was the most serious problem in navigation until the 18th century. The simple way to discover how far one has travelled in an east–west direction is by measuring time against a fixed point of longitude. Unfortunately, Renaissance seamen had only primitive methods of measuring time, and their method of measuring speed was almost equally inaccurate. A floating line, with knots at regular intervals, was paid out to measure the distance travelled, while hour-glasses recorded the time—as long as their sand was not jammed by the sea air. This rough-and-ready method was of little use on long voyages or when the ship was pursuing an indirect course. The plain fact was that distance and longitude could not be calculated satisfactorily until someone invented the chronometer.

Such, briefly, was the equipment of the Renaissance maritime explorer, and if his technical resources appear hardly adequate, results proved them sufficient.

The vast difficulties that confronted the early explorers were met with a mixture of bold determination and bland ignorance. The horrors of ocean voyaging—bad food, discomfort, disease—were for the most part known and expected. Scurvy, a frightful affliction, was regarded as a natural hazard of the sailor's life. If some problems—for instance, the breadth of the oceans—were underrated, others were exaggerated. 'Here

be dragons!', warned one old map, and who could contradict? But above the murmur of medieval superstition could be heard the bold and optimistic utterances of a man like that stalwart merchant of Bristol, Robert Thorne, who asserted in 1530 that 'there is no land uninhabitable and no sea unnavigable'.

Such progressive attitudes were gaining ground. However, Thorne also recommended reaching the rich lands he expected to find in the Pacific Ocean by sailing north from England directly over the pole and so south again. His examination of the globe had revealed this to be the shortest route, and he was blissfully unaware of the Arctic ice. Seventy years later, Henry Hudson was still inclined to favour the transpolar route.

A certain small mammal, lacking the benefit of keen eyesight, is said to pursue its way across land to reach water by a route which, at first painstakingly worked out, it deftly follows by memory alone. If another source of water is artificially introduced nearer its starting point it will at first ignore it, even go round it, preferring to stick to its accustomed route. In a rather similar way, the reaction of Europeans on finding a new, hitherto unknown continent barring the westward route to Asia was to seek a way round the obstacle. The Spaniards had established a monopoly of New World treasure and its other offerings, at first mainly fish, later timber and furs, compared unfavourably with the anticipated trade with the Far East where, it was confidently reported, the very roofs of the houses were tiled with solid gold.

The search for new sea routes was on, and the history of Arctic exploration from the 16th century to the 19th is substantially the search for the Northwest and Northeast Passages.

After John Cabot's failure to bring back the riches he had promised, the English drive to the west languished for a time. There were enterprising men like Robert Thorne, keen to press on, and there were a number of ultimately insignificant transatlantic voyages, but while the Spaniards were carving out their American empire and the Portuguese were expanding the East Indies trade, the English accomplished nothing of lasting importance until the second half of the 16th century.

As the Portuguese had laid claim to the Southeast passage round the Cape of Good Hope, and the Spaniards, thanks to the Portuguese Magellan, had pre-empted the less satisfactory Southwest passage, the English were compelled to look to the north. Navigators in the 16th century preferred to sail along lines of latitude as far as possible, so there were practical reasons also for England's concentration on the northern routes.

The first great exploratory voyage to find a way to Cathay (China) was directed towards the north-east, rather than the north-west, probably on the advice of Sebastian Cabot, first governor of the company of the 'Merchants Adventurers of England for the discovery of lands, territories, isles, dominions and seignories unknown'. Sebastian Cabot had sailed with his father to Newfoundland more than half a century before. He was a rather unreliable character who for 300 years deceived posterity into taking him at his own exalted estimation to the detriment of his father's reputation. Nevertheless, as a result of thirty-six years of service for the Spanish Crown, he was better informed on maritime affairs than anyone else in England and the government lured him home with a substantial pension and the grand title 'Pilot Major of England'.

The expedition sailed from London in May 1553. It was commanded by Sir Hugh Willoughby, an experienced soldier, with Richard Chancellor, well known for his expertise in 'matters touching the sea', as chief pilot and second in command. Cabot was too old for active command, though spry enough three years later to cut a caper with the girls at a send-off party for Stephen Burrough's voyage, but he drew up the expedition's instructions, a blend of sound nautical advice and lofty exhortation. Off the coast of Norway, the ships became separated in a storm. Chancellor, in the strongest ship, discounting the dire warnings of some gloomy Scotsmen who he encountered at Vardö, pushed on into the White Sea, then quite unknown, in the hope that it would carry him through to the Pacific. Instead, he ended up near Archangel, where he was informed that he had reached the territory of the terrible Ivan, Emperor of Muscovy. With great enterprise, Chancellor proceeded by sledge through the Russian winter to Moscow, and was amiably received by the Tsar. From this meeting sprang the Anglo-Russian trade conducted from England by the Muscovy Company which, though economically not very important, yet represented the first significant expansion of English commerce as the direct result of exploratory voyaging. Chancellor himself was drowned when his ship was wrecked returning from his second trip to Russia in 1556.

While Chancellor's exploits had the most important results in terms of commercial expansion, Willoughby's travels were more closely relevant to future developments in Arctic exploration. Having lost contact with his second in command, Willoughby sailed on eastward at about latitude 72° across what was later named the Barents Sea. On 14 August 1553 he sighted an unknown coast lying at right angles to his path. It was the southern island of Novaya Zemlya, but Willoughby assumed it was part of the mainland and boldly turned north. He made slow progress in the face of high winds and coastal ice, and as the weather deteriorated he decided to seek winter quarters before continuing his voyage in the following spring. Novaya Zemlya offered no refuge so he turned back to the Kola Peninsula (the tail on the Scandinavian dog) and found an anchorage there in the mouth of a river. But Englishmen then had no idea of the intensity of

Christopher Columbus – the portrait long thought to be the only authentic likeness, though perhaps not painted from life. His discoveries brought him riches but little else and his character remains the subject of argument: 'to picture him as an unpractical mystic is mere caricature' (J. H. Parry); 'his action, thoughts and writings do at times suggest a man just this side of the edge of insanity' (Salvador de Madariaga).

Sir Hugh Willoughby, in appearance every inch a handsome Elizabethan gentleman (though he died before Elizabeth came to the throne), whose sea voyage in search of the Northeast Passage gives him some claim to be called the first English Arctic explorer. He knew nothing of the conditions he would encounter on his fatal voyage.

the Arctic winter; neither Willoughby nor a single member of his crew survived the ordeal. The bodies were found by Russian fishermen the following spring and some of the cargo, together with Willoughby's journal, was regained by Richard Chancellor in 1555.

In spite of the claims of Sir Hugh Willoughby, the title of first English explorer of the Arctic is usually bestowed upon Sir Martin Frobisher, although that ambitious Yorkshireman would not be much impressed by such an empty honour.

The son of a minor landowner, Frobisher as a boy was given into the care of a wealthy relative, Sir John Yorke. Impressed by the boy's 'great spirit and bould courage, and natural hardness of body', Sir John sent him to 'the hot countrye

right
Sir Martin Frobisher: the
pose is unusual but highly
suitable – Frobisher was
always quick on the draw.
From a painting by Cornelis
Ketel.

of Guinea', where the characteristics that Sir John had remarked on received a thorough testing. On his first voyage to West Africa, under Captain Wyndham, nearly half the crew died in an epidemic. On another occasion Frobisher was captured and held prisoner for half a year.

Besides bartering beads for gold dust, in competition with the Portuguese who claimed a monopoly of West African trade, Frobisher, as the custom was, practised a little piracy. His depredations were not restricted to the ships of Roman Catholic nations, usually considered fair game by English captains, and the complaints of his own countrymen resulted in his spending the best part of one year in an English prison. With arrogant gaze, spectacularly broken nose, and shoulders like a barn door, Frobisher was a tough character; but he was not merely a ruffian. He was educated and intelligent, and stands comparison with his arch-rival Drake both as captain and navigator.

Being primarily interested in his own advancement, Frobisher was not the kind of man to embrace forlorn causes, and his advocacy of the Northwest Passage for many long and unproductive years seems out of character. Whoever or whatever convinced him of the possibilities of the north-west route, his interest was probably sustained by influential friends, in particular Michael Lok, who became his partner and chief backer, and Richard Hakluyt, the invaluable historian and tireless advocate of voyages of exploration. John Dee, Astrologer to the Queen and a man of many parts even by Elizabethan standards, also became involved in the project though initially reported sceptical. These men in turn secured the guarded approval of members of the Privy Council whose influence overcame the objections that resulted from the Muscovy Company's possession of a monopoly covering all northern routes.

In 1576 Frobisher, then aged about thirty-seven, prepared to sail. The size of the expedition showed that financial support was niggardly (most of the capital was provided by Michael Lok). There were two ships, both very small, of which the *Gabriel* was built specially. The other ship became separated from the *Gabriel* in a storm and returned to England soon afterwards. There was also a little pinnace of about ten tons which soon succumbed to the Atlantic rollers.

Frobisher was well equipped with instruments but he relied on the troublesome Zeno map. This was ostensibly the work of two Italian brothers whose claims to have explored the North Atlantic in the late 14th century are rather doubtful. Whatever the truth about their movements, their map was highly inaccurate and was probably a later forgery. Frobisher's efforts to relate his discoveries to the Zeno map were to cause further confusion. From the days of Ptolemy to the days of Sir Alexander Dalrymple, 'men took the plastic stuff of unknown lands and seas and moulded them to their own sanguine

theories', as Jeannette Mirsky gracefully puts it.

The ships weighed anchor at Deptford at the end of May, sailing down river to Greenwich where the Queen, in residence at the palace there, sent a good-luck message and graciously waved a greeting from a window. On reaching the North Sea, Frobisher turned north to the Shetland Isles, then west on latitude 61° North. After five weeks he sighted land, identified by him as the fictional island of 'Friesland' marked on the Zeno map and presumably Greenland. A 'great store of yce' prevented him landing.

Two days later the *Gabriel*, by now on her own, was nearly wrecked, and ship and men were only saved by the quick thinking, courage and agility of their commander. Limping in heavy seas, the ship swung suddenly across the wind and heeled over. Water poured in at the waist and 'she lay still for sunk, and would neither weare nor steare with any help of the helme . . . In this distress, when all the men in the ship had lost their courage, and did despayr of life, the captayn, like him selfe, with valiant courage, stood up, and passed along the ship's side in the chayn wales lying on her flat syde.' He cut away the mizzen with a knife, whereupon the ship slowly righted herself and began to respond to the tiller.

After further buffeting, the Canadian coast was sighted and the *Gabriel* sailed into the bay that now bears Frobisher's name. Anchoring some way up, they came upon some Eskimos, whose appearance was encouragingly Asian, convincing Frobisher that he was sailing up a strait with America on his left hand and Asia on his right. The natives, however, were not friendly, and Frobisher held them responsible for the otherwise unexplained disappearance of five of his men on an exploratory trip ashore.

By a crafty ruse he secured a prisoner in exchange. The Eskimos were fascinated by the articles that the Englishmen had brought to trade, but too suspicious to approach. They paddled about in their kayaks, keeping a safe distance from the *Gabriel*, while Frobisher endeavoured to entice them nearer by displaying various fancy items from the hold. One man seemed especially interested in a brass bell which Frobisher swung to and fro, ringing a cheerful note across the grey waters. The man paddled nearer, as Frobisher leaned farther over the side clanging away and grinning encouragingly. The man came closer until Frobisher, seeming to reach out to give him the bell, let it slip from his fingers. It glimmered for a moment below the surface before it sank out of sight. The Eskimo gazed, disappointed at the place where it had vanished, but as he prepared to turn away Frobisher produced a second bell, which he proffered invitingly. Determined not to lose this one too, the man approached just a little too near. Suddenly letting go of the bell, the powerful Frobisher reached down, grabbed the man with both hands and swung him, canoe and all, over the side of the *Gabriel*. 'Whereupon he found himself in captivity, for very choller and disdain he bit his tong in-twayne within his mouth; notwithstanding, he died not thereof, but lived until he came in Englande, and then he died, of colde which he had taken at Sea.'

After some further investigation at the mouth of the bay, Frobisher set sail for home, arriving in England at the beginning of October. Although people were much interested in the unfortunate Eskimo–the 'Strange Man of Cathay'–and impressed by Frobisher's assertion that he had found the Northwest Passage (he had not sailed to the end of what is now Frobisher's Bay), what aroused public interest sufficiently to make sure of substantial support for a second expedition was the quality of some pieces of 'black rock' that Frobisher had brought back from the shores of Baffin Island. A piece of this mineral was accidentally dropped in a fire, and as it cooled it displayed a most alluring glint. The opinion of London goldsmiths on this phenomenon varied, but at least one of them maintained that the 'black rock' was a rich gold-bearing ore.

It is easy to see why people should so often suppose that the easiest way to get rich is the most straightforward–to go and pick up the stuff. Men have never been able to resist the lure of gold even when the incidental difficulties attending its acquisition are larger than the likely profits. The mere suggestion that Frobisher had discovered gold was enough. The Queen herself provided a ship, the 200-ton *Aid*, for Frobisher's second expedition which sailed under the auspices of the newly founded Cathay Company. Thirty miners as well as craftsmen and metallurgists were among the company, and Frobisher's instructions were to fill the *Aid* with ore and send her back to England. The other objects of the expedition were definitely secondary. Six men were to be landed in 'Friesland'; they were

extracted from jail for the purpose–an early example of the questionable English custom of selecting convicts as colonists. When the *Aid* had been dispatched, Frobisher with the *Gabriel* and *Michael* might, if he wished, continue to search for the passage to Cathay.

Frobisher's second expedition began a year almost to the day after his first. After putting into the Orkneys, where the Englishmen found the inhabitants to be 'very beastlie and rude', they were again unable to land in Greenland, and continued to Frobisher Bay. They did some trade with the Eskimos, but a skirmish followed their attempt to take hostages for the five men lost the previous year. Frobisher himself suffered an undignified but not dangerous wound, being struck in the rump by an arrow. Two Eskimo women were captured; one, old and ugly and suspected of being a witch, was released; the other, a young woman with a baby, was held, but like the captive of the previous year did not long survive the voyage to England.

On one island near the mouth of the bay, the natives said that three of the missing men were still alive and on being questioned further asked for pen and paper. If this surprising request was correctly interpreted, these people could not have been real Eskimos, who had no written language. They were probably the descendants of Icelanders from Greenland.

No further trace of the missing seamen could be found and Frobisher, having loaded his ships with the dubious ore, set sail for England without seriously pursuing his exploration. On the voyage home the ships were caught in a severe storm and all three were for a time in danger of sinking. After the storm had passed, inspection of the damage revealed that the *Aid*'s rudder was split in two and on the point of falling off altogether. In water that was probably not much

A well-observed drawing, perhaps by a member of Frobisher's expedition, of Eskimos hunting with the trident used for birds and fish. From Captain Beste's *Frobisher's Voyages*, 1578.

above freezing point, a dozen men went over the side and 'taking great pains, under water, driving plank and binding with ropes, did well mend and strengthen the matter'.

It is an advantage of relatively simple technology that repairs can often be made the more easily; but the extraordinary skill and enterprise of seamen in the age of discovery is none the less remarkable. Practically nothing seems to have been beyond the ingenuity of ships' carpenters, who often worked, as in this case, in the most trying conditions. There are several examples of shipwrecked sailors constructing a seaworthy vessel with almost no tools and only the wreckage of their vessel as raw material.

All three ships eventually reached home – at widely separated ports – safely, and the *Aid*'s cargo was examined with much interest. Again the reports were mixed, but the optimists prevailed as they usually do when potential riches are at stake, and a much larger expedition consisting of fifteen ships was prepared for the following year. The ore of course was eventually to prove completely worthless, and the whole episode is a revealing example of one of the most striking characteristics of Elizabethan society – a conjunction that seems very curious to us of 'medieval' gullibility on the one hand and 'modern' worldly wisdom on the other. It seems strange that cultivated courtiers and hard-headed merchants were so completely taken in by Frobisher's 'black rock' when a cool appraisal of the evidence must have shown it to be barren.

Frobisher's third expedition was the largest, the best equipped, and – in spite of the dominating search for gold – the most interesting enterprise of its kind that the English had so far launched. Among others the company included a party of 120 who were to start a colony on Baffin Island. The loss of the barque carrying all the building materials prevented the execution of this plan which for the potential colonists was probably just as well. Frobisher did succeed in making a landfall in Greenland, which he had twice tried and failed, and found there evidence of European contacts in the shape of iron tools.

Being anxious to press on to the mainland, he did not stay long in Greenland. He lost his bearings temporarily soon afterwards but successfully disguised the fact from his passengers and eventually struck the coast some miles south of his destination. As a result, probably, of a cold spring, the ice was worse than before and for a time it looked as though the fleet would not be able to approach land. The English still had little experience of the dangers of sailing in far northern waters, but the experiences of Frobisher's third voyage were to enlighten them considerably. As a storm blew up, the ice pressed in upon them. From out of the mists of spray huge floating mountains appeared, while flatter, jagged chunks of ice were suddenly thrust up by the waves, tearing at the fragile hulls of the ships. 'Some of the ships, where they could find a place more

clear of yce, and get a little berth of sea roome, did take in their sayles, and there lay adrift; other some fastened and moored anker upon a great island of yce; and againe, some were so fast shut up, and compassed in amongst an infinite number of great countreys and islands of yce, that they were faine to submit themselves and their ships to the mercy of the unmerciful yce, and strengthened the sides of their ships with junk of cables, beds, masts, planks, and such like, which being hanged overboord, on the sides of their ships, might better defend them from the outrageous sway and strokes of the said yce.'

The excellent Captain Best of the *Anne Francis* was impressed by the bulldog spirit of crew and passengers. It was, he wrote, 'greatly worthy commendation and noting, with what invincible minde every captaine encouraged his company, and with what incredible labour the painefull mariners and poore miners (unacquainted with such extremities), to the everlasting renowne of our nation, did overcome the brunt of these so great and extreme dangers; for some even without boord, upon the yce, and some within boord, upon the sides of their ships, having poles, pikes, pieces of timber, and ores in their hands, stood almost day and night without any rest, bearing off the force, and breaking the sway of the yce, with such incredible paine and perill, that it was wonderful to behold'.

Frobisher fought his way out at last and found himself approaching a strait where a very strong current ran. He sailed up it for a considerable distance, but becoming convinced that it was not the strait he was looking for, he turned about, marking on his map with somewhat ill-founded confidence Mistaken Strait. It was not indeed the opening to the Northwest Passage, as others were to prove; but it was surely a more promising route than Frobisher Bay, and Frobisher's swift retreat is evidence that he was more concerned with gold than exploration. It was left to Henry Hudson to traverse the whole length of the strait and to discover the vast bay to which it led. Thus both bay and strait bear Hudson's name, not Frobisher's.

Few important geographical discoveries were made on Frobisher's third expedition. The little *Gabriel*, making her third transatlantic crossing, sailed round what had been known as Queen Elizabeth Foreland, proving it an island (Resolution Island). Another ship, the *Emmanuel* of Bridgwater, discovered a large island on the way home, but no one could ever find it again; the island remains one of the many minor mysteries created by early voyages of exploration.

On the voyage home the fleet was again scattered by a storm, but except for two small vessels lost earlier, all eventually reached England. They carried several hundred tons of ore, now revealed to be worthless. Michael Lok, who had been compelled to dig deep into his own pockets to get Frobisher under way, was held responsible for the losses and thrown into a debtor's prison. The poor fellow, who had fifteen children, wrote a plaintive letter blaming Frobisher for letting him down, but with how much justice it is impossible to say.

Frobisher himself, though he had not made his fortune, seems not to have suffered much from his failure. He was able to set himself up as a country gentleman in Yorkshire, although it is likely that he augmented his income by a little piracy. At any rate, he kept his nautical hand in and served with distinction against the Armada, being knighted after the battle. In 1594 he led an attack on the Spanish-held port of Brest and was mortally wounded as he led the landing party ashore. He managed to write his report of the action, vigorous though badly spelled, but died soon after returning to Plymouth. His body was sent to London, but first his heart was cut out and buried at Plymouth, the port from which the intrepid captain had often sailed to fight the Spaniards.

The disappointing results of Frobisher's exploits in the north-west did not for long check the aspiration of merchants and courtiers. His work was continued in the 1580s by John Davis. Davis' name is less well known than Frobisher's but his career was no less adventurous, his capacity as a navigator not inferior, and his character on the whole more attractive. In his relations with the Eskimos, for instance, Davis showed a perception and tolerance foreign to the hard character of Frobisher, and he preferred playing games with them (wrestling and football in fact) to fighting them. On one occasion he

The voyages of John Davis in search of the Northwest Passage, from J. Scott Keltie, *The World's Great Explorers* (London 1889). Davis greatly extended the discoveries of Frobisher and showed a more scientific interest in what he saw. He is perhaps the most underrated of Elizabethan captains.

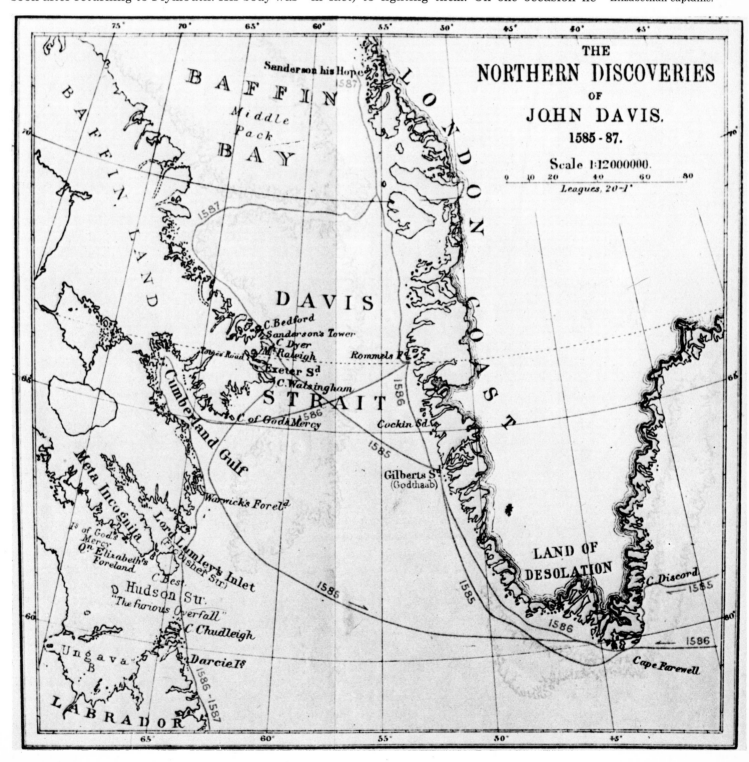

Trouble with bears: an intrepid Dutchman prepares to slip a noose over the animal's head (middle distance), he succeeds (foreground), the bear waxes wrathful, and the sailors suddenly discover something of interest at the far end of the boat. From an engraving by Theodore de Bry.

refused to retaliate when attacked; such forbearance astonished his men and was certainly far from typical of Elizabethan seamen.

Like Hawkins, Drake and many other famous captains, John Davis (he usually spelled it Davys) was a Devon man. It is probable that the Gilbert brothers (Humphrey and Adrian) and Walter Raleigh were among his boyhood companions. In retrospect his choice of career seems inevitable, but little is known of his early life. By the time he married, in 1579, the year after Humphrey Gilbert's first, abortive attempt to establish a colony in Newfoundland, he was about twenty-eight years of age and already an experienced seaman. He would undoubtedly have read Gilbert's confident treatise on the Northwest Passage, and he was among the many periodic visitors to that repository of learning in every branch of science (soon to be wrecked by a superstitious mob) the house of John Dee in Mortlake. Among those interested in the Northwest Passage whom Davis met at Dr Dee's house or elsewhere were Sir Francis Walsingham, Secretary of State, and William Sanderson, a powerful London merchant. With these influential supporters, Davis, Adrian Gilbert and Raleigh secured a royal charter 'for the search and discoverie of the North-West Passage to China', as well as sufficient investment to prepare an expedition.

Consisting of two small ships, with Davis in overall command, the expedition sailed from Dartmouth at the beginning of June 1585. They were held up for two weeks by contrary winds in the Scillies, where Davis employed his time usefully by making a thorough survey of the area, and were further hindered for some days by a dense Atlantic fog. The weather cleared and they made good speed, with occasional diversions to hunt porpoises, whose skins proved too tough for their harpoons. They did catch a 'darbiehead', whatever that was, and found the flesh as good as English mutton.

After three weeks' sailing, they sighted Greenland. Mist hung about them and the grinding pack ice made 'a mighty great roaring'. A dismal place it seemed. Davis called it the Land of Desolation, an apt name perhaps but not one to encourage settlement. The ships then rounded Greenland and sailed up and across the strait that now bears Davis' name, scattering the names of friends and patrons upon significant landmarks, winning the friendship of the Eskimos ('gentle and loving savages') by a display of dancing, and killing four polar bears amid great delight.

At a point just north of the Arctic Circle, Davis turned south again and steered into Cumberland Sound, which he believed might lead to the desired passage. Contrary winds and diminishing supplies forced him to sail for home before completing his examination of the gulf.

He made a favourable report and as a result was commissioned to sail again the following year. This time he had four ships, which he divided into pairs, sending two to explore the seas between Iceland and Greenland while he continued round the southern tip of Greenland. He tried to land there but like Frobisher before him was thwarted by ice. One iceberg was so huge that Davis declined to estimate its dimensions on the grounds that he would not be believed. Having ironically named the inaccessible land Cape Farewell, he sailed on. He carried out the first thorough investigation of the western coast of Greenland with a shallow-draught boat constructed on the spot, and ranged as far north as 63°. He traded with the Eskimos and made a vocabulary of their language, but race relations took a turn for the worse when some of the inhabitants cut his ship's cable and made off with the anchor. Before crossing to the western side of Davis Strait he sent one of his two ships home carrying seamen who had become sick. In the remaining ship he followed the mainland south; strangely, he did not explore Cumberland Sound, the most promising discovery of the year before, but continued to the coast of Newfoundland, where his men made great catches of cod. 'The hook was no sooner over the side, but presently a fish was taken.' By mid-October, Davis was back in England.

He considered his second voyage a success. A large extent of unknown coast had been explored, and although Cumberland Sound had inexplicably fallen from favour, other likely looking inlets had been noted. Davis also brought back a mass of information on other matters. Much more than Frobisher, he was moved by the spirit of scientific curiosity and was interested in everything he saw. He never anchored in a Greenland fjord nor a Labrador bay without attempting to explore the hinterland, investigate the flora and fauna and make contact with the inhabitants.

Support was not so easy to find for a third expedition, but both Walsingham and Sanderson were still interested, and Davis sailed again in 1586. He had only three ships and, anxious to cover his expenses, he dispatched two of them direct from Greenland to the Newfoundland fishery. In the leaky little *Ellen*, Davis himself sailed north along the west coast of Greenland and reached a point 72° 12′ North without serious trouble from ice. At this point a mighty cliff rose from the sea, and Davis named it Sanderson's Hope (i.e. of a Northwest Passage). The water was still clear ahead, but the wind barred progress north, and when the ship turned west she encountered the middle ice pack of Baffin Bay. Forced to retreat for a time, Davis eventually threaded a way through and, striking the coast of Baffin Island near Cumberland Sound, put into it and at last discovered that it offered no through passage. Sailing south again he passed Frobisher Bay but failed to recognize it and renamed it Lumley's Inlet, after a nautical peer of his acquaintance. (Lord Lumley was also known, by reputation anyway, to 'North-West' Foxe as the builder of the pier at Hartlepool: 'At my first coming thither I demanded at whose charge the said pier was builded. An old man answered: Marry, at my good Lord Lumley's, whose soul was in heaven before his bones were cold.') Soon afterwards the ship passed 'a very great gulfe, the water whirling and roring as it were the meeting of the tides'. Like Frobisher, Davis failed to investigate Hudson Strait, perhaps discouraged by the 'furious overfall' of the waters. Failing to contact the fishing vessels off Newfoundland as arranged, the little *Ellen*, much battered after several close calls, sailed for England and dropped anchor in Dartmouth harbour in mid-September.

When Davis returned from this third Arctic expedition England was preparing to repel invasion from Spain, and for the time being voyages of exploration had to be suspended. Davis himself was hardly at the midway point of his career, but his later voyages were in southern waters. His activity as an Arctic explorer was over, although his later writings on the art of navigation were no doubt eagerly read by his successors. Davis had revealed more of the Arctic than any man before him and opened the way for later explorers. In the admiring words of Sir Clements Markham, he 'converted the Arctic regions from a confused myth into a defined area, the physical aspects and conditions of which were understood so far as they were known. He not only described and mapped the extensive tract explored by himself, but he clearly pointed out the work cut out for his successors. He lighted Hudson into his strait. He lighted Baffin into his bay. He lighted Hans Egede (the 18th-century missionary) to the scene of his Greenland labours. But he did more. His true-hearted devotion to the cause of Arctic discovery, his patient scientific research, his loyalty to his employers, his

The route taken by Barents, and Novaya Zemlya, as seen by a contemporary. From 'An Authentic Map made by Gerrit de Veer'.

dauntless gallantry and enthusiasm, form an example which will be a beacon-light to maritime explorers for all time to come.'

John Davis was killed by Japanese pirates off Sumatra in 1605.

The English concentrated on the Northwest rather than the Northeast Passage partly because the example of Willoughby was not encouraging, partly because the Muscovy trade was providing a substitute (if a poorish one) for the dreamed-of riches of Cathay, and partly because 16th-century maps made the prospect of the Northwest Passage look more inviting than the facts warranted. In the year of Chancellor's death Stephen Burrough in the *Searchthrift* tried to pass south of Novaya Zemlya but was stopped by ice. No further attempts were made until 1580, when Arthur Pet and Charles Jackman were defeated by the same obstacle.

The quest for the Northeast Passage was taken up by another seagoing nation of northern Europe, the Dutch, who were preparing to eject their Spanish masters and to build a commercial empire that would challenge Spain's. The Dutch also had their Russian trading company, with a permanent outpost on the Kola Peninsula. From there Olivier Brunel voyaged to Novaya Zemlya in 1584, but the ice barrier thwarted him as it had thwarted his English predecessors. He did succeed in pushing farther east by following an overland route and, in company with Russian guides, he travelled some way east of the Urals.

The search was taken up again ten years later by a man whose name, commemorated in the sea he sailed, stands first among 16th-century explorers of the Arctic – Willem Barents.

Not much is known of Barents' early life. He was born in 1548 or 1549 on a small island off the Dutch coast and, in Ian Cameron's words, his 'whole life from birth to death was played out within sound of the Atlantic waves'. By 1594 he was an experienced and well-known navigator, a natural choice for the States General seeking a pilot for a voyage of discovery in the north. Even in the Netherlands, where the social hierarchy was less rigid than in any other European country, a professional seaman was not put in charge of government-sponsored expeditions, and officially Barents was not the commander of any of the three Arctic expeditions in which he took part. The names of the appointed commanders, however, are hardly remembered now; the combination of Barents' strong personality, long experience and outstanding navigational ability made him the effective leader.

When he sailed in 1594 Barents was well aware of the massive, wind-blown ice barrier that had blocked the way of Pet and of Brunel to the Kara Sea in the strait south of Novaya Zemlya. He therefore decided to investigate the possibility of rounding the north of the island, although that meant sailing some 500 miles nearer the pole. He carried out a close inspection of the western coasts of Novaya Zemlya and discovered that it was not one island but two, divided by a narrow channel (Matochkin Channel). Finding the

northern route impassable, he returned to the south where he found, to his joyful astonishment, that the other ships in the expedition had passed unscathed through the Kara Strait and were cruising in an ice-free Kara Sea. This was an unexpected triumph. Barents was not to know that the mild conditions were highly unusual; if the Northwest Passage was to have been breached in the 16th century, the year of Barents' first expedition was the ideal time to do it.

Information from Russian fishermen was also encouraging. They were quite accustomed to sailing in these waters, they told the Dutch, and had frequently travelled beyond the Yamal Peninsula.

There are of course no records of the movements of the little Russian fishing boats, nor of the travels of the inhabitants of other distant regions in the years before their lands were brought to the notice of Europe. History is probably often unfair to such people, for history is not 'what happened' but 'what is recorded'. Not only is it likely that Russian fishermen explored the northern coasts before western Europeans arrived there, it is also probable that

The Kolyma River near its mouth, under the rays of the midnight sun. The section of coast east of the Kolyma defeated the superhuman endeavours of the Great Northern Expedition and was not satisfactorily surveyed until the early 19th century when Wrangel made the final definitive link with the explorers who had worked northwards to the Bering Strait.

the assistance they rendered to their uninvited visitors was far greater than has been acknowledged.

Barents' Russian acquaintances might have thought it laughably odd that the land and seas on which they had lived and worked for generations were only then being 'discovered'. *They* knew the place well enough. And the same might be said of Eskimos, Maoris, American Indians and many others.

The Dutch were so delighted at their success in reaching the Kara Sea, a feat never accomplished before and not repeated for over 200 years, that they hastened home without sailing farther, prematurely convinced like so many before and after them that a northern sea route to the East had been found. The Dutch government was equally enthusiastic and raised the money for a second expedition consisting of seven ships. It sailed in 1595 with J. H. van Linschoten, better known for his Pacific voyages, as well as Barents among the leaders.

This time they met quite different conditions south of Novaya Zemlya. The strait was choked with ice and, finding no safe way through, the expedition returned ignominiously to Amsterdam. The States General were discouraged by the failure and declined to venture public money in a third attempt; but they did offer a reward to anyone who should find the northern route. Stimulated by Barents' enthusiasm, the enterprising merchants of Amsterdam put up the capital for another attack on the ice.

Barents' momentous third Arctic expedition consisted of only two ships, and a disagreement about objectives led the two commanders, Jacob van Heemskerck and Jan Cornelis Rjp, to separate before they reached Novaya Zemlya. Cornelis Rjp soon returned to Holland, while Barents, in effective command of van Heemskerck's ship, sailed on alone.

So pronounced an impression had the sinister Kara Strait made in the previous year that it was decided to revert to the northern approach to Novaya Zemlya. From Holland the course was set more or less due north, which carried the ships into unknown waters north of the 72nd parallel. On 9 June 1596, they discovered a small island on which they landed. There they found a 'great white bear', which they pursued with the intention of lassooing it. Approaching more closely and observing the great size of the animal, they wisely changed their minds and returned to the ship for reinforcements. There ensued a long and violent hunt '[we] made to her again with muskets, arquebuses, halberts and hatchets, John Cornellyson's men coming also with their boat to help us. And being so well furnished of men and weapons, we rowed with our boats unto the bear and fought with her while four glasses were run out [probably two hours], for our weapons could do her little hurt; and amongst the rest of the blows that we gave her one of our men struck her into the back with an axe which

stuck fast in her, and yet she swam away with it; but we rowed after her, and at last we cut her head in sunder with an axe, wherewith she died'. This gruesome episode is a reminder of the frailty of 16th-century man in the wilderness: a shipload of armed men take two hours to dispose of one wretched bear! Later, the bears were to exact some measure of revenge for the persecution of their fellow.

Having named the new discovery Bear Island (what else indeed?) the Dutch continued northward and in ten days came upon the far larger island group of Spitsbergen.

Spitsbergen – 'pointed mountain' – it is an attractive, evocative name, with echoes of the old days of whaling, before that thrilling though savage occupation became, with modern aids to slaughter, an efficient process of total extermination. Barents and his men, who thought this was part of Greenland, were also favourably impressed by their discovery. To their surprise they found 'leaves and grass and . . . such beasts as live thereon like harts and bucks [reindeer]'.

It is possible to find land farther north than Spitsbergen, but not much farther. The land extends beyond the 80th parallel, and nowhere else is plant life found so far north (Spitsbergen has nearly 150 species of wild flowers). The reason for this relatively mild climate is the same as that which makes the British Isles so temperate – the warm caress of the Gulf Stream.

It was at Spitsbergen that the two ships separated, and Barents and van Heemskerck turned east towards Novaya Zemlya. They passed the northern tip of the island on 17 July, and were at once threatened by the crowding ice. For a month Barents tacked and turned, seeking the inviting but deceptive channels of water that opened up among the pack. Wayward currents swept the ship to and fro, fog obscured the horizon, and blizzards rose from nowhere to swirl about the masts. The Arctic winter approached.

The ship was driven back towards the land where, on a clear day, some of the crew climbed up to an icy promontory to gain a wider view of their perilous situation. Away to the south-east they saw clear water, 'whereat we were much comforted'. Barents set his course towards it, and spent precious days trying to find a way through to the Kara Sea. A persistent mist descended, blinding the sailors' view, as the little Dutch ship nosed perilously along the ice pack.

During the week spent vainly scouting for a passage south, the ice closed in behind them. Barents had left his decision to retire until it was too late. Each time they tried to force their way back along the coast, ice and storms repelled them. Off Ice Haven, the place where they had first landed, they were caught in a jumble of ice floes. The timbers creaked agonizingly, the rudder was sawn off, and blankets of snow swept in from the south-west. The ice, having caught them in its vice-like grip, began to extend its frozen fingers underneath the hull, until the patch of

water that the ship floated in was frozen hard and she reared up suddenly, marooned on the ice pack. The pressure on the sides increased, and planks splintered with a sound like a rifle shot. 'It was most fearful both to see and hear, and made all the hair of our heads to rise upright with fear.'

The ship was finished, that was obvious. Help, and the nearest human being, were a thousand miles away. No European had yet lived through an Arctic winter. The prospect was almost hopeless.

But not quite hopeless. They could save the ship's stores, which were substantial, and the ship's boats, in which they might make a break for safety when summer came again. In the meantime, they had to stay alive on the bleak shores of Novaya Zemlya for eight or nine months.

The first great epic of survival in the polar regions began. There have been many similar stories since–stories of physical endurance and moral courage so extraordinary they are barely credible. Yet the survival of Barents and his companions, partly because they were the first to come through the ordeal of an Arctic winter, is perhaps the most extraordinary of all. Barents himself, approaching fifty, was the oldest of the party and for much of the time he was so ill and weak he could not stand. Yet it is clear from the account of one who survived to tell the story that he was at all times the unquestioned leader, and his inspiring leadership and determination was, for most of his men, the difference between life and death.

They also had some luck. Not far away along the shore they discovered 'certain great trees

roots and all, as if God had purposely sent them unto us, and these served not only to build our house but also to burn all winter'. The house that they constructed from this far-travelled driftwood was, in the circumstances, a large and elaborate building. It consisted of one room, 32 feet long, 20 feet wide and 11 feet high, with three doors and a central chimney. It was also equipped with a Turkish bath, made from wine barrels, where each man bathed once a week. Wooden bunks were ranged along the walls, with heated stones and bearskins to supplement the thin woollen clothes of the sailors. Animals also provided fat for burning in lamps and, of course, meat.

In the first week of November the sun hauled itself reluctantly above the horizon, hovered there briefly, and sank out of sight, not to be seen again for three months.

The long Arctic night closed in upon them, and with it came the cold. A deadly, killing cold. Cold that paralyses the muscles and saps the will. Cold that overcame all the frail defences the shivering Dutchmen could raise against it.

'Today we washed our shirts, but it was so cold that they froze stiff, and although we laid them by a great fire yet only the side that lay next to the fire thawed, the other remaining frozen as hard as a board.'

'December 12: extreme cold, so that the walls inside our house and our bunks were frozen a finger thick with ice; yea, and the very clothes upon our backs were white all over with frost and icicles.' The clock stopped and the wine froze solid.

At night the Arctic foxes pattered over the

roof, barking noisily. Then there were the bears: 'Came another great bear, as if she had smelt that we would be gone and desired first to have a taste of us; for this was the third day running that the bears set so fiercely upon us that we were obliged to leave our work and run for the house.' But they would not have survived without the odd bear that they killed, nor without the foxes and the fat-bearing walrus.

Two men died; the others were weak with scurvy, poor food and exhaustion. Barents himself was prostrate and helpless. Spring came slowly and winter fought stubbornly against retreat; but in May the ice began to break up fast. The boats were made ready. Early in June a fair spell set in. They loaded the boats with supplies and on 13 June they set forth.

There were fourteen men in the two boats, which were open to the weather and vulnerable to every jagged ice floe. When a storm blew up they just managed to reach land, saving their little craft from being smashed to pieces among the tossing ice. But they had well over a thousand miles to travel, across the open sea. 'Every minute of every hour we saw death before our eyes.' When it grew calm they launched the boats again. As they rounded the north cape of Novaya Zemlya, Barents asked two of his men to raise him up to take a last glance at the 'cursed land' where he had spent ten terrible months. Later the same day he asked for a drink and having swallowed it he suddenly fell back. The pupils of his eyes turned up. He was dead.

Two more men died on this amazing voyage, but the unheralded commander of the expedition, Jacob van Heemskerck, remained and, late in August, he led them to a landfall on the Kola Peninsula where they met Jan Cornelis Rjp, who had come to look for them. In October they were back in Amsterdam. 'Men wondered to see us, having believed us long ago to have been dead and rotten . . . and in our homes men were wont ever after to call on us to rehearse our journey, both our voyages and our adventures, and marvel.'

Barents's well-built house stood alone on the shores of Novaya Zemlya. The blizzards howled around it, the planks warped at last and snow filtered in. The bears came and scattered the contents.

A Norwegian fishing boat, 282 years after the death of Willem Barents, took advantage of a mild year to sail round the north of Novaya Zemlya and, caught by a sudden change in the weather, she put into Ice Haven. There her crew found the remains of Barents' house. There, still, were pots and pans, swords and guns, even musical instruments and the old, long-defunct ship's clock. Later investigation turned up Barents's log, pathetically hopeful books about China, and a trunk containing religious prints to assist the pagans of Cathay into the true way of Christianity. Perhaps some objects were overlooked; if so, they are probably still there.

The failure of Barents' expedition to find the Northeast Passage coincided with a successful Dutch voyage to the East Indies and the establishment of the Dutch East India Company. Freed from the confining grip of Spain, the Netherlands embarked enthusiastically upon the southern trade routes. The short but spectacular Dutch assault upon the Arctic seaways was over.

Eskimos in kayaks approach a visiting ship off the western coast of Greenland. Relations between their 16th-century forbears and the early English explorers were not always friendly though Davis (who reached a point not far south of this spot) showed that a little common sense and forbearance were more effective than Frobisher's guns and bluster.

The Quest for Trade Routes: the 17th Century

Choked by bureaucracy and sick from over-indulgence on the fruits of empire, the glittering giant that was Habsburg Spain was already staggering when, to the English, he seemed most menacing. The Armada was the beginning, not the end, of Spain's war with England, but after the ships of 1588 had been scattered, Philip II was never able to mount a new assault. As the threat from Spain receded, the English renewed their search for the Northwest Passage. The treaty of 1604 that closed hostilities marked no triumphant victory for the English but, like many diplomatic documents, it was significant for what it failed to mention. In particular, nothing was said of the Spanish monopoly in the New World. The first English colony in North America was founded soon afterwards, and the search for the North-west Passage was intensified.

In 1601, the East India Company commissioned 'one George Waymouth, a navigator', to search for 'the North-West passage to the East Indies'. Waymouth (or Weymouth) was not successful in this endeavour and his voyage is of no great interest in itself. But it happens that the organization of his expedition, which may be regarded as representative of the many similar expeditions in the following thirty years, is well recorded.

The project was first put before the Council of the East India Company by Waymouth himself. It was well received, and a committee was appointed to take charge of equipping the expedition. On a vote, it was decided that members of the company should subscribe what sum they liked, and should be rewarded proportionately from the profits of the voyage. In conference with Waymouth, the committee decided that two ships, one of fifty tons and one of forty, would be enough, with total crew of thirty. The cost was estimated at £3,000, 'or thereabouts'.

Legal problems then arose. The Muscovy Company still claimed exclusive rights in northern routes and proved awkward when the East India Company suggested a combined operation; both sides no doubt suspected financial skulduggery. The opinion of learned counsel was obtained, and complaints were lodged with the Privy Council. Finally, the Muscovy Company backed down.

Two ships were hired that fitted the agreed specifications, the *Godspeed* and the fifty-five-ton *Discovery* (of which more will be heard). Another committee was appointed to oversee their fitting out.

Waymouth was allowed £100 to spend on navigational instruments. This was probably adequate, although rather less than the sum expended on beer (£120 3s. 0d.). The total expenditure on provisions appears to have been in the neighbourhood of £800, a surprisingly large sum (the expedition was expected to be away 'one year at the least'). Clothing was also costly: '31 pairs of leather breeches, furred with white lambskins, at 18s 6d per pair; and 6 pairs of another description at 5s 8d per pair; 30 cassocks of the like material and similarly furred, at 19s each; with 30 hoods to fasten to the cassocks, at 5s 3d each; 30 leather gowns lined with frieze, at £1 2s 9d each; 30 pairs of leather mittens, furred, at 1s 6d per pair', and so on, down to '£6 for chest and cords' and '48 dozen of leather points at 1d per dozen'. Pay for the crew varied from £6 for William Cobreath, second in command, to 28s. for the lower-paid mariners. Waymouth himself was to get £500 for finding the passage; if he failed he would get nothing. But he was allowed expenses–£6 for journeys between London and Devon to hire seamen. Other incidental expenses included £6 13s. 4d. to 'Mr Seger for writing her Majestie letters to the Emperor of China and Cathay'.

At the beginning of May 1602 Captain Waymouth brought his two little ships down the Thames and set out for Greenland, which was sighted in mid-June. They reached Davis Strait, where the weather gave them a rough welcome. Violent storms were followed by dense fog and, in the evening, 'a great noise as though it had been the breach of some shore'. On closer inspection, Waymouth 'found it to be the noyse of a great quantity of ice, very loathsome to be heard'. The sails and tackle were 'so hard frozen that it did seem very strange, being in the chiefest time of summer'.

Waymouth had undertaken not to return for at least a year, but his crew had seen enough of the conditions in two months–and in 'the chiefest part of the summer' at that – to regard the prospect of winter in these inhospitable climes as intolerable. Not unreasonably they told Waymouth they would go no farther. A thousand miles from home and civilization, with no witnesses and the possibility of retribution distant, the risk that ill-paid, undisciplined seamen would mutiny was always present in the age of discovery. It took a remarkably strong personality, a Drake or a Frobisher, to maintain undisputed authority, and even those captains had disciplinary problems at one time or another.

The mutiny against Waymouth was led by his own second in command and – of all people – the ship's chaplain; as they were supported by the entire crew he had little choice but to follow their desire to return to England. In his report, Waymouth says: 'I sent for the chiefest of those which were the cause . . . and punished them severely.' But as 'North-West' Foxe remarked, some years later, 'This doth not appear [reasonable] that he could punish, and yet suffer them to carry the ship back.' There are one or two other remarks in Waymouth's account which arouse a faint suspicion that he was not so reluctant to give in to the mutineers as he wanted his employers to believe.

As Waymouth returned ignominiously to Dartmouth less than four months after sailing from the Thames, the ships of another northern nation were about to appear in the North Atlantic sea lanes. Christian IV, the young, ambitious, attractive, but maddening King of Denmark, had only twenty-two ships in his navy in 1596; fourteen years later he had three times as many, some of them built to his own design. Among the less disastrous of his plans for advancing the power of Denmark was his effort to re-establish contact with the lost Icelandic settlements in Greenland. Beginning in 1605, a number of Danish expeditions were sent to Greenland. Navigators could not be trained as quickly as ships could be built, and Christian's commanders were often English or Scots. James Hall sailed on three expeditions and mapped parts of the west coast, but his promising work of exploration was diverted by the same silly notion that had sidetracked Frobisher – except that Hall's 'precious' ore was supposed to be silver rather than gold. In 1612 Hall made a fourth voyage, to Greenland; this was an English voyage, with William Baffin as pilot. Hall was recognized by a relative of one of the Eskimos he had killed or kidnapped six years before, and stabbed fatally through the liver.

Another professional sailor who worked for the Danes and the English was John Knight. He was hired by the East India and Muscovy Companies to make another search for the Northwest Passage, and sailed in the *Hopewell* in 1606. He was accompanied by that tireless Dutchman, Olivier Brunel, who had sailed the Barents Sea before Barents and possibly travelled more miles in unknown waters than any other man of his

The grim end of Henry Hudson, abandoned with his son and loyal members of his crew in the bay he discovered. No one knows what Hudson really looked like. From a painting by J. Collier.

The title-page of Captain Fox's account of the search for the Northwest Passage.

NORTH-VVEST FOX,
OR,
Fox *from the North-west passage*.
BEGINNING
VVith King ARTHVR, MALGA, OCTHVR,
the two ZENIS of *Iseland, Estotiland*, and *Dorgia*; Following with briefe Abstracts of the Voyages of *Cabot, Frobisher, Davis, Waymouth, Knight, Hudson, Button, Gibbons, Bylot, Baffin, Hawkridge* : Together with the Courses, Distance, Latitudes, Longitudes, Variations, Depths of Seas, Sets of Tydes, Currents, Races, and over-Falls; with other Observations, Accidents and remarkable things, as our Miseries and sufferings.

Mr. IAMES HALL's three Voyages to *Groynland*, with a *Topographicall description of the Countries*, the Salvages lives and Treacheries, how our Men have beene slayne by them there, with the Commodities of all those parts; whereby the Marchant may have Trade, and the Mariner Imployment.

Demonstrated in a Polar Card, wherein are all the Maines, Seas, and Ilands, herein mentioned.

With the Author his owne Voyage, being the XVIth. with the opinions and Collections of the most famous Mathematicians, and Cosmographers; with a Probabilitie to prove the same by Marine Remonstrations, compared by the Ebbing and Flowing of the Sea, experimented with places of our owne Coast.

By Captaine LVKE FOXE *of* Kingstone *vpon* Hull, Capt. and Pylot for the Voyage, in his Majesties Pinnace the CHARLES.

Printed by his Majesties Command.

LONDON,
Printed by B. ALSOP and THO. FAVVCET, dwelling in *Grubstreet*, 1635.

time, except Hudson. Unfortunately, the voyage 'did not prove one of discovery. The results were the loss of the master and of some of the crew: peril, excessive toil, with severe hardship to the rest of the people; and unmitigated disappointment to the projectors'. In other words, it was not untypical of voyages in search of the Northwest Passage at the time. The precise details of Knight's end are not known. He disappeared

An alleged 'true portrait' of Captain Thomas James, looking just a little frayed after numerous calamities during his voyage to Hudson Bay.

along with two companions on an island in Labrador; foul play was suspected.

The London merchants, not discouraged, looked about for another captain to renew the task. The man they picked was Henry Hudson; it is safe to assume that he was an experienced navigator, but apart from that nothing can be said about the man who, between 1607 and 1612, established his reputation as perhaps the greatest English maritime explorer before Cook.

The record of Hudson's voyages confirms his reputation as a skilful navigator, and from that record, some of it compiled by persons of doubtful integrity, his character must be inferred. He is generally said to have been a mild and amiable man. He certainly treated the Algonkins with greater consideration than was common, and the fights that did take place between his men and the Indians may have been another symptom of what was obviously Hudson's gravest fault as a captain–his inability to retain control of his men in times of stress.

Hudson's greatest discoveries were made in regions south of the Arctic Circle, but all his voyages were in search of a northern passage and in the course of them he added more to men's knowledge of the Arctic fringes than any man

between Barents and Baffin.

Like all good explorers, Hudson was a man of ideas. His theories about the northern passage may have been wrong, but geographical discoveries are often made in the pursuit of erroneous notions. Once the discoveries have been made, the original theory is unimportant anyway. Thus in 1607 Hudson, in the employment of the Muscovy Company, aimed to reach the Far East by sailing directly north. This may seem a mad idea now, but there was a common belief at the time that the Arctic ice was a barrier beyond which lay clear water with the North Pole, whether or not in the form of a great black rock as Nicholas of Lynn had believed in the 14th century, situated in the middle of a mild and placid sea. (This belief was still current 300 years later.)

Following the edge of the ice pack, Hudson sailed north along the east coast of Greenland and across to Spitsbergen, where he crossed the 80th parallel. This was the farthest north that any man had ventured in that part of the world, and Hudson's record stood unbroken for over 150 years. Having failed to find a likely passage farther north, he turned for home and on the way discovered Jan Mayen Island, named after a later Dutch explorer. Hudson's name for the island was 'Hudson's Touches'; he had a gift for attractive names (Isles of God's Mercy, Hold with Hope Bay, and Desire Provoked–a land that he liked the look of but did not visit) although like all his contemporaries he felt compelled also to label the globe with the names of his patrons (Salisbury's Foreland). On arriving in England, Hud-

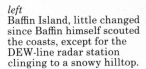
son submitted an enthusiastic report on the prospects for whaling and fishing in the area of Spitsbergen, which gave a sharp impetus to the infant whaling industry.

In the same ship, the *Hopewell*, Hudson sailed the following year in search of the Northeast Passage. One advantage he had over Barents in this region was his possession of Barents's own charts (just as Barents had an advantage over *his* predecessor, Pet, in the shape of Pet's log). Attempting the northern passage, he was blocked by ice, and in sailing down the coast of Novaya Zemlya he somehow missed the narrow Matochkin Channel. The third alternative was the southern route, but the crew, in spite of the pleasant sight of a cruising mermaid (possibly a friendly seal) were unwilling to hazard their lives in more battles with the ice and Hudson returned defeated. One of the leaders of the mutineers on this ominous occasion was the ship's mate, Robert Juet. It seems strange that Hudson should have ever sailed again with this man who, apart from being mutinous, was no longer young. Yet Robert Juet, along with Henry Greene, a young layabout whom Hudson took along as an act of kindness, was among the leaders of the mutiny in Hudson Bay four years later.

The Muscovy Company was slow to renew Hudson's contract after his second failure to find the passage, and he was lured across the North Sea by the Dutch geographer Plancius, backed by the money of the Dutch East India Company. The project was for another attempt on the Northeast Passage, round Novaya Zemlya. In the gelid Barents Sea Hudson's crew again became restless, but rather than return so soon to Amsterdam, they agreed to their captain's suggestion that they sail west and look for the North*west* Passage. In high northern latitudes, the distance between Europe and America is, of course, relatively small, yet this was surely an extraordinary change of plan, as if the technicians at Cape Kennedy, having fired a rocket to Mars, should decide when it was half-way there to switch it to Venus instead.

Hudson was personally more interested in the Northwest Passage than the Northeast which had defeated him two years earlier, and he was probably anxious to investigate the theory, warmly advocated by Richard Hakluyt among others, that a passage existed in Virginia (the name then encompassed a far larger region than the modern state). He thought he had found this passage in the river that bears his name, but having sailed up it nearly as far as the site of Albany, he realized his error and returned. The Dutch were later to found New Amsterdam (New York) on the pleasant, wooded island of Manhattan at the mouth of Hudson's river.

On his way back, Hudson put into an English port and was prevented from returning to Holland. The Dutch were becoming powerful rivals to English commerce and the authorities could at least prevent English captains assisting them. Hudson's voyage had made a great impression in England, and he was promptly hired to make another attempt at the Northwest Passage. This was the voyage on which the *Discovery* (Waymouth's old ship) sailed the length of Hudson Strait, which had frightened off many a bold captain since Frobisher, and down Hudson Bay to its south-east corner, where Hudson was compelled to spend the winter. When the ice melted in June (1611) the *Discovery* floated free, but long-simmering discontent among the crew broke into mutiny. Hudson, his young son and five others were abandoned in an open boat, without oars, in the middle of the bay. Nothing was ever heard of them afterwards.

The thirteen mutineers sailed back to England, pursued by vengeful Fates. The story of their grim voyage might have inspired Coleridge's *The Rime of the Ancient Mariner* (in fact said to be based partly on the experiences of Captain James in 1631–32 as well as the Pacific voyage of the privateer *Shelvocke* in 1718–22 during which the albatross incident occurred). Four were killed by Eskimos and Robert Juet died of starvation. Nine scarecrows survived in the creaking *Discovery* to reach an Irish port. They were sentenced to hang, but the sentence was never carried out and one of them, Robert Bylot, an experienced sailor who may have been a reluctant participant in the mutiny, survived to take a prominent part in later voyages. So did the *Discovery*.

In fact, both sailor and ship took part in Sir Thomas Button's 1612–13 expedition in search of Hudson and the passage. Button found no trace of the missing explorer, but on this and a second voyage in 1615 he ranged the western shore of Hudson Bay, wintering at Port Nelson and losing one of his ships. He found no exit to the Pacific from Hudson Bay, and appropriately named the point where he reached its western shore Hopes Checked. Hopes were checked but not destroyed, and for fear that rivals might make use of Button's discoveries, his employers suppressed all news of his voyage including his own report, which has never turned up, depriving Button of the attention he deserves. Meanwhile, other voyages were taking place. The *Discovery* made the least eventful of her numerous Atlantic crossings under the command of Captain Gibbons, a man untroubled by aspirations to fame, who sailed into a secure though icebound Labrador bay and was so reluctant (or unable) to leave it that his crew named the place 'Gibbons' Hole'.

The great Baffin, whose early life (like Hudson's) is a complete blank, was also building up experience in two voyages to Spitsbergen, where the whaling was proving as profitable as Hudson had reckoned and the English were doing their best to keep out all foreigners, chiefly Dutch and French, who trespassed on what they chose to regard as their private property.

Baffin is known to history only in the last ten years of his life (1612–22), but it was an eventful decade, covering seven important voyages. Although the first five of these were all in Arctic waters, the great advances he made in polar exploration belong chiefly to the fifth voyage, in 1616. Unfortunately, the records of this voyage are far from complete. The Reverend Samuel Purchas, unworthy successor to Hakluyt as chief chronicler of English voyages, noted in his edition of Baffin's travels that the 'map of the author, with the tables of his journal and sailing were somewhat troublesome and too costly to insert', a remark that Sir Clements Markham described, with admirable restraint, as 'exasperating'. As a result of this injudicious editing, the true extent of Baffin's discoveries

was soon forgotten. In a map published in 1818 'Baffin's Bay' is vaguely indicated with a note 'according to the relation of Wm Baffin but not now believed', while in Sir John Barrow's *History of Arctic Voyages*, also published in 1818, Baffin Bay is not shown at all. Not until Ross and Parry followed the same route did Baffin regain his place as one of the greatest of Arctic explorers of the early period.

With Bylot as captain and Baffin as pilot, the *Discovery* (her sixth transatlantic voyage) left England in March 1616. The expedition was mounted by the North-West Company, formed after Hudson's voyage of 1612, and its object was to search for a Northwest Passage off Davis Strait. (The same team had exhausted the possibilities of Hudson Bay the previous year.) By the beginning of June, the *Discovery* was at Sanderson's Hope, 'the farthest land Master Davis was at'. Cautiously, Baffin navigated farther north, exchanging iron and beads for skins and meat provided by Eskimos, observing many 'sea unicorns' (narwhals) and finding a dead whale from which the sailors removed most of the whalebone before a storm broke the ropes binding the great corpse to the ship. In July they passed a cape named for Sir Dudley Digges, one of their chief backers; then on past Wolsten-holme Sound and to the place they called Whale Sound (for obvious reasons), where the ship was damaged in a violent storm. Farther north, Baffin observed a compass variation of 56°, 'a thing almost incredible and matchless in all the world beside'. He must have been close to the magnetic pole.

'On the eighth day it cleared up, and seeing a company of islands lie off from the shore twelve or thirteen leagues, we minded to go to them to see if there we could anchor. When we were something near, the wind took us short, and being loth to spend more time, we took opportunity of the wind, and left the searching of these islands, which ... the map doth truly describe [this is the map that Purchas could not be bothered to print]. So we stood to the westward in an open sea, with a stiff gale of wind, all the next day and

A gigantic double-stemmed mushroom cruising off the coast of Baffin Island. Early Arctic explorers were more impressed by the physical force of icebergs than by the beauty of their forms.

till the tenth day of July at one or two o'clock in the morning, at which time it fell calm and very foggy, and we near the land in the entrance of a fair sound, which we called Alderman Jones Sound.' Baffin had sailed through – or round – the ice in Baffin Bay, a feat not repeated until the 19th century. His plain account makes it seem absurdly simple; in fact he was incredibly lucky – as well as skilful.

The *Discovery* sailed south until 'On the twelfth day we were open of another great sound, lying in the latitude of 70°20′ [Baffin's measurements were nearly always astonishingly accurate], and we called it Sir James Lancaster's Sound; here our hope of passage began to be less every day. . . .'

An unconsciously ironic remark – for Lancaster Sound is the opening to the Northwest Passage, for what it's worth. In fact, the result of Baffin's great voyage, in which he sailed round the limits of the huge northern bay named after him, was to convince him that the passage did not exist. In a letter to Sir John Wolstenholme he wrote, 'I intend to show the whole proceeding of the voyage in a word: as namely, there is no passage nor hope of passage in the north of Davis Straits.'

This was the end of Baffin's Arctic explorations. He made two voyages as pilot for the East India Company, on the second of which he was 'slain in fight with a shot', characteristically, 'as he was trying his mathematical projects and conclusions'.

Baffin, as his recorded measurements and one surviving map show, was a navigator of outstanding skill and resource – a really constructive explorer in the mould of Hudson. In particular, he was more successful than any of his predecessors in calculating longitude by astronomical measurements in conjunction with a set of nautical tables. He appears to have been the first to take lunar observations at sea.

It would be tidy to end the first assault of the English upon the Arctic with William Baffin, the most accomplished explorer of the age whose negative report dampened interest in the Northwest Passage for two hundred years, but it is impossible to ignore completely the voyages of Luke Foxe and his rival – and inferior – Captain Thomas James.

Luke Foxe, or 'North-West' Foxe as he preferred to be called, is one of the most endearing of the supporting players in the cast of Arctic explorers. He was described by a 19th-century editor as 'a native of Yorkshire: a shrewd man, somewhat conceited and given to pedantry, but of a generous disposition'. He was also a wit; but his eccentricities did not extend to matters of seamanship. Indeed, few men have prepared more thoroughly for an expedition of discovery than Foxe did during the long years he spent trying to raise support for a voyage to the north-west.

Thanks to the influence of Sir Thomas Button

he was eventually provided with a royal ship, the *Charles*, and set off on his quest in May 1631. He sailed through Hudson Strait and across the bay, having some trouble with icebergs on the way, and made a thorough inspection of the Bay. Among other places, he gave Wellcome Island its name. In September he turned north again, passing through Foxe Channel and into Foxe Basin as far as 67° North. But it was a 'scurvy voyage', a remark meant literally: half his crew were sick. Towards the end of the month he turned back and reached England without further incident. It was an exemplary expedition which, though failing like all others to discover the passage, nevertheless added a sizeable chunk to the map of northern Canada.

While Foxe was preparing to fulfil his lifelong ambition, the merchants of Bristol commissioned Captain Thomas James to undertake a voyage to the same quarter. It was suggested that the two expeditions might combine, but in the event James sailed separately, leaving England two days before Foxe. Unlike Foxe's, James' voyage was an unmitigated disaster. He reached Hudson Bay after several close calls and sailed south into James Bay. To prevent his ship being crushed by ice, he was forced to sink her in shallow water and spent the winter on Charlton Island. Several of his men died of scurvy, and James himself was almost killed in a fire which got out of control after being lit as a signal. He finally reached England in a ship that was on the point of falling to pieces. No doubt he had bad luck, but Foxe's judgement that his rival was 'no seaman' seems to be based on accurate observation.

For James and Foxe had met in Hudson Bay before the worst of James' troubles had begun, and although the meeting was superficially friendly, 'North-West' Foxe's entertainment to dinner on James' ship was, from his account, something of a shambles. As there was not room enough in the cabin they dined between decks and, the ship being poorly stationed, water poured in freely. As Foxe acidly remarked, 'sauce would not have been wanted if there had been roast mutton'. Yet Foxe was not sure that the continual drenching of James' men was bad for them. He wondered 'whether it were better for James' company to be impounded amongst ice, where they might be kept from putrefaction by piercing air, or in open sea to be kept sweet by being thus pickled'. Their ship, he observed, took 'her liquor as kindly as themselves, for her nose was no sooner out of the pitcher, but her neb, like the duck's, was in't again'.

Although Foxe was a far better captain than James, he was a poorer, or at any rate a slower, writer. James brought his well-written account out swiftly and was acclaimed as a great hero. Foxe was ignored, and when he at last published his book, an intriguing mixture of euphuistic descriptions, practical seamanship and humorous asides, it made not a ripple. He died soon afterwards, a disappointed man.

The Russians in the North

The English and the Dutch, in their search for trade routes, were compelled to probe the Arctic for a sea passage but they entered Arctic waters with reluctance. There was one country in the 17th century with a closer interest in the Arctic – Russia, through whose northern lands the Arctic Circle runs for over 5,000 miles. Siberia became Russian in the late 16th century, although vast stretches of country were still unaware of the existence of St Petersburg 200 years later. The Cossacks pushed steadily farther east and were established on the Pacific coast by the end of the 17th century. The story is no less exciting (and no less bloody) than the conquest of the American West, although it is not so well known. No doubt many great pioneering journeys are lost to history, or linger only in local folklore; some doubt still hovers about the voyage of Simon Dezhnev, the first man to sail round the East Cape (Cape Dezhnev) and through Bering Strait.

In the summer of 1648 Dezhnev journeyed from the Kolyma River to the Anadyr River. The question is: did he go by sea or did he travel overland – a much shorter and easier journey? For a hundred years after 1648 Dezhnev's voyage was lost to view (Bering probably never heard of him) and his claim was only uncovered by a historian named G. F. Muller working in Yakutsk in the 18th century. What has made many people doubt the Dezhnev story is the extreme difficulty of such a voyage. Dezhnev's boat was a flat-bottomed *koch*, a simple vessel not much larger than a sailing dinghy and untouched by anything so modern as an iron nail; the distance, assuming Dezhnev stuck close to land, is over 2,000 miles and he seems to have made a perilously late start. Until the days of steam power, no one else was able to accomplish the voyage.

If Dezhnev is granted benefit of the doubt, then his voyage is one of the most extraordinary in the

Arctic Siberia near the mouth of the great Yenisey River. In 1737 Ovtzin and his crew, having rounded the Gydaskiy Peninsula, became the first men to sail into the Yenisey from the Arctic Ocean.

Peter the Great (1672–1725) looking as thoroughly Western as he wished his country to be. His famous order to Bering in 1724, phrased with characteristic directness and determination, laid the basis for Russia's sustained and tireless exploration of her great northern territories.

history of Arctic exploration, but just as the English knew nothing of the Vikings who had preceded them in Greenland waters, so the great exploration of Siberia by the Russians in the mid-18th century was carried out in ignorance of the feat of the Cossack Dezhnev.

Peter the Great was determined to force his people into the 18th century if he in person had to cut off the ancient beards of his councillors to emphasize the necessity of being up to date. He travelled in western Europe, observing, inquiring, learning; he heard how French and English, Portuguese and Spanish, Dutch and Danish ships were expanding the boundaries of the world. Back in his new capital, Peter regarded with interest the pelts sent back from eastern Siberia by pioneering Cossacks and encouraged the extension of Russian authority over the Siberian tribes. The conquest was not easy: the Koriaks, living in the region of the Anadyr River, fought to the last man, woman or child; they had acquired guns and were better fighters than the Russians.

Peter was interested in knowledge as well as power. Like the most learned geographers of western Europe, he was intrigued by the unsolved problems of the northern Pacific (an area that appeared on contemporary maps in many forms–all wildly wrong). Several men were sent to investigate; the orders of two who travelled east in 1719 stated: 'You are to go to Kamchatka and farther . . . and determine whether Asia and America are united; and go not only north and south but east and west, and put on a chart all that you see.' They chose to go south first, to the partly explored Kuril Islands, but lost their anchors in a storm and returned. The Tsar was soon planning another expedition, and the man he chose to lead it this time was a Dane, Vitus Bering.

Bering was born in 1681 and entered the naval service of Russia at the age of twenty-three. In the twenty years that passed before his appointment by Peter the Great, he acquired great experience in navigation, a knowledge of Far Eastern waters, and a number of influential friends. He was to prove a man of great determination and courage although not a dynamic leader. His two chief assistants were Martin Spanberg, another Dane who was later to complete the charting of the whole chain of the Kuril Islands, and a bold Russian, Alexei Chirikov.

Peter the Great's instructions to Bering were drawn up at the end of 1724 in a memorandum that has become one of the most famous documents of Arctic exploration. It was simple and to the point:

1. To build in Kamchatka or in some other place one or two decked boats.
2. To sail on these boats along the shore which runs to the north and which (as its limits are unknown) seems to be a part of the American coast.
3. To determine where it joins with America. To sail to some settlement under European jurisdiction, and if a European ship should be met with learn from her the name of the coast and take it down in writing, make a landing, obtain detailed information, draw a chart and bring it here.

Within a few weeks of signing this order Peter the Great died, and for most of the next eighty years Russia was ruled by a series of more or less extraordinary women. The plans that Peter had made for opening up the Far East were carried forward and eventually extended considerably.

Bering left St Petersburg shortly before the Tsar's death. He contemplated a difficult voyage in unknown but assuredly dangerous waters, but the voyage was as yet a distant prospect. Before

left
Bering's map (1729) of his
first expedition to the strait
named after him, attrac-
tively embellished with
scenes from the life of
Siberian tribes. Bering's
map helped to fill in the
enormous blank of the
northern coastline, soon to
be determined by the Great
Northern Expedition.

it could begin, he had to travel the entire breadth
of Russia, from the Baltic to the Pacific, and he
had to take with him virtually everything bar the
actual wood that he would need to build his ships.
He travelled by water as far as possible, in long
stages. The winter of 1725–26 was spent at
Ilimsk; Yakutsk, the only sizeable town in the
whole of Asian Siberia, was reached at the
beginning of June 1726. This was the last place
for loading up with raw materials, so the hardest
part of the journey–from Yakutsk through
swamps and over mountains to the Sea of
Okhotsk–had to be undertaken with the most
cumbersome baggage train. Most of the horses
died, either of cold or starvation, but by 1 October
Bering had reached the little group of huts that
was the settlement of Okhotsk, where he spent
the second winter watching his carpenters build
a boat. In August 1727 he crossed the Sea of
Okhotsk to the Peninsula of Kamchatka though,
oddly, he elected to sail to the western edge of
the peninsula and to proceed overland to the
place chosen for the starting point of his voyage
on the south-eastern coast. It would have been
simpler to go the whole way by sea, but the route
was not known and Bering, for all his bravery a
cautious man, did not wish to take unnecessary
risks. Another boat, the *St Gabriel*, sixty feet
long, was built in Kamchatka and in July 1728,
nearly three and a half years since leaving St
Petersburg, Bering ventured into the sea which
was to be named after him.

For about four weeks he sailed north-east
along the coast, keeping near the land and making rather slow progress, until contact was made
with a group of Chukchi in the Anadyr Gulf.
Bering invited them on board and after some
hesitation one man, bolder than the rest, swam
over to the *St Gabriel* on inflated bladders. He
told Bering that the coast they were following

would lead them eventually to the mouth of the
Kolyma, which flowed into a sea that 'always
had ice in it'. Bering continued to sail north and
a day or two later discovered, and named, the
island of St Lawrence. Having reached 65°30′
latitude without sighting more land, and with
the knowledge that winter was approaching,
Bering consulted with his officers. Should they
sail on or turn back? Spanberg was in favour of
continuing north until the middle of the month
in the hope of reaching the 66th parallel;
Chirikov pointed out that 'as we have no positive
information as to the degree north latitude
Europeans have ever reached in the Arctic
Ocean on the Asiatic side we cannot know with
certainty whether America is really separated
from Asia unless we touch at the mouth of the
Kolyma, or at least the ice, because it is well
known that there is always ice in the Arctic
Ocean'. He was for pressing on.

Perhaps predictably, Bering preferred the conservative advice of his fellow countryman, and
on the appointed day turned about and set his
course for Kamchatka. The *St Gabriel* was then
at a position 67°18′ North and 193°7′ East, well
to the north of East Cape. He had thus passed
through the Bering Strait, and but for persistent
mists he would have had the exciting experience
that Captain Cook enjoyed half a century later of
seeing America on one hand and Asia on the
other.

The following summer the *St Gabriel* made a
short voyage to the east in search of an island
that was spoken of by the natives of Kamchatka.
Bering narrowly missed seeing the island now
named after him, on which he was to land in less
happy circumstances thirteen years later. Instead he returned to Okhotsk and began the
journey back to St Petersburg to deliver his
report.

His reception was mixed. He had been commissioned, his critics said, to establish whether
or not Asia and America were joined, but he had
failed in his task. His *impression* that the coastline fell away to the west north of 67° latitude and
the report of local tribesmen did not add up to the
definite proof that was required. In a fit of pique,
the government held back Bering's salary. Still,
Bering had friends at court and plenty of supporters among the young scientists, mostly
imported–like Bering himself–from abroad,
whom Peter the Great had installed in the
capital. When he produced plans for a second
expedition they were accepted, in fact they were
considerably enlarged, and Bering found himself put in overall charge of the project that became known as the Great Northern Expedition,
the largest exploratory expedition in polar
regions until Operation Highjump.

Meanwhile, Bering's ship the *St Gabriel* had
made another voyage in the Bering Sea.

This strange exploit began with an attempt by
a Cossack leader named Shestakov to augment
his political prestige by volunteering to suppress

the Chukchi of north-eastern Siberia. The government provided him with 1500 men, a mathematician and geographer Michael Gvosdev, and a co-commander, Pavlutsky, with whom he exchanged insults if not blows all the way across Russia. Shestakov's confidence was not well placed. He met the Chukchi in the neighbourhood of Penzhinsk Bay and was decisively defeated. Wounded in the neck by a Chukchi arrow, Shestakov managed to scramble on to a reindeer sledge, but the animal being the property of the Chukchi it carried the protesting Cossack straight to the Chukchi camp where he was swiftly dispatched. Pavlutsky, meanwhile, was still in Yakutsk; although he was to prove a far more capable subjugator of the Chukchi than his rival, he came to the same end – the Chukchi kept his head for a long time as a trophy. Gvosdev, with others, was at Okhotsk, whence he continued with the other aims of the expedition, one of which was to sail in search of the 'Large Country' vaguely said to lie north or east of Siberia. (The persistence of rumours concerning the 'Large Country' suggests that the Chukchi knew of the existence of the mainland across the Bering Strait long before the Russians discovered it.)

His superiors being sick, Gvosdev was in effective command of this part of the expedition, and he set out in Bering's *St Gabriel* in 1732. He was gone two months, and there seems little doubt that he did indeed reach the 'Large Country', which he supposed to be an island but which was in fact the American mainland. Gvosdev's report was lost and his voyage might have vanished from history but for the chance remarks of a sailor at a court martial in St Petersburg which prompted inquiries by the Imperial Admiralty College. Gvosdev then wrote a second

report, but in the interval ten years had passed and Bering had completed his voyage to Alaska.

The suggestions that Bering put forward regarding a second expedition were largely concerned with economic matters – mining in Siberia, cattle-raising in Kamchatka, etc. The lines he suggested future exploration should pursue were: a voyage from Kamchatka to determine how far America was from Asia; a search for a sea route to the Amur River and Japan (later carried out by Martin Spanberg); thirdly, Bering said, the Siberian coast from the Ob to the Lena could be mapped, 'if it should be considered wise', either by small boats or by land.

In common with many other explorers before and since, Bering had suffered from the tendency of officials leading a comfortable life in a large city to expect superhuman efforts from those sent forth to battle with nature in her fiercest aspect; no man has ever had to contend with more inefficiency, jealousy, selfishness and general idleness than Bering on his second expedition. Yet Bering did not have to struggle with a government intent on saving money or 'playing safe'; he was not treated, as ambitious explorers usually are, as a wild and unreliable fellow whose plans outreached his capacity. On the contrary, Bering had the uncommon experience of seeing his suggestions enthusiastically embraced.

Some of his propositions were modified in the light of the advice given by Chirikov; for example, it was decided that the boats should be built not in Kamchatka, as Bering preferred, but at Okhotsk. But Bering's rather half-hearted remarks about exploring the northern coast from the Ob to the Lena 'if it should be considered wise' were turned into a mighty project to explore the entire coast from Archangel to the Anadyr. Bering, promoted to captain-commander, was given overall charge of this project except for the stretch between Archangel and the Ob, which was under the direct control of the Imperial Admiralty College, but as he was increasingly preoccupied with his own effort to reach America he had little to do with the other sectors.

The work of mapping the northern Siberian coast was divided into five sections: the first from Archangel to the Ob; the second from the Ob to the Yenisey; the third and fourth were to converge on the forbidding Taymyr Peninsula from the Yenisey and the Lena respectively; the fifth was to tackle the stretch between the Lena and the Anadyr. The Imperial Admiralty College allowed two years for the completion of this enormous task, a highly optimistic estimate. The job was not finished in ten years, but during that time the young Russian officers who undertook it came very near to complete success in what was one of the largest and most difficult explorations ever attempted. 'Nowhere,' said Fridtjof Nansen, 'have travellers gone through so many sufferings, or evinced so much endurance.'

A Chukchi today with a young reindeer. Though more friendly to visitors, the Chukchi still live in northeast Siberia in a manner not much different from that of their forefathers, although industrial developments are inevitably bringing changes.

The first section, from the White Sea to the Gulf of Ob, was assigned to Lieutenants Muravyov and Pavlov, who left the Dvina River in two seventy-foot boats in mid-July 1734. The Kara Sea was comparatively ice-free and by late August, when they turned back for winter quarters, they had covered a large part of the western coast of the Yamal Peninsula. Next year the ice was worse, and they advanced less than a hundred miles farther. Progress was also hindered by the unfortunate fact that Pavlov and Muravyov were at each other's throats whenever they were not quarrelling with their men or the inhabitants of the town where they spent the winter. The Imperial Admiralty College impatiently reduced the pair of them to the ranks and put Lieutenant Malgin in charge. He started badly by losing one of his boats in the ice, but replacements were provided and next year he set out again.

That year, 1737, was the salvation of the Great Northern Expedition; it was a particularly mild one and seas that were normally choked by ice were free and clear. Malgin found an ice-free lead that he followed all the way to the tip of the Yamal Peninsula, rounded it at the beginning of August and in mid-October triumphantly dropped anchor at Berezovo on the Ob. From there he hastened to St Petersburg to report his victory, leaving his subordinates with the thankless task of sailing the boats back again (it took them two years).

Lieutenant Dmitri Ovtzin had a comparatively short length of coast to define from the Ob to the Yenisey, but as it took that determined young officer three years to get out of the Gulf of Ob it is evident that the journey was not an easy one. In the winter of 1735 he returned to St Petersburg to request better officers and better boats, both of which were granted. The new boat did not arrive until the spring of 1737, but in that amiable summer Ovtzin and his crew of thirty-five (crews were large in these little boats because they depended on oars as much as on their inadequate sails) rounded the cape and sailed into the Yenisey. When Ovtzin arrived in St Petersburg he received, instead of the anticipated promotion, a sharp reprimand and reduction to the ranks as a result of his association with a 'political undesirable' in Siberia (*plus ça change* . . .). He made his way east and joined Bering on his voyage to America in the *St Peter*. He survived that voyage and is last heard of fifteen years later in command of the ship *Poltava*.

The pilot of Ovtzin's ship was placed in charge of the assault on the Taymyr Peninsula from the west. He made three unsuccessful attempts in the years 1738–41, and ultimately shared the fate of many of his colleagues in losing his commission. His assistant, Strelegov, failed to accomplish the journey overland, and hopes for the conquest of Taymyr were placed in those approaching it from the east.

This part of the programme had begun earlier. In command was an uxorious young officer named Pronchishev, who was accompanied by his wife on the hazardous journey that ended in their deaths. They started in 1735 from Yakutsk. (The vast distances travelled by these explorers before they reached the coast—Ovtzin started from Tobolsk on the Irtysh—is a reminder of the utter wilderness of northern Siberia.) Reaching the sea at the beginning of August they made their way, 'steering between icebergs, polar bears and walrus', along the coast to the west. They attained a latitude of 77°30′, not so far short of their destination though they did not know it, before they had to turn round. They threaded their way back to the Olenek River, where Pronchishev and his wife died. The senior officer left was the pilot, Chelyuskin, but he did not know what to do next, since the two years originally allotted had passed. He decided to visit Bering in Yakutsk for new instructions, but on arriving there he found that Bering had moved on to Okhotsk. Chelyuskin's feelings on discovering that the commander was absent are not recorded, but after a rugged journey of nearly a thousand miles he must have been a bit cross.

At this time (1735–36) the prospects of the Great Northern Expedition were looking rather poor. By that winter, none of the five northern surveys had been completed. But in St Petersburg there was no gloomy resignation, only renewed determination: the various commanders were impressed with the necessity for success; rewards were dangled before their eyes; every effort was made to fulfil their demands for more or better equipment. Khariton Laptev, appointed as Pronchishev's successor, was told that time was unlimited, that if he could not pass the Taymyr Peninsula by sea he should try to reach its farthest cape overland. Above all, he must not fail.

Boats were overhauled, more men supplied, food stockpiled at the river mouths. In 1739 Laptev renewed the attempt. Having reached the sea without incident, his boat was at once assaulted by the Arctic. She forged through the ice, dipping left and right to avoid its jagged teeth. She reached the Khatanga, where provisions were stored, and felt her way carefully along the eastern shore of the peninsula, but at about the point where the coast turns sharply to the west, progress ended. Laptev looked for a place to spend the winter, but there was no comfort on that barren coast. His men could not even find driftwood.

They returned to the Khatanga for the winter, and in the following year set out again. Fighting a constant battle with the ice, it took them a month to reach the sea, and they had not progressed far when the boat was seized by the ice in an unbreakable grip and carried inexorably onward by a northern current. Checked by a great ice floe, the contorted vessel suddenly

began to fill with water. Efforts to lighten her failed to stop the leak, and now the boat began to drift helplessly out into what is now called the Laptev Sea. They had no choice but to abandon her, and spent a terrible night, wet, half-frozen and full of dread, upon the ice. With the morning, faint hope appeared, for the coast could be seen some fifteen miles away. They hauled themselves towards it and after a two-day trek staggered to safety of a sort. Another slight but decisive stroke of luck – the ice floe in which the boat was caught remained close to land for two weeks, and they were able to rescue what was left of their stores.

Still they would have died without the vigorous leadership and encouragement of Laptev, one of the unsung heroes (except in Russia) of the Arctic. Ill and exhausted and suffering from frostbite, they struggled back to their base where, unfortunately, several died before good food and warmth could restore them.

Laptev was not beaten. If he could not accomplish his objective by sea (which the loss of his boat had made impossible) he would do it by land. He divided his company into three teams, each accompanied by dog sledges. All were eventually to reassemble on the Taymyr River after carrying out their various assignments. The most vital journey, to the North-East (Chelyuskin) Cape, was to be undertaken by Chekin; Laptev himself and Chelyuskin led the other parties. The latter two carried out the plan successfully, but Chekin was immobilized by snow-blindness when still a long way short of his objective and had to retire. As autumn approached, the whole expedition withdrew down the Yenisey to winter at Turukhansk.

Laptev had surveyed the Taymyr Peninsula fairly thoroughly but the northernmost cape had still not been reached. For a final effort to finish the job, Laptev chose the pilot Chelyuskin, who had proved so capable a leader in 1740. Chelyuskin made an early start, and by March 1742 he was at the mouth of the Khatanga. Making good progress with his dog sledges he reached the cape that now bears his name on 17 May. By his reckoning, it was 77°34′ North, by some way the farthest point north on the Siberian mainland (though this was not yet known for certain). On his return, the triumphant Chelyuskin met Laptev coming to meet him with fresh supplies, and together they retreated for the last time up the Yenisey River, Laptev continuing on to St Petersburg and out of the pages of Arctic history.

His brother, Dmitri Laptev, arrived in St Petersburg at roughly the same time, though he had a less satisfactory report to make to the Imperial Admiralty College. Dmitri Laptev had been chosen by Bering to take charge of the fifth – and most intractable – sector of the northern coast in 1735, after the first expedition in that sector had been stricken by scurvy while wintering in Buorkhaya Bay. Laptev made little advance in 1736, and then found himself in the same quandary as Chelyuskin at that time, and with the same result: he journeyed to Yakutsk to ask Bering whether he should carry on but – no Bering. Instructions to continue eventually reached Laptev while he was on his way to make further inquiries in St Petersburg, but by the time he resumed his work he had missed the favourable summer of 1737.

In 1739 Laptev succeeded in rounding Svyatoy Nos, the first important objective in his sector. He continued east to the Indigirka, and the following year ventured some way east of the Kolyma. In 1741, with no less than forty-five dog teams, he marched overland to Anadyr. His instructions were to sail from Anadyr back to the Kolyma, rounding the notorious East Cape and finally confirming that Asia and America were separated by water, but no boat was available at Anadyr (Bering had been supposed to send one, but by this time no one knew where Bering was) so Laptev, whose own opinion was that the voyage was impossible owing to the hostility of the Chukchi and the shortness of the

Brilliant crystal splinters thrust up by the force of the spring thaw descending a Siberian river to the Arctic Ocean.

season, with some relief returned by the overland route to the Kolyma and thence to St Petersburg.

Meanwhile what of the Captain-Commander, that dogged Dane, the great Bering himself? The story of his second expedition is one of the sagas of maritime exploration, but as he sailed no farther north than latitude 60 it is only of marginal relevance to Arctic exploration.

The *St Peter*, under Bering, and the *St Paul*, under Chirikov, left the little port of Petropavlovsk (named after the ships) in June 1741, seven years after leaving St Petersburg. The ships soon became separated and proceeded independently. Bering reached Alaska in late July, but the sight of it brought him little satisfaction. Old, exhausted, scurvy-ridden and thoroughly fed up, he guided his ship back in a horrific voyage along the Aleutian chain until she was wrecked on Bering Island. The crew wintered there and got back to Kamchatka the following year in a boat they constructed from the carcass of the *St Peter*; but they left their captain on the island, where he had died in November 1741. Chirikov also reached Alaska and returned safe but not unharmed; his health was ruined and he died three years later.

Although some work continued until 1749, the Great Northern Expedition was for all practical purposes over in 1742. It was the first nationally directed, long-sustained effort in Arctic exploration, carried out to a large extent in a scientific manner. It had been costly, both in lives and money. But it was extraordinarily successful. Oddly, the one question that had not been answered was the question that, above all others, had set it in motion: were Asia and America joined or separate? Bering had never really believed they were joined and his first expedition had proved it to his satisfaction if not to that of his critics. It was generally people of a somewhat academic cast of mind who, in the years between Bering and Cook, kept insisting that the two continents had not been proved to be separate. But, in the words of F. A. Golder, apart from this unsettled controversy, 'nearly everything else of geographical interest which was undertaken was successfully carried out'. The Imperial Admiralty College had much to be proud of.

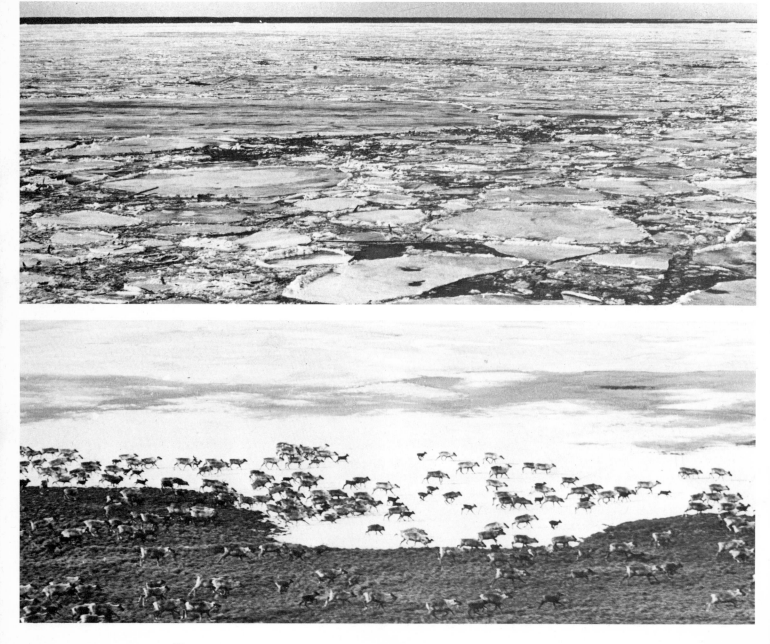

The Approach to Antarctica

'Geography is a science of facts,' wrote Louis de Bougainville in 1770, and 'in studying it, authors must by no means give way to any system formed in their studies, unless they would run the risk of being subject to very great errors which can be rectified only at the expense of navigators.' The warning would have been useful three centuries earlier. Just as the early exploration of the Arctic followed from the search for hopelessly inaccessible northern sea routes, so the European approach to the Antarctic arose from the desire to exploit an almost totally mythical continent.

Not everyone believed in *terra australis*: a rival school of thought in the 15th century held that the earth was entirely surrounded by water. But there were apparently good reasons for the existence of a large land mass in the southern hemisphere; it seemed necessary in order to balance the land in the north and prevent a lopsided world toppling over. So the myth persisted, in one form or another, for about 2,000 years. Even now, after reading the compelling arguments of its adherents, one feels a faint sense of deprivation in the knowledge that *terra australis* does not exist; as if in a detective story the murder turns out to be accidental death after all.

As Christopher Lloyd wrote, 'the curious thing about the persistence of the belief [in the Southern Continent] is not its logic, but the fact that it was held far more strongly *after* men began to sail the Pacific than *before*'. Every piece of negative evidence only stimulated men like Alexander Dalrymple, to whom proving the existence of the Southern Continent was 'the great passion of my life', to greater effort, and every voyage that lopped one piece off the 'continent' by sailing through seas where it was supposed to lie also produced new evidence that could be interpreted as suggesting its existence in another part. Thus, the famous voyage of Tasman and Visscher in 1642 proved that Australia was not part of the Southern Continent–but discovered a new land that *was* taken to be the coast of the Southern Continent; not until Cook destroyed the whole myth over a hundred years later was the true outline of New Zealand understood.

The matter would undoubtedly have been cleared up much sooner but for the peculiar difficulties of exploring the Pacific south of the tropics. Before the 19th century nearly every voyage across the Pacific went from east to west, entering the South Sea, as it was more often called, from Magellan's Strait or Drake's Passage (through which Drake did not pass, however), round Cape Horn; Tasman's voyage was a rare exception. Off southern Chile, the Humboldt Current surges steadily northward; the prevailing winds are westerly and, more often than not, very strong. It was almost impossible for a sailing ship to make any westward progress in this latitude, and more than one vessel accomplished the slow and dangerous passage of the strait only to be blown all the way back to the Atlantic. The involuntary procedure for trans-Pacific sailors therefore became–through the strait and hard a'starboard. Not until the ship approached the 30th parallel could she take advantage of the trade winds which, their direction being north-easterly, carried the ship still farther from the south.

The first man to make this journey, Magellan, believed correctly that the land on his left as he passed through the strait was an island. Nevertheless, most of the maps made after his voyage show Tierra del Fuego as a cape of the Southern Continent. When Drake repeated the feat sixty years later he was blown south by a storm, and although his *Golden Hind* did not, as once was thought, reach Cape Horn, Drake formed the opinion, whether based on observation or inference, that below South America the waters of the Pacific and the Atlantic rolled together. The weighty opinions of Magellan and Drake were nevertheless insufficient to divorce Tierra del Fuego from the Southern Continent. Of course, these early voyages, taking place in an atmosphere of intense international rivalry, were secret operations. To this day, Drake's purposes in 1577–80 are far from clear. The sailors themselves often did not know where they were going until, with their homes well behind them, their captain announced his secret instructions. This served a double purpose, for besides preventing unguarded talk before the ships sailed, it prevented hasty desertion by men reluctant to sail

into the vast and distant South Sea: both
Magellan and Drake had to quell incipient
mutinies before they could get their men to sail
through the strait, and nearly 200 years later
John ('Foul-Weather Jack') Byron, on giving his
men the bad news that they were not bound for
India but round the world, though it advisable at
the same time to double their pay (to the later
derision of Bougainville).

Gossip could be prevented before the voyage –
but not after it; by one means or another any
significant new information soon percolated to
interested parties around Europe, and the
secretiveness of governments cannot alone account for the persistence of legend in the work of
cartographers.

The first explorers of the Pacific were Spaniards,
often with Portuguese pilots like Magellan and
Quiros. Mendaña discovered the Solomon Islands
in 1568 but located them incorrectly and they
were not found again for 200 years. The elusive-
ness of the Solomons illustrates the sheer vast-
ness of the Pacific, whose total area is greater
than the world's land mass. In 1606, Quiros landed
in the New Hebrides, which he supposed to be part
of the Southern Continent, and his assistant,
Torres, on his way to the Philippines, passed
between New Guinea and Australia, proving that
New Guinea was not part of the continent. This
voyage *did* remain a secret, and Torres' exploit
was not repeated before Cook (a phrase that
occurs so frequently in the history of the Pacific
that it is tempting to write 'BC').

After the Spaniards came the Dutch. They
discovered Australia, which did not impress them
favourably, and, ignorant of Torres Strait, supposed that Australia and New Guinea were
joined east of the Gulf of Carpentaria. In 1616
Schouten and Le Maire, determined to break the

monopoly of known routes owned by the Dutch
East India Company, reached the Pacific south
of Tierra del Fuego, discovering Cape Horn (and
ramming a 'sea monster'). However, they passed
west of what is now known as Staten Island and
assumed that it was part of the Southern Continent. Finally, Tasman and Visscher proved that
Australia was not part of *terra australis*, whose
northern extremity they believed they had located
in North Cape, on New Zealand's North Island.

There followed a short interval. Spanish zeal
had languished, the Dutch were making enough
profit from the spice islands to keep even them
content, and the burgeoning commercial rivalry
of France and England had not yet reached the
South Pacific.

The prolonged dying of the last Spanish Habsburg brought matters to a head in Europe, where
the English were aghast at the prospect of French
succession to the Spanish throne and – worse –
the Spanish Empire. Interest in the South Seas
was also stimulated by the publication of several
books about that region, in particular the works
of William Dampier, a remarkable ex-buccaneer
and a rolling stone to halt all rolling stones (he
circumnavigated the globe three times, taking
eight years over the first journey alone). The
new enthusiasm for the Pacific had commercial
manifestations too – in the South Sea Company.
Founded in 1711, its connections with the South
Sea were in fact tenuous, and it collapsed in the
famous 'Bubble' of 1720. New voyages were
organized (not very efficiently) by the British
Admiralty but made few discoveries bearing on
the Southern Continent, though they furnished
the raw material for the geographical fantasies of
Swift and Defoe. In France, the Southern Continent had a hopeful advocate of immense influence in Charles de Brosses (the only man, says

Lytton Strachey, to win an argument with Voltaire), whose *Histoire des Navigations aux Terres Australes* was published in 1756. In 1764, Bougainville planted his colony in the Falkland Islands (not much compensation, perhaps, for the loss of Canada) and eight months later the British, unaware of the existence of the French settlement, set themselves down a few miles away. The British colonists were forcibly, though temporarily, expelled by Spain, but poor Bougainville had been compelled to sell French rights to his beloved colony as part of a rather involved diplomatic manœuvre of Choiseul.

There was a crescendo in Pacific exploration after the Seven Years War, with the British and the French intent on laying first claim to the Southern Continent, among other objectives. The capable Wallis on the well-equipped *Dolphin* and the determined Carteret in the decrepit *Swallow* were no more able than their predecessors to hold to a western course after Cape Horn, though Carteret sailed farther south than anyone yet and so carved a slice off the theoretical continent through some 60° of longitude. Hot on their track came the dumpy and amiable figure of Bougainville, making good speed in the newly built *Boudeuse* and finding ample compensation for sacrificing the pleasures of civilization, to which he was greatly attached, in the hospitable reception of the islanders of Tahiti, not at all exhausted by their entertainment of the English a short time before.

All these voyages, spanning 250 years, added to Europe's knowledge of the Pacific in some way or other. By the time the exhausted Carteret guided his rotting vessel home to England, many of the chief islands were known and, looking at the situation in retrospect, the theoretical Southern Continent had been much reduced in size and shown to be altogether a rather dim possibility. And yet in 1768 the credibility of the Southern Continent had never stood higher. It was widely believed to stretch beyond 60° latitude in every quarter, with its greatest northward extension, in the Pacific, from 90° to 190° East, running roughly along an east–west parallel a few degrees short of the Tropic of Capricorn. The demolition of the myth and the revelation of the true 'Southern Continent'–Antarctica–was about to be accomplished by the greatest maritime explorer of the century and perhaps of any other century, James Cook.

The outstanding characteristic of James Cook is his professional competence. In spite of the many and detailed records of his voyages, as a man he remains something of an enigma–a reticent Yorkshireman, intelligent, humane and sharp-tempered. But the results of his exploration in lands discovered, seas charted, and in lives saved (for Cook was always concerned with the well-being of his crew) place him far above any other explorer of the 18th century.

Except among naval men and geographers, Cook was not especially famous in his own day; the reports of the safe return of his first expedition barely mention him while dripping tributes over his famous passenger, Joseph Banks. For Cook was socially a nobody–the son of a farm bailiff who enlisted in the Royal Navy, after ten years in merchant shipping in coastal waters, at the advanced age of twenty-seven. But there is something to be said for a naval administration which, however corrupt, did recognize Cook's abilities and did allow him to make the best possible use of them.

Not that even Cook could have gone far without influence. He was fortunate in serving under an intelligent officer, Sir Hugh Palisser, later

Governor of Newfoundland and eventually Comptroller of the Navy, who gave a careful push to his career on occasions, while the Whitby coalshippers who had formerly employed him put in a word with the local M.P. But his rapid promotion was the result of his obvious ability; the tall, erect figure and cool intelligence of the young Cook must have made a strong impression among the motley crew of able seamen who were his first shipmates.

Within two years, he was master (a non-commissioned rank) of a ship. In the sixty-gun *Pembroke*, he joined Amherst's expedition to North America which ended in Wolfe's famous conquest of Quebec (Bougainville was also present at this engagement, having run the British blockade of the St Lawrence). In the difficult work of charting the approaches to Quebec, which had defeated an earlier British expedition during the War of the Spanish Succession, Cook first proved his uncanny talent as a pilot–a talent nurtured during his nine years on North Country colliers off England's east coast. His commanding officer, Colville, informed the Admiralty that in Cook they had 'a man of genius and capacity'. After five years in North America, Cook returned to England in 1762, picked up £300 back pay, and married a girl of twenty-one, who began to produce children regularly every autumn (two sons survived long enough to die on active service). He spent the summers off Newfoundland, charting the coasts with minute accuracy.

Cook's appointment to lead a naval expedition to the South Seas in 1778 marks the beginning of the dominance of British polar exploration by the Royal Navy. He was still uncommissioned and clearly his naval reputation had long outstripped his rank. Alexander Dalrymple, self-appointed prophet of the 'Southland', had expected to get the command; but he was not a naval officer and ruined his chances by taking a domineering tone with the Admiralty. The Admiralty had a poor opinion of scientists as commanders, their only experience being the unfortunate one of Edmund Halley, who had led a troubled expedition in 1698. Cook was also to be much pestered by scientists, like the Duke of Wellington by writers; an idle remark before his third expedition that it was a pity no scientists were sailing with him provoked him into damning and blasting the entire breed.

His orders were first to proceed to Tahiti to observe the transit of Venus across the sun, forecast by Halley and unlikely to occur again for many years. Subsequently he was to sail in search of the Southern Continent in the Pacific. Cook himself kept an open mind (one of his chief attributes as an explorer) about the existence or otherwise of the Southern Continent; on the whole he was doubtful. The voyage was decided on before the return of Wallis and Carteret, though Carteret did arrive before Cook sailed, and acquired some urgency through the apparent interest of the French, notably Bougainville, in the continent.

The French had also been making voyages in the murky regions of the South Atlantic and Indian Ocean. Their discovery of Madagascar ('South India') was regarded as a preliminary claim to the Southern Continent. In 1739 Bouvet had discovered the island named after him and caught a glimpse of the Antarctic ice, which he had correctly guessed encircled a continent very different from the pleasant fantasies of a de Brosses or a Dalrymple. Then Bougainville appeared, settling the Falkland Islands just before the British and visiting Tahiti just after them. When Cook was in New Zealand, de Surville was within 100 miles of him, and du Fresne was killed by the Maoris not long after Cook's visit.

As in so many other matters, Cook set new standards with his choice of ship (if he *did* choose her). The 368-ton *Endeavour* was a former Whitby collier, of the type that Cook had sailed in during his merchant-navy days. She was not very beautiful, being broad (and therefore roomy) in the beam and round-bottomed, but she was tough and of shallow draught. Cook was not interested in flashing across the Pacific like Bougainville in his speedy frigate; he wanted a ship that could be handled in shallow and uncharted seas, would not be wrecked at the first touch of a sandbank, and was large enough to take plenty of provisions. 'These properties,' he said, 'are not to be found in ships of war of forty guns, nor in frigates, nor in East India Company's ships, nor in large three-decked West India ships, nor indeed in any other but North Country ships such as are built for the coal trade.'

Although he was never a popular hero, Cook was admired by his men as well as his superior officers. By the standards of his day he was a firm but not harsh disciplinarian; only the worst miscreants received more than twelve strokes of the cat. He was fair and tolerant, although he was not, of course, the seaborne saint since portrayed by patriotic writers: it is pleasant no doubt to think of him smiling and patting the heads of the Maoris, but light-fingered Tahitians also felt the touch of naval discipline and one Hawaiian islander had his ears cropped. Yet Cook was a humane man, more tolerant of seamen's peccadilloes and more perceptive of non-European cultures than anyone might have expected in the light of his education (or lack of it) and experience. And Cook, as he signalled the bo'sun's mate to lay on, could often say sincerely that the punishment was for the man's good: those who refused to eat the food Cook ordered or traded iron nails for Tahitian erotic delights really were endangering their own lives. So far as ordinary seamen were concerned the greatest of Cook's achievements was no geographical discovery but his splendid conquest of the ancient menace of scurvy. Although the juice of citrus fruits had been used for medicinal purposes since about

1600. Cook was convinced of the importance of a decent diet of fresh meat and vegetables whenever possible, and when not he made do with such ingenious inventions as his 'portable soup' (on the same principle as a beef cube). He was also aware of the importance of cleanliness, both of ship and men, and this he rigorously enforced.

After spending three months in Tahiti and cruising among the Society Islands, named by Cook for the Royal Society, of which Joseph Banks was – at twenty-four – a member, under the guidance of a Tahitian chief, Cook sailed south to look for the eastern shore of the dubious cape that Tasman had identified as part of the Southern Continent.

The first contact with the New Zealand Maoris was unhappy, as most later contacts were to be also. The Maoris regarded all strangers as foes and attacked fiercely. By horrid experience they learned the superiority of European weapons; it was, said Banks, 'the most disagreeable day my life has yet seen'. In spite of this inauspicious start, friendly relations were eventually established and Cook began his masterly, six-month survey of New Zealand's coasts, a dangerous and difficult exercise that remains a classic of good seamanship.

Cook's explicit tasks were then completed; his crew and ship were in good shape and he contemplated making a run for the Horn, which would have finally settled the question of the Southern Continent, but it was late in the year for such a voyage and instead he set his course for Australia. There followed the famous voyage along the east coast of the island-continent *inside* the Great Barrier Reef; a narrow shave when the *Endeavour* was caught and held for two tides by the coral; and the westward passage through Endeavour Strait which lies to the south of the Strait of Torres, the only other man to have made this passage. At the Dutch port of Batavia in Java, the luck of the *Endeavour* ran out as the entire crew, with the single exception of the ancient sailmaker, went down with fever. Many died, and Cook was forced to take on Dutch and Scandinavian seamen to fill the sad vacancies. But when he dropped anchor in the Downs on 13 July, 1771, Cook still had fifty-six left of the crew of ninety-five who had begun the three-year voyage. Another survivor was an English goat. This durable creature had actually circled the world twice, having been inherited by Cook from Wallis of the *Dolphin* shortly before sailing. It is said that on her return in the *Endeavour* she was granted honourable retirement along with an encomium from the pen of Dr Johnson, a gentleman notoriously bored by human explorers.

Cook had not finally proved or disproved the existence of the Southern Continent, as its proponents, somewhat defensively, were quick to point out. He suggested another voyage to make certain. His idea for the voyage, like many good ideas, was blindingly simple: he would sail to a high southern latitude and circumnavigate the world in that latitude. Such a voyage could be accomplished in less than six months, assuming no land were discovered, but delays for one reason or another were inevitable so that Cook's basically simple plan was augmented by diversions to the Pacific.

Cook's ships at anchor in Prince William Sound, east of the modern Anchorage, in Alaska. Far from finding a passage to the east, Cook found he had to travel a long way to the west before he could sail north.

His experience on the Barrier Reef had convinced Cook that two ships are better than one (had the *Endeavour* gone down all would have drowned), and for his second expedition he was provided with the *Resolution* and the *Adventure*. They were of similar type to the *Endeavour*, but the *Resolution*, 462 tons, was considerably larger. Banks had demanded a ship of the line and when that was refused, insisted on elaborate modifications to the *Resolution* for his considerable suite (which included his mistress disguised as a man – a tradition begun by one of Bougainville's officers whose 'servant's' disguise was immediately penetrated by the sexually aware islanders of Tahiti). The result of the alterations was that the *Resolution* could barely stand upright in the placid waters of the Thames, so the installations were all ripped out again and the self-centred but rather endearing young Banks took himself (but not his mistress) off to Iceland instead. Another scientist, the tiresome J. R. Forster, took Banks' place; he was a great irritant to Cook and not much use to anyone, although he did sacrifice his pet dog to make a tempting soup when Cook was sick.

The expedition left Plymouth exactly a year after the *Endeavour*'s return. In order to reach the Antarctic in summer a fairly swift voyage to the Cape of Good Hope (108 days) was required. A brief search was made for Bouvet's island but without success as the French captain had not located it accurately. Cook had already shown himself, with the aid of the recently published *Nautical Almanac*, an expert navigator whose longitude reckonings on his first voyage were never more than one degree out, but the *Resolution* and the *Adventure* were equipped with chronometers, those invaluable instruments for which sailors had waited so long. He might have had one on the *Endeavour*, but although Parliament had offered a substantial prize for an accurate watch, its inventor, a Yorkshire craftsman named John Harrison who had spent most of his long life on the work, had difficulty in getting his invention accepted and his reward paid. King George himself, for whom Harrison had made a watch, had to intervene ('Harrison, I'll see you righted'). The accuracy of Cook's chronometer, made according to Harrison's design though not by him personally, was almost perfect. Harrison's four chronometers can be seen, still ticking away, in the National Maritime Museum, Greenwich; it is fascinating to observe their progress from a large and ungainly, Heath Robinsonish contraption to a chunky oversized pocket watch. A Frenchman, Julien Leroy, produced a satisfactory chronometer shortly after Harrison.

In January 1773 the two ships reached 60° South and, a week or two later, Cook's men became the first to cross the Antarctic Circle. The scene was impressive, if not comforting. Now indeed they were in unknown waters, several hundred miles from the farthest south of the French captains. In the freezing air the sails stiffened and became as rigid as glass. The ropes grew hard as iron bars and a man who handled

The *Resolution* passing to windward of a giant iceberg, having just become the first ship to sail south of the Antarctic Circle.

them carelessly suffered a burn as if they were red-hot. The seamen worked with bleeding hands, their beards white with frost and the spit freezing on their lips; their feet crunched on the deck. All around in the grey ocean drifted the great icebergs, huge frozen islands, flat-topped, like great sugared cakes. On a clear day more than a hundred could be seen. Among them swam ice floes large and small, and many weirdly contorted shapes, shed by the Antarctic in its summer moult. Abstract sculptures, beautiful and frightening, dipped and drifted past: one like a vast mutating mushroom, another like a Gothic arch, some drilled with holes, some cracked and cavernous. As the *Resolution* ploughed cautiously still farther to the south, the ice increased. High above the deck men struggled with the rigging, as Cook strove to find his way between the menacing obstacles that drifted into his path: 'we discovered Field or Pack Ice . . . and had so many loose pieces about the ship that we were obliged to luff for one and bear up for the other'. Every man stuck to his task, but even among this carefully selected crew, many of them veterans of the Arctic Ocean, anxious glances were exchanged.

At length, Cook decided he could go no farther. He ordered an extra nip of brandy for every man coming down from the rigging, and changed course to the north.

In the 40s he looked without success for the island of Kerguelen, named after the French navigator who had discovered it, then headed

south and east between 58 and 60° South, spanning the whole Indian Ocean section of the Antarctic. He found no land. In a snow-storm, the *Resolution* lost touch with the *Adventure*, but they came together at a prearranged meeting place off Cook Strait in May. (The two ships again became separated in November and the *Adventure* made her way back to England independently.)

Now it was winter in the southern hemisphere, and Cook's next task was to explore that area of the Pacific, north and east of New Zealand, that he had not covered in the *Endeavour*. He worked his way north without incident, spent some time in Tahiti and the Society Islands, and discovered the attractive Tonga group. In October he headed back to New Zealand and at the end of November began his second journey towards the South Pole.

In the summer of 1772–73 he had traversed the Indian Ocean section; this year he was to cover the Pacific. The course on which he set out would have taken him almost to what is now known as Ross Sea; this is the Antarctic's most vulnerable point and Cook might have gone even farther south had he not been driven by easterly winds off the line of his original course.

Once more, the ordeal of the ice began, and the sturdy *Resolution* played her game of catch-me-if-you-can with the ponderous icebergs. On Christmas Day they were beyond the 70th parallel and the crew, having first made all safe, celebrated in the accustomed manner by getting as drunk

The *Adventure* (in the foreground) and the *Resolution* taking on ice to be melted for drinking water. The location is latitude 61 degrees south of the Equator, during Cook's first venture into the Antarctic. Watercolour by William Hodges.

as possible. The captain looked on with an amiable eye; he was not a drinking man.

The pack soon forced him north again. 'I who had Ambition not only to go Farther than any one had done before, but as far as it was possible for man to go, was not sorry at meeting with this interruption as it in some measure relieved us, at least shortened the dangers and hardships inseparable with the navigation of the Southern Polar Regions.' Cook did not often acknowledge the demon ambition, but it was there sure enough.

He was farther south in February 1774 than at his nearest approach the previous year, and when he crossed the Antarctic Circle again on his way north he crossed it for the last time: his 'farthest south' record was to stand for nearly half a century. There was still time to run for the Horn and take a quick look at the southern Atlantic before returning home. But that was not Cook's way. He had supplies for a year, friendly bases in the Pacific, and no serious trouble with ship or crew. He decided to continue his exploration of the Pacific and pass into the Atlantic in the following year. According to his journal, his officers fully agreed with this decision and his crew greeted it with great satisfaction; nothing can better illustrate Cook's stature than the credibility of that remarkable statement (though it must be said that the scientist Forster, who was definitely not enjoying himself, describes the crew's attitude as one of sullen acceptance).

During his voyage through the Pacific in 1774, Cook correctly located Easter Island (first discovered half a century earlier by the Dutchman Roggeveen), visited the Marquesas (not seen since Mendaña discovered them in 1595) and his favourite Tahiti; charted the New Hebrides (thought by Quiros to form part of the Southern Continent), discovered New Caledonia (where the inhabitants forgot to say that the fish they sold him were somewhat poisonous until the English had already discovered the fact), the Isle of Pines, and Norfolk Island, before reaching his New Zealand base in October–not a bad winter's work!

His final run across the South Pacific towards Cape Horn in about 55° South proved that the Southern Continent was not lurking there. He spent a couple of weeks surveying the bleak and rocky coasts at the tip of the South American continent and finally exploded another long-lived legend–that the men of Patagonia were giants. Only one short stretch remained, across the South Atlantic. The weather continued good, and the *Resolution* veered south round the Horn to search for land reported by a Spanish ship in the 1750s. It was found and named South Georgia. Creeping carefully through the pack ice at about 60° South, Cook sighted more land, the South Sandwich Islands, but the ice prevented a close inspection. Farther east he swung north again to look for Bouvet's Island, but it eluded him as it had on his southward voyage. On 23 February 1775 he crossed his own track of 1772: his circumnavigation of Antarctica was complete. He sailed for Cape Town, then England, where he arrived on 29 July, just over three years after he had left. He had lost four of his 112-man crew in that time; none had died of scurvy.

The Southern Continent was no more. Cook's voyage had proved that if any continent existed it was no larger than Antarctica, for although large areas of ocean still remained unexplored, and large islands might still exist somewhere in those southern latitudes, Cook's careful survey had ruled out the possibility of a major land mass north of the Antarctic Circle. Visibility from the *Resolution* had often been down to nothing, but the uninterrupted swell of the ocean murmured of thousands of miles of ceaseless motion. The presence of big icebergs suggested that there was land beyond the ice barrier. Cook himself was sure of it; but although he had twice sailed within about seventy miles of the coast he had not actually seen Antarctica.

The Admiralty felt that Cook, now aged forty-seven, had done enough, and gave him a sinecure appointment. But another voyage of discovery, to search once more for a northern sea route, was under discussion. It was inevitable that Cook, appointed captain at last, should be consulted and perhaps inevitable that he should volunteer to lead it. Men like Cook do not take to retirement.

The British had made no great advances in their efforts to find the Northwest Passage since the voyages of James and Foxe, but time had not stood still. The Hudson's Bay Company had become disillusioned with exploration after the disastrous voyage of James Knight in 1719, and two subsequent voyages were no more successful. But the company's fur traders gradually pushed into northern and western Canada overland and in 1768–70 Samuel Hearne reached Coronation Gulf, on the northern coast of Canada, from Hudson Bay. By that time it was certain that no westward exit from the bay to the Pacific existed, but it was widely believed that a route might exist to the north, in the direction pioneered by 'North-West' Foxe. The land between the Coppermine River (Hearne's route) and the Bering Strait was unexplored: Alaska might be just a collection of islands, for Bering had not carried out a survey of the coast.

The *Resolution* was again nominated for the voyage and she was to be accompanied by the 300-ton *Discovery*, another ex-collier, under Lieutenant Clerke, a good officer who had unfortunately contracted consumption in a debtor's prison after his return from Cook's previous expedition.

The purpose of Cook's third voyage was to seek the Northwest Passage from the opposite direction. As no one had been able to find a route west of Hudson Bay, perhaps better luck might be had in looking for the exit rather than the entrance. Also, by approaching from the Pacific side, Cook would be able to look for a Northeast Passage past Bering Strait if he failed to locate the Northwest Passage. The idea was not new: it seems to have been part of Drake's plans to seek the Pacific opening of the passage in 'New Albion' (California) in 1578–the same year in which Frobisher was exploring his bay. Had everything turned out as desired, Frobisher would have joined Drake in the Pacific and the two of them would have sailed back to England through their newly discovered passage, thus saving Drake the bother of going round the world. Cook was to sail via the Cape of Good Hope and, after various calls in the Pacific, to aim for the American coast at about the point where Drake had turned away. He would then follow the coast to the north looking for a passage.

The *Resolution* was refitted in the naval dockyards on the Thames at Deptford. The work was not done well. According to Cook himself the equipment of commercial vessels cast aside as worn out was more reliable than the new equipment installed in the Royal Navy's docks. The inefficiency, idleness and corruption that characterized 18th-century naval administration were wasteful not only of money but men's lives. Throughout his third voyage, Cook was hindered by broken masts, fragile rigging and leaky hulls. So, no doubt, were all captains, and Cook's

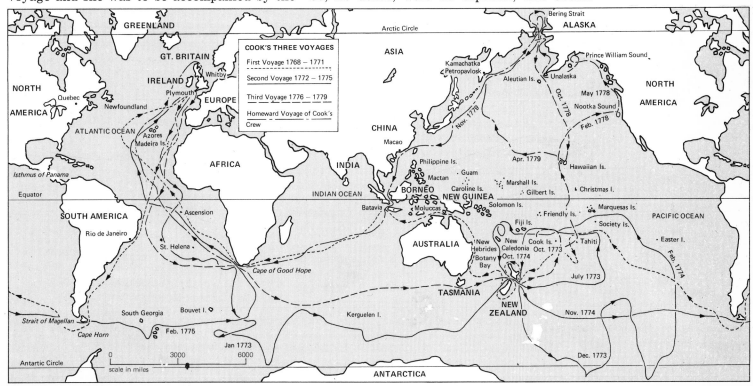

earlier voyages were not trouble-free; but on this occasion the work was shoddier than usual and by compelling him to put back to the Hawaiian islands at an inopportune moment, indirectly brought about his death.

Cook sailed on 12 July 1776. As usual, the creaking of the rigging and the lapping of the waves–those pleasant nautical sounds of romantic imagining–were entirely drowned by the complaints of the numerous livestock that had not yet found their sea legs. The *Resolution* was carrying a greater number of animals than usual as gifts for the South Sea islanders, and Cook, shouting his orders above the bleats, moos and whinnies, felt more like Noah than an officer of His Britannic Majesty's Navy. At Cape Town he was delayed by the gaps that had opened up in the ill-caulked planks of both the *Resolution* and the *Discovery*. Having checked, this time successfully, on various tiny French-discovered islands on the Antarctic fringes, Cook made for New Zealand, but had to put into Tasmania first to replace a shattered mast. In March he was among the islands, discovering those now named after him and getting cured of rheumatism by the vigorous massage of a team of large Tahitian ladies.

In order to make the best use of the prevailing winds, Cook sailed due north from Tahiti to pick up the trade winds north of the Tropic of Cancer. This course brought him to the Hawaiian Islands, perhaps his most important discovery from a strategic point of view (which was, naturally, the point of view of the Admiralty). He sighted the North American mainland opposite what is now the state of Oregon in March 1778, and began to follow the coast to the north.

This was undiscovered territory, but probably the reports of Hudson Bay trappers and the outline of the mountains convinced Cook that there was little hope of a passage in this area. At any rate, his inspection was somewhat cursory: he kept well clear of the land and thus overlooked the strait south of Vancouver (subsequently discovered by one of his midshipmen). Gradually the coast turned away towards the west, and after sighting Mount Elias, Cook began to search more closely for a useful inlet, though his desire to find a passage was for the moment secondary to his need to find a safe anchorage to patch up his ships. Such a place was found in Prince William Sound, although it was not a friendly spot: a band of Eskimos tried to capture the *Discovery*, but the sailors fought them off with swords (Cook did not like to use firearms except when necessary). Beyond the sound, the coast took a discouraging turn to the south, but when they had passed the cape they found themselves in the mouth of a large and promising inlet. Already they were 1,500 miles from Hudson Bay and getting farther all the time: Cook Inlet was the first hopeful opening they had found. Unfortunately, its promise was chimerical. The *Resolution*'s master, Mr Bligh (later Captain of the *Bounty*) took a boat up the inlet and soon found the water becoming shallow and brackish. Something better was needed.

Cook left this anchorage (now Anchorage) and sailed south-west along the peninsula that gradually dwindled into a chain of islands (the Aleutians). The inhabitants traded salmon and furs for iron, and raised their hats politely when they encountered the Englishmen, a custom learned, perhaps, from the Russian fur traders in these parts, whom Cook soon encountered. One man, Ismailov, was particularly helpful and showed Cook his charts of the Bering Sea. In fog and gloom they sailed on, eventually passing north between two rocky outcrops by lucky chance; Cook remarked that he would never have attempted to navigate between such obstacles if he had been able to see where he was going. In the Bering Sea, Cook followed the irregular line of the coast minutely, but without success. Already, as he reached Icy Cape (named by him), the Arctic summer was on the wane. The water had opened broad chinks in the *Resolution*'s hull, but Cook pushed her on, up to the very edge of the ice (almost level with Point Barrow) where the sound that Elizabethan sailors described as very loathsome to be heard – the grinding and cracking of ice floes – filled the foggy air with threats.

Baulked at last, Cook turned west, crossing the north of Bering Strait to challenge the ice again on the Siberian side. Here too his way was blocked, but as he retreated through Bering Strait he observed with satisfaction a sight that the Danish explorer had never seen: 'The weather becoming clear, we had the opportunity of seeing, at the same moment, the remarkable peaked hill, near Cape Prince of Wales, on the Coast of America, and the East Cape of Asia, with the two connecting islands of Saint Diomede between them.'

With winter upon them, the ships withdrew hastily to the islands they had discovered on their voyage north, and there, in a wretched incident that resulted from mutual misunderstanding, Captain James Cook was killed by the Hawaiians. Clerke, himself a dying man, took command, and showing a devotion to duty worthy of Cook himself, repaired the ships and proceeded to Petropavlovsk in Kamchatka, from where he made another attack on the Arctic Ocean in the following summer. The ice was worse then before; he failed to pass Cook's limit and died soon afterwards. The expedition returned to England by way of China, arriving in October 1780 amid some gloom, as the news of Cook's death had preceded them.

The best tribute to Cook's achievements is the opinion of his successors, especially those of rival nations. 'A sailor,' said the generally critical Dumont d'Urville, 'in the fullest sense of the word.' 'That great explorer' was Bellingshausen's verdict, and most glowing of all, the opinion of Jean-François de Galaup, Comte de la Pérouse, 'No one will ever again equal that immortal navigator.' Yet the man who came nearest to Cook in that period was the gallant La Pérouse himself.

La Pérouse gained his reputation between 1778 and 1783 in the war against England, when he captured various settlements east of Hudson Bay. When the French king (who, incidentally, had ordered free passage for Cook during the Anglo-French War) decided to mount a great round-the-world expedition in 1785, La Pérouse was chosen to command. His brief was large. He

Captain Nathaniel Palmer (1799–1877), the Connecticut sealer who discovered Deception Island and was perhaps the first man to see the mainland of Antarctica; he described the scene as 'sterile and dismal'.

was to seek the Northwest Passage from the Pacific and explore the Asian and American coasts in that region; then he was to proceed south to investigate the Pacific, including the seas around Japan and China, and the prospects for whaling in the far south. He was to examine tides, currents, the formation of icebergs, magnetic variation and atmospheric pressure, and he carried a variety of scientific equipment including balloons for measuring air currents. His ships, the *Boussole* and the *Astrolabe*, carried a British chronometer and other instruments used by Cook, as well as more luxurious items that Cook might have envied; the ship's library contained 1,200 volumes.

La Pérouse did not make any important new discoveries but rather confirmed Cook's findings in certain respects, for instance that no Northwest Passage existed on the Canadian or west Alaskan coasts. He made one or two minor discoveries, and completed significant surveys in the Far East; on some maps, the strait north of Japan still bears his name. Early in 1788 he was in Australia where 'he interchanged courtesies with some of the English pioneers', but after that no more was heard of him. Thirty-four years later the wreckage of two ships was found on a reef north of the New Hebrides – all that remained of the *Boussole* and the *Astrolabe*. Dumont d'Urville erected a monument near the spot in 1828.

Cook had reported that whales and seals were plentiful in the Antarctic and his words were not unheeded in Atlantic fishing ports. Marine mammals have always been peculiarly vulnerable to man. In spite of the primitive weapons and fragile ships, whaling in the Atlantic was almost finished by the end of the

Middle Ages, and that was why reports like Hudson's of whales around Spitsbergen sent the whalers hastening thither as soon as they heard the good news. In the days 'before Standard Oil became the light of the world' (as Stefansson puts it), whales were immensely valuable, not only for their oil but for a host of other products including of course that peculiar substance whalebone, which has properties not found elsewhere in nature. In the Middle Ages, a stranded whale washed up on the beach was as good as a treasure chest, and many complex (and comical) legal battles were fought for the possession of such a carcass.

Hunters for whales, walrus and seals were extraordinarily quick to follow up the reports of the discoverers. Within a few years of Cook's Antarctic voyage, British and American sealers were hunting in waters that, before Cook, had never been visited by man. The French Revolutionary and Napoleonic Wars temporarily interrupted this traffic, but by 1820 it was reaching a peak. No doubt American whalers, unaffected by European conflicts, had made many unrecorded visits in the meantime; the commercial nature of these voyages plus the need to keep good hunting grounds secret has meant that the movements of the sealers are difficult to trace. Much confusion surrounds the actual 'discovery' (i.e. first sighting of the mainland) of Antarctica and some rather unedifying chauvinistic disputes have arisen. Yet, really, these events are of minor importance. The sealers were not particularly interested in geographical discovery or scientific research, and although Bellingshausen was probably not the first man to identify the Antarctic continent as the Russians seem to think, his work was vastly more significant than the chance sightings of the sealing ships, at least until the British firm of Enderby began to be interested in where their sealers were going.

In 1819 the brig, *Williams*, Captain William Smith, was blown far south of Cape Horn and sighted land in 62°42′ South. Returning later the same year, Smith landed on what came to be known as the South Shetland Islands. Next year Smith sailed again with Captain Edward Bransfield to survey the islands and plant the British flag among the penguins. On this voyage they sighted what they called Trinity Land which, there is little doubt, was the tip of Graham Land and thus part of the Antarctic mainland.

Graham Land does not appear on some American maps. There it is called Palmer Peninsula, and the reason is that an intrepid Yankee sealer, Nathaniel Palmer of Stonnington, Connecticut, discovered it in the same year, though some months later. (Lately a compromise seems to have been reached, with the narrow, northern part of the peninsula named Graham Land and the wider, southern part Palmer Land.) Like his British predecessors, Palmer was unable to land because of the ice, and the first man to set foot on the continent appears to have been Captain John Davis of the *Huron*, another Yankee sealer, in 1821.

From these rather confusing and somewhat incidental advances in Antarctic exploration it is a relief to turn to that Estonian aristocrat and no-nonsense sailor, Baron Bellingshausen. Not that the sealers lacked courage and enterprise; on the contrary, the fact that comparatively little is known of their movements is one more example of how history tends to ignore ordinary people going about their business, however extraordinary, in favour of politically supported enterprises led by comparatively favoured persons. Still, Bellingshausen is no doubt rightly regarded as the first great Antarctic explorer after Cook.

When the Napoleonic Wars were over and Napoleon safely put away on St Helena, the British looked around to see who next would threaten their predominance as a world power. The United States was obviously a future rival, but at the moment the chief danger seemed to

A dark and angry sea, a lifeless rocky coast, ice and a freezing wind – Antarctica was not an inviting place for the first men who visited it (Hope Bay, Graham Land).

come from the Russia of Alexander I. It was Russian naval activity largely that prompted the renewed British assault on the north-west by Ross and Parry. Although the Russian attempt on the Northwest Passage, from Bering Strait, was a failure and added nothing to men's knowledge of those regions, the Antarctic expedition launched simultaneously had greater success, although it did not lead to the hoped-for Russian bases that earlier expeditions had sought in more temperate climes.

Bellingshausen sailed in July 1819 with two ships, the *Vostok*, and the *Mirny* which carried the bulk of the supplies and unfortunately proved much slower than the command ship. One advantage they had over ships of Cook's generation was copper-plated bottoms (Cook could have had copper sheathing but preferred an extra layer of wood rather than risk an unproven device that might make repairs a serious problem). The expedition was prepared in a very short time, and the German scientists appointed to it made the short notice their excuse to withdraw, to Bellingshausen's lasting disgust. Most of the instruments and charts were purchased in London, perhaps the best source still.

By the end of the year Bellingshausen was off South Georgia, where he took the opportunity to cross-question two British sealers and complete Cook's survey of the coast. Sailing south and east, he proved that the South Sandwich Islands were indeed islands, as Cook had thought but not proved, and cleared up a number of additional navigational queries before crossing the Antarctic Circle. Off Queen Maud Land, the ice barrier forced him north again (if Bellingshausen is to be considered the 'discoverer' of Antarctica this is the moment, for Williams and Bransfield sighted Graham Land only two days later). Continuing round the continent eastward, Bellingshausen stuck pertinaciously to the ice but without knowing that he was in fact following the continental coastline quite closely, and he does not seem to have claimed the discovery of Antarctica even though on a rare fine day he observed mountains in the distance. At about 40° East he turned off to the Pacific, returning to the Antarctic in November 1820. In January he discovered Peter I Island and soon afterwards Alexander Land, which is actually an island although Bellingshausen thought, not surprisingly as the maps shows, that it was part of the mainland. While surveying the South Shetland Islands with characteristically speedy efficiency, he met an American sealing ship captained, as it turned out, by none other than Nat Palmer, who told him of the profitable sealing in which he was engaged. Bellingshausen did not think that it would be worth while sending Russian sealers to these islands, and for a very good reason: 'As other sealers also were competing in the destruction of the seals there could be no doubt that round the South Shetland Islands just as at South Georgia and Macquarie Island [discovered by the Australian Frederick Hasselborough in 1810] the number of these sea animals will rapidly decrease.' Bellingshausen's prophecy was borne out with ugly swiftness. The seal population of the South Shetlands in 1820 cannot be accurately estimated, but possibly exceeded a million. They were killed with the utmost ease: Palmer told Bellingshausen that Smith of the *Williams* had taken 60,000. By 1822, just three years after the industry began, the sealing boom in the South Shetlands was over: there were so few seals left. The contemplation of this crude slaughter is sickening.

Bellingshausen had completed the circumnavigation of the Antarctic continent, and in a latitude generally farther south than Cook. It was a remarkable voyage and a striking success. But the Tsar was disappointed. He refused to sanction the publication of Bellingshausen's maps on the grounds that it would be too expensive.

The most notable exploratory voyages of the sealers were made by employees of the British firm of Enderby, whose proprietors placed knowledge before profit, encouraged their captains to make new discoveries and, most admirable of all, freely published their findings. 'There is, perhaps,' wrote Hugh Robert Mill in 1905, 'no other instance of a private mercantile firm undertaking so extensive a series of voyages of discovery without much encouragement in the way of pecuniary returns.' In 1822 James Weddell, an Enderby captain and a Royal Navy veteran, sailed far into the dangerous sea named after him and established a record for 'farthest south' of 74°15'. It was clearly a freak year, for in average conditions Weddell's two little ships could never have advanced so far. Another Enderby captain, John Biscoe, eager to prove his theory that Antarctica was not a new continent but merely an enormous formation of sea ice, completed its circumnavigation in 1832, in a latitude to the south of Bellingshausen's route. With the brig *Tula* and cutter *Lively*, Biscoe persevered in the face of terrific gales, ice and scurvy. It is amazing how these little sealing ships survived, when one solid blow from an ice floe could send a perceptible ripple along the length of the ship. When the *Lively* (having been separated from the *Tula*) reached Tasmania in the autumn of 1831 only the Captain, one seaman and a boy were on their feet (youngsters of thirteen and fourteen regularly made these voyages). It was Biscoe who gave Enderby Land its name and placed the disputed label of Graham Land (after the First Sea Lord) on the Antarctic Peninsula.

There were many other voyages by sealers that added something to men's knowledge of the Antarctic. Kemp Land and the Balleny Islands are two places whose names commemorate their discoverers in this period. Less well known are the ships that failed to return—at least seven in the South Shetlands in 1820–22, when Weddell was doggedly charting his discoveries.

Opening the Canadian Arctic

The activities of sealers in the Antarctic were the southern counterpart to the voyages of Arctic whalers, of whom the most notable were the William Scoresbys, father and son. In 1806 the elder Scoresby established a new 'farthest north' in the Spitsbergen region of 81°31', beating the previous record held by Phipps in HMS *Racehorse* since 1773 – an expedition now remembered chiefly for the contest between a polar bear and a somewhat rash young midshipman named Horatio Nelson.

On the elder Scoresby's record-breaking trip his son sailed as mate. He was then seventeen years old and within five years he was the most experienced captain in Arctic waters. His two books, published in 1820 and 1823, have been described as 'the most important contributions made to a scientific knowledge of the Arctic Regions'. The Scoresbys managed to combine research and profit more successfully than the most famous captains of the Enderby brothers; between them they mapped nearly a thousand miles of the east coast of Greenland. Both of them had creative minds. The elder Scoresby, born like Cook of Yorkshire farming stock and virtually uneducated, invented the crow's nest which made the job of the look-out a great deal less uncomfortable, and taught his crew to roll the ship free of young ice by a concerted dash from one side of the vessel to the other.

The younger Scoresby had the double advantage of a good education and long experience under his father. Not all his ideas worked well (his suggestion of reindeer to pull sledges was a failure) but he was undoubtedly the best-informed authority in the country at the time of the renewed British assault on the Northwest Passage. When Parry met him in 1819 he had apparently never heard of him and was surprised by his knowledge. The Royal Navy's jealously guarded control of polar exploration is perhaps responsible for Scoresby's comparative neglect as a popular hero of the Arctic. He should, for instance, receive at least equal credit with Sir John Barrow for stimulating the burst of Arctic exploration that began with John Ross's expedition of 1818.

It was Scoresby who wrote to Barrow (a secretary to the Admiralty from 1804 to 1845) in 1817 drawing his attention to the comparative lack of ice in northern Greenland waters that he had observed for two consecutive seasons, and suggesting that this was the time to discover if or where the Northwest Passage ran. Barrow, who was also concerned about Russian activity in the Arctic and aware that, the Napoleonic Wars being over, the Royal Navy had many ships idle, in turn approached the First Lord of the Admiralty, Lord Melville. If Scoresby was right about the disappearance of the ice, it did not follow that it would be equally clear in the following season, but there was a widespread belief that this was more than a seasonal variation. Sir Joseph Banks, Cook's old shipmate who was still going strong after nearly forty years as President of the Royal Society, pointed to the sputtering flame in his oil lamp and theorized that the whales were finding the sea too warm and hence producing unsatisfactory blubber.

In the 200 years since Baffin, little advance had been made in the Canadian Arctic. The most recent voyage of much interest had been that of Captain Middleton in 1746, which had added some details (Wager River, Repulse Bay – though the latter was doubted) to the north-west of Hudson Bay. Hearne had followed the Coppermine to the sea and Alexander Mackenzie had imitated his achievement farther west on the Mackenzie River (1789). Apart from these two isolated river mouths, the Arctic coast was a blank from Cook's Icy Cape to Davis Strait.

The Admiralty decided to send two expeditions of two ships each, the first towards the pole between Greenland and Spitsbergen, the second to look for the Northwest Passage off Davis Strait. Nearly all the major British names in polar exploration during the next thirty years appeared among the officers of this expedition. The north-west ships were commanded by Captain John Ross, a breezy sailor then about forty years old; his second in command was Lieutenant Edward Parry, and one of the midshipmen was his seventeen-year-old nephew James Clark Ross. The Spitsbergen ships were commanded by Captain Buchan with, as second in command, an amiable, round-faced man who looked like a

CAPT^N SIR JOHN ROSS. R.N. KN^T K.S. &c. &c.

Truly Yours John Ross

country doctor, Lieutenant John Franklin. Buchan and Franklin failed to make any new breakthrough in 1818; they were blocked by ice not far from Spitsbergen and though they brought back some valuable charts, that was all they could do.

Ross's side of the expedition was not much of a success either, but it was to lead to greater things. The ships followed roughly the path of Davis and, once north of Sanderson's Hope, of Baffin. They were carrying the journals of their predecessors and were fascinated to see how far the Elizabethans had travelled and how accurately they had recorded their route. Parry was particularly enthusiastic about 'those *darling* old fellows, Baffin and Davis'. They crossed to the Canadian shore within sight of Smith Sound, observed the ice-blocked Jones Sound, and so came at the end of August 1818 to Lancaster Sound. Baffin had rejected this sound as a possible opening to the passage but Parry, observing the uninterrupted swell, was more hopeful. Ross, however, thought he saw mountains at the end of the strait (he had observed the same phenomenon, equally fictitious, blocking Smith Sound and Jones Sound) and gave the order to withdraw. After taking possession of what was later named Bylot Island (after Baffin's captain) and glancing hopefully at Cumberland Sound, they headed for home, the ships becoming separated on the way in the inevitable South Greenland storm.

Ross reported that there was no passage to be found in Davis Strait or Baffin Bay, but the Admiralty paid more attention to Parry's views. Parry had returned feeling somewhat disgruntled at what he privately regarded as Ross's 'blunder-

ing'. He had not seen the mountain range which Ross believed marked the end of Lancaster Sound, and recommended a closer look. A second expedition sailed the following year, with Parry in command.

There are some resemblances between Parry and Scott. Each was, fundamentally, a first-rate naval officer of a conventional British type. Like Scott, Parry was always the blue-eyed boy of the naval establishment; if he had been any kind of a rebel he could not have retained the benevolent patronage of his somewhat conservative employers. Yet Parry was both literally and metaphorically a great breaker of new ground – and not only as an explorer. In later life he was to be one of the chief proponents of the screw propeller against the paddle wheel. He had most of the virtues of the good officer – unassailable confidence, a capacity for making decisions (usually the right ones) in difficult conditions, an unstuffy but unassailable command of his men. But he had something more – a gift found in varying degree in all successful men of action – a capacity for adapting to circumstances, a flair for innovation. Men like Parry, with no particular intellectual or artistic pretensions (though Parry was a fair violinist) can truly be called creative. This talent was shared by other (though by no means all) polar explorers: Peary is an obvious example.

Parry's Arctic explorations are for ever associated with the name of his ship, the *Hecla*. She was a barque-rigged, 375-ton bomb (a small warship of rugged construction for carrying mortars). Such ships had long proved their capacity in icy seas: Middleton and Phipps had used similar vessels. On his 1819 expedition the second ship, the 180-ton brig *Griper* showed more gripe than grip: 'a vessel', said Parry later, 'of such lubberly, shameful construction as to baffle the ingenuity of the most ingenious seaman in England'. The *Griper* was commanded by Lieutenant Liddon, Parry's choice, and the younger Ross sailed with Parry. Apart from Edward Sabine, an army officer (but holding a temporary naval commission at the Admiralty's insistence) with a reputation as a scientist,

left
John Ross, first of the great British Arctic captains of the 19th century. A vigorous red-haired Scot, he quarrelled with Assistant Secretary Barrow after his voyage of 1818 and was never again given command of a Royal Naval expedition.

above
Samuel Hearne inscribed his name and the date on a rock near Churchill, Hudson Bay, before setting out on the journey that took him down the Coppermine River to the Arctic Ocean.

opposite, top
The Americans in the Antarctic: a painting from a drawing by Captain Wilkes of seamen from the *Vincennes* frolicking on the icy slopes of an island off the continental coast. Apart from such light-hearted moments, the atmosphere on board was not happy, but Wilkes was determined 'not to give up the cruise until the ship was totally disabled, or . . . it was impossible to persist any longer'.

opposite, bottom
The narrow escape of *Erebus* and *Terror* between two icebergs on their way north in March 1842. Their survival was due to the great navigational skills of captains Ross and Crozier. The artist, Beechey, one of the ships' officers, has convincingly captured the nightmare quality of the scene.

The Eskimos, without maps themselves, were able to identify features on British maps and to draw in fairly accurate details from memory, but misunderstandings – sometimes no doubt the result of language difficulties – prevented the fullest possible use of local knowledge.

Parry at twenty-eight was the oldest member of the expedition, and five years above the average age of his officers. It must have been the youngest polar expedition ever assembled.

Parry soon showed his mettle by deciding to take a direct route through the ice pack to Lancaster Sound, which if accomplished would give him more time to explore before winter closed in. After two failures he managed it, although at times the ships had to be towed by their boats or warped along by pulling on anchors cast into the ice ahead of them. Though starting later, Parry reached the sound a month earlier than Ross in the previous year and finding it clear, speeded towards the west. The ships (*Griper* as usual hanging behind) were now in an unknown region.

At the beginning of September they passed 110° West of Greenwich, earning the prize of £5,000 offered by Parliament for that achievement north of the Arctic Circle. But for some time they had been fighting a running battle with ice and at 112°51′ Parry decided to turn back and seek winter quarters at Winter Harbour, on the south side of Melville Island. Except for the ice, the voyage from Lancaster Sound had been astonishingly easy. In two months they had travelled over 600 miles (as the crow flies), farther west than anyone had gone before. They had sighted the Beaufort Sea, although McClure Strait had proved impassable (as elsewhere in this book, the modern name is used for the sake of convenience although it did not yet appear on maps). They had escaped illness or serious accident; they had not even had any really cold weather.

At Winter Harbour, Parry organized the first planned Arctic wintering. He had supplies for three years and he had already thought out ways of defeating the cold. He was carrying a large quantity of waterproof cloth to form a tent-like roof over the deck, and the galley fire was kept burning constantly; a makeshift arrangement of pipes conveyed the warmth around the ships (next time, Parry was to have his pipes built in before sailing). When the snow came, it was

banked up against the sides of the ships to provide insulation. Strict discipline was enforced to keep the men healthy, with weekly medical inspections for signs of scurvy, regular airing of bedding, and careful diet. A hole in the ice near the ships was kept permanently open for the prompt dousing of fire – one of their greatest fears. A hut was built on land to house the instruments, and the pickaxes needed for the job were made in a forge on shore. The men were able to bake their own bread and even – until it grew too cold – to brew their own beer. Game was fortunately not scarce and a supply of fresh meat was available most of the winter. As the temperature dropped and the light faded, Parry's men were ready for the winter.

Parry realized that one of the worst hazards of the long enforced stay in Winter Harbour would be boredom, especially for those possessing, as he put it, 'little resource within themselves'. (Most could not read; Parry later organized classes to teach them.) A record was kept of all interesting phenomena, and observations were made all round the clock. It proved necessary to wrap the metal parts of the instruments in cloth to avoid cold burns. More entertaining ways of passing the time were also found. A play was produced once a fortnight, and it is a mark of Parry's authority that he felt able to take part without endangering it. The pretty-faced Ross usually played the girls' parts. Parry also assisted in

writing new plays for the company; one had seven characters—five seamen, an Eskimo and a polar bear. And he suggested that they should start a newspaper. Thus began *The Winter Chronicle and North Georgia Gazette*, forerunner of many similar literary diversions in the polar regions, whose facetious humour and even, occasionally, wit helped to keep the morale of the crews at such a level that Parry could write, 'I verily believe there never was a more merry and cheerful set of men than ours, and I must in justice add that they seem fully sensible of attending to the precautions adopted for the preservation of their health.'

These precautions included daily exercise, and when it became too cold to exercise on shore, the men ran round the decks, singing songs taught them by the old whalers among the crew. Parry looked on with an amiable and satisfied eye. 'All sailors,' he remarked with fatherly candour, 'are somewhat like children, and require constant looking after.' It is not an attitude that would work well in, say, a modern factory, but in Parry's time it was one reason for his success.

In January and February, snow fell in thin drifting showers, covering the ground. One day the thermometer registered —55 °F. A case of scurvy was cured by 'a very nice salad' made of mustard and cress which Parry grew in a box of earth above the warm pipes. There were some bad cases of frostbite, and Parry ordered the making of large, loose canvas boots, to be worn over several pairs of socks. April was the snowiest month yet, but it fell in soft comfortable flakes, heralding the approach of summer. In May they had rain. On *Hecla* and *Griper* the men began to caulk the timbers, patch the canvas, and repair the rigging, while Parry prepared to make an overland journey across Melville Island.

All explorers are entitled to expect a fair share of good luck, and they usually receive it in proportion to their own capacity. It so happened that Parry set out to cross Melville Island at what is—though he did not know it—its narrowest point. With Sabine and ten others, he reached the northern coast and returned, by a different route, in the space of two weeks. Like Robert Peary later, Parry elected to travel at night (although so far as the light was concerned there was little difference), and supplies for the party were carried in a handcart. On the journey back the well-travelled cart finally broke down and they made a warming fire of it. Thirty years later, McClintock could still follow the tracks made by Parry's cart.

Back at Winter Harbour, the ships were surrounded by ice that showed no sign of shifting. By mid-July, even Parry was mildly apprehensive and he gave orders to prepare for sailing not because it was possible but because the anniversary of their arrival was less than two months away and the men might soon be wondering if they were to be marooned for good.

On the night of 31 July the ice quite suddenly drifted away and the following day the *Hecla* and the *Griper* moved out into the sound. They turned at once to the west in an endeavour to break through the pack ice in McClure Strait which had barred their way the year before, but they only managed a few miles farther and the ships took a severe battering. They named their farthest point Cape Dundas after the First Lord of the Admiralty (it is some relief that they chose Lord Melville's family name on this occasion, as the frequency with which that nautical peer occurs on the map of the Canadian Arctic can lead to confusion). Turning back to the east, the *Hecla* scouted for possible outlets to the south, but ice barred their way everywhere until they came to Prince Regent Inlet, part of which Parry had explored on the voyage west while waiting for the *Griper* to catch up. After a survey of Bylot Island, previously carried out by John Ross but – in Parry's opinion – inadequately, they sailed for England, where their arrival at the end of October 1820 caused much excitement.

As Parry's great-great-granddaughter and biographer says, Parry's expedition to Melville Island was 'perhaps the most successful of all Arctic voyages'. He had not managed to deliver his papers to the Russian authorities in Kamchatka, as his orders had optimistically suggested he should do if he found the Northwest Passage. He had not found the passage. But he had accomplished far more than any previous explorer in that region. He had mapped more miles of unknown coasts than any navigator since Cook, and he had cut a substantial swathe through the utter mystery of the lands and seas of Arctic Canada. Perhaps more important, he had set an example to a whole generation of British naval explorers who learned from his experience and copied or adapted his methods.

Meanwhile, the Russians themselves were not idle in the Arctic. Following the achievements of the Great Northern Expedition further discoveries had been made, though without government sponsorship, by interested Siberian merchants. The name of the Lyakhov Islands is a memorial to one of these men. An Englishman, Joseph Billings, lavishly equipped, was commissioned to chart the north-eastern peninsula in 1788, but failed to make any progress. The formidable stretch between the Kolyma and the Anadyr held out unconquered until the expedition of Ferdinand von Wrangel, later Governor of Alaska, in 1820–24. He travelled by dog sledge overland, rounding Cape Shelagskiy, which had defeated many before him, in the first year and in the subsequent two summers exploring the sea north of the Chukot Peninsula. In the fourth year he followed the coast again from the Kolyma to North Cape, seen by Cook on his voyage to Bering Strait, and so added final confirmation to the fact that no land link existed between Siberia and Alaska. He tried and failed to reach

the island now named after him, and in the course of that attempt travelled by sledge 1,500 miles in eleven weeks – a record that makes James Ross's journeys in 1830–31 seem less astonishing.

When Parry returned from his first voyage he was not yet thirty years old and his career was just beginning. He was still only a lieutenant, although promotion soon came ('late but I trust not ingloriously', as he said). He was soon commissioned to lead another expedition.

The great mass of ice floes in McClure Strait, jammed together with great ridges and outcrops yards high, had convinced Parry that no outlet to the sea could be found there. His second expedition was therefore made in more southern latitudes, via Hudson Strait, although Parry was none too hopeful of finding a way there either. For the progress of polar exploration his expedition is important for its discovery of Fury and Hecla Strait, between Baffin Island and Melville Peninsula, which even the tough combination of Parry and the *Hecla* could not break through (modern ships do not find it easy), and for Parry's two successive winters in the Arctic (the first just south of the Arctic Circle) in close contact with the Eskimos of the Melville Peninsula.

Although Parry did not learn all the Eskimos could teach him he did learn a great deal. He appears to have regarded the Eskimos in much the same manner as he regarded his sailors, with affectionate patronage, but his admiration for the way they adapted to life in the Arctic was genuine. He learned how to paddle a kayak and drive a dog sledge, but overland journeys even with dogs did not accomplish much because they started too late in the year. Having waited in vain for another summer to see if the ice cleared from Fury and Hecla Strait, Parry's second expedition returned to England just in time to prevent a relief expedition setting out to look for him.

Parry's third expedition (1824–25) was designed to investigate an earlier theory of his – that the passage would most likely be found through one of the waterways to the south of Lancaster Sound. Prince Regent Inlet was regarded as the most hopeful.

There is some evidence that Parry began his third expedition with rather less enthusiasm than he had begun his first. He complained to a lady at a dinner party that while he might know the Arctic pretty well he had seen nothing of the rest of the world, and the ice of McClure Strait had made him wonder if there really was a free Northwest Passage. Nevertheless, he was as energetic as ever in his preparations and found the hours from 6 a.m. until midnight not enough for everything he had to do.

The *Hecla* and *Fury* got off to an unfortunate start in Davis Strait where the ice was much worse than usual. At the beginning of August, when on his first expedition Parry had been entering Lancaster Sound, the ships were besieged and the *Hecla* driven over on her side by

London, Published (for the Proprietors of the European Magazine) by the Executors of the late Ja.ᵗ Asperne, 32 Cornhill 1ˢᵗ March 1821

Capt.ⁿ W. E. Parry – R.N.
Commander of the Polar Expedition
1819–20.

Cutting a passage with ice saws for *Fury* and *Hecla* to reach a safe winter anchorage off Melville Peninsula during Parry's second expedition.

a gale. By the time they reached Prince Regent Inlet the winter's young ice was already forming, and a westerly gale drove them back almost to Davis Strait. Fortunately, the strong winds also broke up the ice and with a more favourable breeze the ships were able to enter Prince Regent Inlet and find a place to spend the winter at Port Bowen, some fifty miles south of the sound, which Parry had briefly surveyed in 1819. Not until late July 1825 was Parry able to continue his exploration of Prince Regent Inlet, and even then the offshore ice made his work extremely hazardous. On 1 August, which seems to have been an eventful date for Parry, the *Fury* was badly damaged after being driven hard into the ice. In stormy weather, with the constant threat of the ice treating the *Hecla* as it had treated the *Fury*, Parry reluctantly decided to abandon the ship, and both crews crammed into the *Hecla* for the voyage back to England. In accordance with naval regulations, an officer who lost his ship had to be court-martialled. It happened that there were not enough captains available for the court, and Parry found himself in the peculiar position of sitting in judgement on his subordinate who had abandoned the *Fury* at his orders! Of course, the hearing was a formality, ending with an absolute discharge and hearty congratulations all round.

So ended Parry's last expedition in search of the Northwest Passage, though not his last expedition to the Arctic. It is now necessary to return to the year when he set out on his first

voyage and to trace the fortunes of another expedition sent out by the Admiralty in the hope, never fulfilled, that it might link up with Parry.

The overland expedition timed to coincide with Parry's voyage of 1819 was to explore the northern coast to the east of the mouth of the Coppermine, discovered by Samuel Hearne. Command of this expedition was given to John Franklin, Buchan's second in command on the voyage to Spitsbergen the previous year.

Franklin was thirty-three years old in 1819, with nearly twenty years of experience in the Royal Navy. He had been present at the Battle of Copenhagen and had sailed under his cousin, Matthew Flinders, to Australia. It was probably on that voyage that he learned much about navigation. The orders for his 1819 expedition defined his task but left the choice of route to him, and Franklin elected to make his decision after consulting the traders of the Hudson's Bay Company at York Factory, which he reached in the *Prince of Wales* on 30 August. The advice he received there determined his plan to make for Great Slave Lake and thence take boats down the Coppermine to the Arctic Ocean.

Franklin's career nearly ended before it had properly begun when 'I had the misfortune to slip from the summit of a rock into the river betwixt two of the falls. My attempts to regain the bank were, for a time, ineffectual owing to the rocks within my reach having been worn smooth by the action of the water; but after I had been carried a considerable distance down the

stream, I caught hold of a willow by which I held until two gentlemen of the Hudson's Bay Company came in a boat to my assistance.' The calm prose is characteristic of Franklin.

The first winter (1819–20) was spent by the main party at Cumberland House, a post established by Hearne on the Saskatchewan River, while Franklin and Midshipman George Back (who proved to be an excellent artist as well as a first-rate assistant) pushed on, staggering uncomfortably on unaccustomed snowshoes, to the North-West Company's post at Fort Chipewyan on Lake Athabasca, 1,550 miles from York Factory. Looking back on this trek, Franklin reckoned there had been more disagreeable than agreeable incidents. He disliked the bad language of the voyageurs (employees of the fur companies) and their cruelty to their dogs, and commented unfavourably on the effects the 'fur war' between the rival companies was having on the society of the Indians, whom both sides bribed with cheap liquor.

In July, the reunited expedition set off to the north again, making good speed along the broad Slave River in canoes. At Great Slave Lake they were met by an experienced employee of the North-West Company, Frederick Wentzel, and a group of Copper Indians who had volunteered to act as hunters and guides. In this region they were moving through land unknown to Europeans. Their canoes took them along the Yellowknife River, though there were many places where canoes and supplies had to be lugged laboriously over obstacles. At the end of August, some signs of the approaching winter were observed. Franklin wanted to go on down the Coppermine, but Chief Akaitcho refused to accompany him on what he considered a foolhardy venture. As he was dependent on the Indians for meat and guidance, Franklin reluctantly gave up his plan. They built up their store of reindeer meat, some of it pounded into pemmican (dried meat with an admixture of fat) which became staple polar fare after Franklin's first expedition, caught fish from the lake, and built a solid wooden house, Fort Enterprise. That December was the coldest month that Franklin experienced during the three years of his first expedition, and even inside the house, where the fire was always kept burning, the thermometers often dropped below 0 °F.

The last stage of the journey to the Arctic Ocean began in June 1821. At first the going was very difficult: each man's pack weighed about 180 lb, and they had to struggle across part-frozen lakes in heavy rain. 'The surface of the ice, being honeycombed by the recent rains, presented innumerable sharp points, which tore our shoes and lacerated the feet at every step. The poor dogs, too, marked their path with their blood.' When they reached the Coppermine travel was easier, or at any rate swifter, for the current swept the canoes along at a risky pace. The skill of the bowmen and paddlers kept them clear of jagged rocks, and birch-bark canoes proved again that what they lose in fragility they

Parry's plan for his assault on the North Pole in 1827 was to mount boats on sledges for use over ice (or land, if any) and in water. For men – or animals – to draw such heavy loads across the ice ridges and hummocks proved too hard a task.

make up for in ease of repair. At the mouth of the river the Indians and some of the French-speaking voyageurs left them, along with the invaluable Wentzel whose commitment ended at the ocean. The Eskimos of this region were suspicious, and the only one they were able to talk to was an old man who could not run away as fast as his friends and relatives. Franklin found bones that looked like the remains of the ghastly massacre perpetrated by Hearne's Indian companions on his journey to this spot. No wonder the Eskimos were apprehensive.

After more than two years, the real purpose of Franklin's expedition—to explore the Arctic coast—could be carried out. With his remaining companions, who numbered about twenty, he embarked upon the northern ocean—in birch-bark canoes! The temperature was generally in the 40s, but there was plenty of ice about and many times the little boats narrowly escaped being crushed. On land, the mosquitoes swarmed unmercifully.

In these extraordinary circumstances, they made good progress. Many days were spent sailing into and out of the Great Fish River before they realized it *was* a river and not a bay, but by mid-August they were paddling along the southern side of Kent Peninsula. The voyageurs were terrified by the appearance of the ocean (which they had never seen), with its enormous waves and icebergs swinging along on the tide. They grew more restless as Franklin led them farther and farther from the nearest settlement. Keen as he was to go on, and increasingly inclined to think he had struck a western part of the Northwest Passage, even Franklin reluctantly decided, on 22 August, that if he was to return the way he had come he would have to turn back at once. He named their farthest point, Point Turnagain. As he discovered later, Parry was 500 miles away at this time in Repulse Bay, which Franklin had hoped to reach.

Their objective now was to regain Fort Enterprise as soon as possible: the state of their supplies was critical and summer was fast receding, taking with it, they feared, the game. They boldly crossed Melville Sound, which took them out of sight of land in the heavy swell, and entered the Hood River: Franklin reckoned they could not risk retracing their voyage along Coronation Gulf (named by him to commemorate the coronation of George IV). They discarded all but essentials, constructed lighter canoes for easier porterage, and set off. The distance was only about 150 miles as the crow flies.

The horror of that journey and its sequel, as recounted in Franklin's faintly pontifical prose, has become part of popular mythology. The end of the food supplies and scarcity of game forced the men to scratch up a kind of lichen called *tripe de roche*. The terrain was murderous, the weather vile. Old boots and leather trousers were eaten by the starving men. The voyageurs lost heart, the canoes were broken and beyond

left, below
A near thing for H.M.S.
Terror under Back's
command in 1837, near the
end of his expedition to
northern Canada which had
begun as a search for the
Boothia expedition of John
Ross. The *Terror* drifted
safely into the Atlantic
eventually and survived
many more perils before the
ice claimed her for good in
Victoria Strait in 1846.

repair, a river perilously crossed by raft. Discipline cracked. The party became split up and the first men died. One man vanished and his companion reappeared with strange meat that he said he had chopped from a dead wolf. Disaster piled upon disaster. Midshipman Hood was murdered and his murderer shot by Dr Richardson who feared he was marked down for destruction next. One man died within earshot of others who were too weak to go to his aid. When at last Franklin and three companions, limbs swollen, eyes protruding, reeled into Fort Enterprise, they found nothing there – no supplies and no Indians, who had promised to stock up the settlement (the Indians themselves had fallen on hard times and their failure to supply Fort Enterprise was not entirely their fault).

Undoubtedly Franklin, Richardson, and the remaining members of the expedition would all have perished but for the grit of Midshipman George Back and the humanity of the Coppermine Indians. Back, with three of the voyageurs, had been sent ahead by Franklin and finding Fort Enterprise deserted had pressed on at once, although in no better condition than the rest of the party, to Fort Providence. One man died on the way, but Back eventually made contact with Chief Akaitcho, who sent a group of his braves to bring the meat that saved Franklin from death at Fort Enterprise. The Indians did not always behave exactly as Franklin wished, but he paid them a deserved tribute at this time: 'The Indians treated us with the utmost tenderness, gave us their snow-shoes and walked without themselves, keeping by our sides that they might lift us when we fell . . . [they] prepared our encampment, cooked for us, and fed us as if we had been children; evincing humanity that would have done honour to the most civilized people.'

Perhaps still more remarkable is the attitude of Chief Akaitcho. On the journey north Franklin had impressed upon that clever man the importance of the power he represented – the 'Great Father across the seas', etc. – in order to gain the Indians' co-operation. He reappeared destitute, saved from death by Akaitcho's men, with no presents to offer, most of his men left dead in the wilderness, and altogether cutting a very different figure from that which he had presented on his first appearance, rigged out in ceremonial naval uniform. Franklin wrote: 'We discovered at the commencement of [Akaitcho's] speech to us, that he had been informed that our expected supplies had not come. He spoke of this circumstance as a disappointment . . . but without attaching any blame to us. "The world goes badly," he said, "all are poor; you are poor, the traders appear to be poor, I and my party are poor likewise; and since the goods have not come in, we cannot have them. I do not regret having supplied you with provisions, for a Copper Indian can never permit white men to suffer from want of food on his lands, without flying to their aid . . . and at all events," he added in a tone of good humour, "it is the first time that the White People have been indebted to the Copper Indians". . . . Akaitcho afterwards expressed a strong desire that we should represent the character of his nation in a favourable light to our countrymen,' and to give Franklin his due, he did that.

On 14 July, Franklin and his remaining companions reached York Factory. 'And thus terminated our long, fatiguing, and disastrous travels in North America, having journeyed by water and by land (including our navigation of the Polar Sea), five thousand five hundred and fifty miles.'

The tongue probes an aching tooth, murderers return to the scene of their crime and explorers who feel their work is unfinished are impelled to revisit the place of earlier ordeals. Thus, in 1825, Franklin returned to the Canadian north. And not only Franklin: Dr Richardson, Lieutenant Back and the amiable and courageous Eskimo interpreter whom they called Augustus were with him. The purpose of the new expedition was to explore the coast west of the Mackenzie River, linking up, if all went well, with a ship sent to the Alaskan coast, while a second party, led by Richardson, was to explore east of the river. Franklin also hoped to link up with Parry in the Arctic. The two men met often in London and took to each other.

Franklin's second expedition was better organized than his first. Birch-bark canoes, however useful in rivers, had not proved ideal vessels for voyages in the Arctic Ocean and he had more suitable boats built to his specifications. He was to have only two casualties during the two and a half years of the expedition, both occurring on Back's homeward journey to York Factory. The men were never dangerously short of food,

though sometimes hungry, and travelled much faster. Franklin's capacity as an explorer has often been criticized, and as two of his three expeditions, while making many new discoveries, failed in their purpose and suffered heavy casualties he cannot be regarded as an outstanding success. Still, some of the criticisms offered by Stefansson, for example, seem a little narrow. It is true that Franklin and his fellow officers displayed almost total inability to 'live off the land' in 1822; but as they were at all times accompanied by professional hunters and trappers their failure to bag their share of reindeer seems insignificant: the voyageurs were not able to acquire meat where none existed and the British officers could not have done so either. It is also true that Franklin travelled more slowly than Hearne or Mackenzie, but those pioneers added little to scientific knowledge (and Hearne did not determine his position very accurately) while Franklin, to mention a single item in his research, listed 663 plants in the notes to his account of his second expedition.

In fact, Franklin surprised the fur companies' representatives by arriving in the far north much earlier than expected. Without serious mishaps, the whole party descended the Mackenzie River and in August 1825 reached the ocean and landed on Garry Island.

'The sun was setting as the boat touched the beach, and we hastened to the most elevated part of the island . . . to look around; and never was a prospect more gratifying than that which lay open to us. The Rocky Mountains were seen from SW to WNW; and from the latter point, round by the north, the sea appeared in all its majesty, entirely free from ice and without any visible obstruction to its navigation. Many seals and black and white whales were sporting on its

right, below
Franklin's men reach the Coppermine River, September 1820, from Franklin's *Narrative of a Journey to the Polar Sea.*

below
George Back (1796–1878) from a portrait made long after his exploratory days. Among his talents was a considerable artistic skill, and the excellent engravings that accompanied Franklin's account of his Canadian travels were made from Back's drawings.

waves; and the whole scene was calculated to excite in our minds the most flattering expectations as to our own success and that of our friends in the *Hecla* and the *Fury*.' Franklin raised a flag woven by his wife (who, he had since heard, had died a week after he had sailed) and left a message for Parry, should he reach that point, conspicuously marked. As the season was late, the expedition then retired by the same route to the base that had been prepared beforehand on Great Bear Lake and named, in spite of the leader's modest deprecation, Fort Franklin. Between March and August 1825 members of the expedition had journeyed a total of 5,800 miles.

After wintering without serious discomfort at Fort Franklin, the expedition set out on its task, splitting into two groups at the mouth of the Mackenzie. The cheerful and capable Dr Richardson followed the coast east to the Coppermine River, thus linking up with the area covered in Franklin's first expedition, and made a successful (thanks to helpful Indians) overland trip to base. It was nearly a year before Richardson and Franklin met again. Franklin himself set out in his boats to the west, hoping to reach Icy Cape before he was iced up. A tense and dangerous incident with Eskimos at a place which Franklin called Pillage Point to commemorate a larcenous attack on his boats ended, to the credit of Franklin and his men, without a shot being fired. Other Eskimos were more amenable. One of them expressed surprise that Franklin's party should attempt to explore the icebound coast in boats. 'We wonder that you are not provided with sledges and dogs, as our men are, to travel along the land when these interruptions [from ice] occur.'

They made slow progress because of storms, ice and above all fog: 'Fog is of all others the most hazardous state of the atmosphere for navigation in an icy sea,' commented Franklin, perhaps unnecessarily. Delays on Foggy Island convinced him that Icy Cape could not be reached; he named his farthest point westward Beechey Point, after the Captain of the *Blossom* whom he had hoped to meet in Bering Strait.

The crew of the *Blossom* had in fact made a substantial contribution themselves. A party in a barge had followed the coast east from Icy Cape as far as Point Barrow, which they named after the secretary to the Admiralty. The two parties were therefore within about 150 miles of each other (or would have been if Franklin had reached Beechey Point two weeks earlier).

After numerous adventures, some 'disagreeable', Franklin returned safely to his base and thence, via New York, he sailed to England.

By this time, the burning enthusiasm of the Admiralty for the Northwest Passage had flickered and gone out. The next expedition to the Arctic was financed by a City of London merchant, Felix Booth, whose name was soon to join those of explorers and naval celebrities on the map of northern Canada. But it was again led by naval officers experienced in polar exploration, none other than John Ross, eager to restore his reputation after his ill-rewarded efforts of 1818, and his nephew, James Clark Ross. The latter, having taken a prominent part in all Parry's expeditions, was perhaps more knowledgeable than any man in England in the ways of polar exploration.

But what of Parry himself? Although no one, certainly not Parry, regarded his eight years in search of the Northwest Passage as a waste of time, he shared the opinion of his superiors that the passage, if it existed, was not worthy of further searching (its practical value had long

A thunderstorm at Point Ogle, near the mouth of the Great Fish River, which George Back reached in 1834 after a running duel with disaster along most of the river's 500-odd tortuous miles.

been known to be minimal). Still, Parry was an Arctic man, and during the long winter night he had considered other exploits that might usefully be undertaken in the Arctic. The plan he had evolved was for an assault on the North Pole, and it was accepted by the Admiralty in 1826. It was the first scientific expedition aimed directly at the pole.

After a pleasant eighteen months in England, during which he found the courage to ask for, and obtain, the hand of an attractive sprig of the formidable Stanley family of Alderley (said by Nancy Mitford to regard the Earl of Derby as head of a junior branch of the family), Parry's *Hecla* sailed for Spitsbergen. His intention was to find a harbour in the north of Spitsbergen, from which he would travel towards the pole in boats fitted with steel runners.

Off Smeerenburg–the old Dutch whaling station of 'Blubbertown'–the *Hecla* was caught in a violent storm and to dodge the wind Parry deliberately sought out the ice pack, which at least offered some shelter. It was easier to get into the ice than get out again, and by the time the ship was safely settled at an anchorage on the north-east tip of west Spitsbergen, Parry was three weeks behind schedule.

The two boats, commanded by Parry and James Clark Ross and each containing one other officer and five men, began their journey on 21 June. The reindeer that, at Scoresby's suggestion, Parry had brought with him were amiable

creatures but proved useless as draught animals, and they were consigned to the *Hecla*'s butcher. Thus the men had to drag very heavy loads across the ice, which was not as level as they had expected. Parry elected to travel by night which at this time of year was not dark, sleeping when it was warmer (occasionally the thermometer reached 60 °F) and travelling when the surface was firmer. On average, they travelled for ten hours out of twenty-four. At the time appointed for rising in the evening, the man on watch

right
Dr John Rae (1813–93), perhaps the most accomplished overland Arctic explorer of the Franklin period. As he was a bit of a lone wolf – and not a navy man – he never became a popular hero.

below
An awkward incident during Franklin's second journey to the Arctic Ocean, when a group of 'Eskimos' (Indians?) plundered his boats. To his credit, major violence was avoided. From a drawing by George Back.

sounded a bugle. Parry never forgot that, first and foremost, he was a naval officer.

This expedition was important, more perhaps for what was learned from it than for what was actually achieved. Reindeer were ruled out; boats converted into sledges proved too heavy and cumbersome (though their use persisted); the daily ration of 10 oz of biscuit, 9 oz of pemmican and 1 oz of cocoa proved insufficient; expectations that the ice would become solid nearer the pole were disappointed; and finally Parry discovered the Arctic drift.

Progress was sometimes extremely difficult, clambering on and off ice floes, struggling through freshwater pools a foot or more deep, surmounting ridges and circumventing rifts, and on some days they only advanced three or four miles. But it soon dawned on Parry that the distance they travelled northward by the compass was considerably greater than the distance they actually advanced as revealed by his daily observation of latitude. On 22 July he noted in his journal; 'We were in latitude 82°43'5" or not quite four miles to the Northward of yesterday's observation, instead of the ten or eleven we had travelled!' During the next four days they gained only a mile, and Parry decided to reveal the sad truth to his men, whom he had not informed of his discovery, that while they advanced the ocean was carrying them back.

They had reached 82°45', considerably farther north than anyone had previously achieved

and not to be surpassed for nearly fifty years. Though they were still the best part of 500 miles from the pole, Parry ordered the return. Having made careful observations they headed back, a shorter journey as the drift was in their favour but not a pleasant one. They suffered from snow-blindness, chilblains and constant hunger – until Ross shot a polar bear, whereupon some of them endured the effects of overeating on a starved stomach. To Parry's amusement, for he had warned them of the danger, they attributed their discomfort not to the quantity of meat they had eaten but to its quality. They rejoined the *Hecla* on 21 August and reached the Orkneys a month later. Offered passage to Inverness in a Customs vessel, Parry left his tough little *Hecla* for the last time. The eventual fate of that famous vessel is unknown.

Parry's career as a polar explorer was over, but less than two years later, in 1829, the tireless James Clark Ross was back in action, this time with his uncle who had been his commander during his first experience of the Arctic eleven years earlier. The goal was once more the Northwest Passage and, building on Parry's work, the expedition was to seek a westward exit from Prince Regent Inlet. John Ross's ship, the *Victory*, was something new in polar exploration, but her novelty was, as things turned out, premature. Ross, a rather progressive skipper, soon came to survey with feelings of disgust her two giant paddle wheels and her large, noisy and ineffective steam engine which 'was not merely useless; it was a serious encumbrance since it occupied with its fuel two-thirds of our tonnage'. The engine was eventually dumped on the ice and the *Victory* reverted to sails alone.

Following Parry's route, the *Victory* passed down Prince Regent Inlet to the spot off Somerset Island where the *Fury* had been wrecked in 1823. No trace of Parry's ship remained, but her ample supplies were still neatly packed on the beach as he had left them. Ross was to find them very useful. Proceeding south, Ross proved that his ability to distinguish between a bay and a strait had not improved since 1818 by identifying Bellot Strait, in fact the only channel leading to the west, as a bay. Such mistakes are, of course, easy to make in a polar landscape where the coastal regions are low; Parry had found it necessary to dig through fourteen feet of ice to salt water in order to establish that he had passed the northern coast of Melville Island in 1820, and James Ross was soon to make an error of this kind more serious than his uncle's.

Proceeding south, Ross found an anchorage in Felix Harbour. He guided the *Victory* in, bedded her down for the winter – and there she stayed. Like the *Fury* before her, the *Victory* was never to escape from the ice. But the two winters during which the Ross expedition was confined to that grim harbour were not spent idly – particularly by James Ross. Friendly Eskimos came and built their igloo village nearby, and although the

British seamen still thought that the way they swathed themselves in layers of furs was comic rather than common sense, James Ross studied with interest their manner of building snow houses with windows of clear ice and joined them in travelling far afield by dog sledge. During the second winter he established a landmark in polar exploration when, at a spot on the west coast of Boothia Peninsula, his magnetic dipper needle pointed to 90° while the horizontal needle swung aimlessly. He was standing at the magnetic pole. Fondly thinking, perhaps, of the illusions of Nicholas of Lynn, he observed regretfully that 'Nature had erected no monument to denote the spot which she had chosen as the centre of one of her great and dark powers.' Just as well, perhaps, as the position of the magnetic pole is not constant.

On another journey overland he reached Victory Point, on the west coast of King William Island, but did not realize that in doing so he had crossed a strait (now named after him, ironically). Thus when Franklin approached King William Island in 1847, he chose the fatal westward side (Victoria Strait) because his maps showed land connecting King William Island with Boothia Peninsula.

After two winters in Felix Harbour, the *Victory* moved again, but she moved sluggishly and not far. The third winter was worse than the previous two as supplies were running low. In the summer the men struggled to Fury Beach, where Parry's supplies got them through a fourth winter. In the *Fury*'s boats, they managed to reach Lancaster Sound in the summer of 1833 and there they had the good fortune to be picked up by the whaler *Isabella*, a ship that oddly enough had once been commanded by John Ross.

They returned to England in the elderly *Isabella*. Their unprecedented four-year sojourn in the Arctic (with only three casualties) was generally acclaimed, and John Ross joined his younger rivals, Parry and Franklin, as one of that distinguished band of polar knights.

There were no more major naval expeditions until Franklin's last voyage in 1845, but the work continued if with less fanfare. George Back was sent on a relief expedition to find Ross in 1833; learning of Ross's rescue, he decided to continue exploring the Great Fish River (sometimes called Back River) and charted its course for 500 miles. Three years later Back sailed in the *Terror* to fill in, if possible, a serious blank on the map of Canada's northern coastline, by striking westward from Repulse Bay. The year 1836 turned out a bad one for ice and Back not only failed in his objective but narrowly avoided losing his ship which, on the voyage home, just reached Ireland without sinking.

Other journeys in the regions that Franklin had pioneered were undertaken by members of Hudson's Bay Company, in particular Peter Warren Dease, who had played a prominent part in Franklin's second expedition, and the youth-

ful Thomas Simpson, a man of almost daemonic determination. In fact Simpson, who died at thirty-one and is not well remembered today, was one of the most remarkable of all Arctic explorers.

Dease and Simpson set out to fill in the gaps on the mainland coast left by Franklin, Back and Ross by exploring the remaining 150-odd miles between Franklin's farthest west and Point Barrow, and by completing the journey between Franklin's farthest east and the mouth of the Great Fish River, reached by Back. Both objects were achieved.

Descending the Mackenzie, Dease and Simpson reached the Arctic Ocean at the beginning of July 1837. In their two twenty-four-foot boats, they followed Franklin's route along the coast, encountering the same difficulties and discomforts that he had described. They reached approximately the point where Franklin had turned back, and from there Simpson and five companions completed the journey along the shore to Point Barrow. By the end of September the whole party was back at winter quarters on Great Bear Lake. The following year, after Simpson had reconnoitred the ground during the winter, they hauled their boats overland to the Coppermine, which they descended to the sea. Struggling through massed ice, they reached Franklin's Point Turnagain where, again, Simpson with a small group struck out on foot. They reached Victoria Island, which Simpson named for the new British queen, before turning back. On the way to Fort Confidence, they hauled their boats up the Coppermine, a feat that Franklin had regarded as impossible. In 1839 Simpson pursued his discoveries still farther, into the strait named after him and on to the sandy estuary of the Great Fish River. He hoped to reach Fury and Hecla Strait next year but he was shot while returning from Red River settlement, 2,000 miles from Fort Confidence, to which he had walked to pick up the mail. Whether he was killed by one of his companions or committed suicide remains a mystery. The kindest explanation is that his mind gave way after the terrific physical and mental strain of his journeys.

His work was continued by Dr John Rae who, not being a naval man, has also been underrated as an explorer; his physical stamina almost matched Simpson's. From his base at Repulse Bay Rae, who was ill-equipped with supplies and but meagerly supported by his employers, advanced at the second attempt to Committee Bay, the southernmost part of Prince Regent Inlet. To the north-west he linked up with the farthest southward that Ross had explored and, after a short rest at his base, advanced almost as far as Fury and Hecla Strait. Rae thus completed the major outline of coasts and seas in the area between Melville Peninsula and King William Island, and ruled out the lingering hope that a strait might exist turning Boothia Peninsula into an island.

The Search for the South Magnetic Pole

In a little over a decade the coast of the Canadian Antarctic, from being almost a complete blank, had been charted almost end to end from Baffin Bay to Bering Strait. Many of the waterways and islands to the north had been mapped as well. This sudden advance, the most remarkable in polar exploration since the days of Bering, had been achieved almost entirely by the British, or more accurately, by British and Canadians.

By comparison, Antarctica was little known, and the three expeditions launched in the late 1830s, though revealing more than all previous voyages, were not to penetrate beyond the fringe of the great white continent. Unlike the Canadian Arctic, Antarctica was not predominantly a British interest; the three expeditions were dispatched by three different countries–France, the United States, and Britain–and a note of international competition was sounded across the southern seas.

J. S. C. Dumont d'Urville was born in 1790 into an old Norman family with aristocratic connections, which at that time had suddenly become rather undesirable. His early childhood was disorganized by the family's flight from their home and the death of his father, but he eventually

Jules Dumont d'Urville (1790–1842), the remarkable French navigator who so irritated his contemporaries that his tomb was inscribed with the disgraceful words (subsequently erased), *Point de deuil, Un peu de cendre, Un peu de terre, Beaucoup de bruit.* (No mourning, a little ash, a little earth, a lot of fuss.)

entered one of Napoleon's new lycées where he displayed an unusual intellect, a disinclination to play games and a solitary disposition. He is said to have bet a schoolfellow that he would be an admiral by the time he was fifty (he lost the bet by a matter of weeks), and joined the navy at sixteen. He was, he says, always more interested in voyages of discovery than warfare, of which he disapproved, and although this may sound like a retrospective comment it is probably true. He was an intellectual–well read in the classics, a remarkable linguist, and an able botanist and ethnographer. But voyages of discovery were not high on the schedule of Napoleon (whom d'Urville hated) nor of the Bourbons ('unspeakably disagreeable').

The most remarkable incident in his career, perhaps as well known as his explorations, occurred while he was engaged in hydrographic research in the Mediterranean in 1820. An old statue was discovered in one of the Greek islands. Dumont d'Urville at once recognized it, though no one else did, but his captain would not let him buy it (it was going for 400 francs) because it would take up too much space. Dumont d'Urville thereupon drew up a learned report urging acquisition of the statue which he sent to the French Ambassador at Constantinople. Impressed by the tone of the document, the Ambassador followed his advice and procured the work on behalf of the French nation. It was the Venus de Milo.

D'Urville's naval career took an upward turn soon afterwards. He sailed on the *Coquille* as second in command of a scientific expedition that covered 73,000 miles, and in 1826 he commanded the same ship, renamed *Astrolabe*, in the search for La Pérouse. This three-year voyage established his reputation as an outstanding navigator, although the government's failure to reward his officers as he requested aroused his bitterness and marked the beginning of mutual hostility between Dumont d'Urville and the scientific-naval establishment which continued until his death, and finds frequent expression in Dumont d'Urville's massive publications.

Dumont d'Urville was not especially interested in the Antarctic but when he was offered command of an expedition to the Antarctic and the Pacific in 1837 he felt he would not refuse: 'When I examined the proposal from every aspect I came to the conclusion that an attempt to reach the South Pole would appeal to the public as something so novel, so great and even so astounding that it could not fail to attract attention.'

In September 1837 the *Astrolabe* and the *Zélée* left Toulon. Four months later they were in the Antarctic. The ships, usually described as corvettes, were not suitable for polar waters and their survival is a tribute to their commander's seamanship and gritty determination. King Louis-Philippe was primarily interested in *la gloire* and had instructed Dumont d'Urville to beat Weddell's record for farthest south. No extensive exploration was called for. After sighting Graham Land and naming Joinville Island among other places, Dumont d'Urville retired to the Pacific to pursue the ethnological studies that he preferred.

The following summer, however, he decided to make another foray into the Antarctic, this time approaching from the direction of Australia rather than South America. Such a venture was in excess of his instructions and on the face of it seems strange, given Dumont d'Urville's lack of interest, lack of preparation, and the perils of the Antarctic Ocean – not to mention the gout that was making the Captain even crankier than usual. With customary frankness, he explained his motive in his account of the voyage: the hope of finding the south magnetic pole and thus beating the rival expeditions of Wilkes and Ross to the punch. Perhaps he also remembered a sailor's remark, overheard when he took command of his ships. 'This old fellow won't take us far.' He approached the circle in fine weather, though surrounded by tabular icebergs, but before reaching it sighted land – a high plateau stretching away on either side without any distinctive features. Taking advantage of the

good weather, a boat from the *Astrolabe* landed on a rocky islet close to the coast and ran up the tricolour. Dumont d'Urville, a good family man, named the place Adélie Land 'to perpetuate the memory of my profound regard for the devoted companion who has three times consented to a long and painful separation in order to allow me to accomplish my plans for distant explorations'.

Having followed the land eastwards for two days the ships were caught in a sudden and savage storm, which ripped the mainsail of the *Astrolabe* to shreds. They weathered the storm and a few days later encountered one of the American Wilkes' ships. Subsequently, both captains accused the other of deliberately not signalling, but it seems that the brusque nose-in-the-air attitude that each ship displayed arose from mutual misunderstanding: Wilkes' captain thought Dumont d'Urville was trying to avoid him, and the Frenchman replied by levelling the same accusation at the Wilkes expedition. The French ships continued to follow the ice cliffs for some days but conditions on board were deteriorating, with Dumont d'Urville himself among the sick. Encountering pack ice, he decided to withdraw, and by November 1840 he was back in France. No other French ship was to venture into Antarctic waters until the 20th century.

Eighteen months after his return, Dumont d'Urville allowed his much-loved wife and one remaining child to persuade him to take a short break from his work. They wanted to see the fountains at Versailles. Their train crashed and burst into flames, and Dumont d'Urville, who had fought his way through gales, storms, icebergs and coral reefs, was burned to death with his family.

American sealers in the Antarctic had outnumbered those of other nations since the early days, and there were many who advocated greater national activity in the south polar regions.

On 21 January 1840 a party from the *Astrolabe* planted the French flag on a rock just off the inaccessible coast of Adélie Land, which remains the centre of French Antarctic research today.

A member of the race native to Adélie Land – an Adélie penguin with her ugly but charming chicks. It was Dumont d'Urville who observed that penguins looked like little old gentlemen in evening dress. They are curious and comparatively fearless creatures, a combination of characteristics that did them no good when they came into contact with men and dogs.

James Clark Ross (1800–62), telescope in his hand, explorer's fur cloak over his shoulder and determined gaze in his eyes: the most accomplished British polar explorer of the 19th century.

Edmund Fanning produced his somewhat over-imaginative account of Antarctic discovery in 1834. John Reynolds complained that American discoveries in Antarctica were being appropriated by the British and persuaded the House of Representatives to petition the President to send out an expedition.

These pressures eventually resulted in the Wilkes expedition of 1838, which in characteristic American fashion was the largest Antarctic expedition yet mounted but, less characteristically, was badly planned and badly equipped. Wilkes set out in a frame of mind hardly conducive to success: 'It required all the hope I could muster to outweigh the intense feeling of responsibility that hung over me. I may compare it with that of one doomed to destruction.'

He had every excuse for feeling so gloomy; the preliminaries to sailing had been characterized by bungling, ill-feeling, ignorance and pig-headedness on a startling scale, providing much evidence for the European belief that democracy tended to make men quarrelsome. Charles Wilkes himself had originally been appointed to a subordinate position: he was only a lieutenant and a comparatively junior one at that. Later he resigned when he found that he was listed as a member of the scientific side rather than the executive staff (his opinion of civilian scientists was contemptuous) and he had finally been appointed to overall command of the squadron of five ships after one officer had resigned and three more had refused.

He finally sailed rather hastily, in August 1838, because public opinion was becoming exasperated by the delays and his men were showing a tendency to desert in droves (throughout, the expedition suffered the astonishing desertion rate of 40 per cent). He was fully aware that his ships and supplies were inadequate. His own ship, the 780-ton sloop *Vincennes*, was equipped with large gun ports that, while hardly

necessary for guns since Wilkes was not going to shoot at anyone, let in the sea spray abundantly. The 650-ton *Peacock* was, in the opinion of her commander Lieutenant William L. Hudson, 'fitted out . . . with less regard to safety and convenience than any vessel I ever had anything to do with'. As for the equipment of the Wilkes expedition, the citizens of Sydney, where the winter was spent in 1839, asked some telling questions: 'They enquired whether we had compartments in our ships to prevent us from sinking? How we intended to keep ourselves warm? What kind of anti-scorbutic we were to use? And where were our great ice-saws?' To these questions, Wilkes was obliged to answer that they had none and to agree that the Americans were embarked upon a decidedly risky cruise. 'Most of our visitors considered us doomed to be frozen to death.' In these circumstances, the achievements of Wilkes and his fellow officers, though falling short of their superiors' sanguine expectations, were none the less remarkable.

In the first season, one of the smaller boats reached 70° South – not so far as Cook but a commendable effort for a vessel of ninety tons. Wilkes' ships sighted the Antarctic mainland at several points although, unfortunately, some of these sightings were shortly afterwards proved false by James Ross, bringing more discredit to Wilkes than he deserved. It was impossible to land because of the ice barrier, but the crews did enjoy themselves skating on a pond on one of the large ice islands. Although his charts were inaccurate, Wilkes is rightly credited with the discovery of Wilkes Land, close to which he sailed from about 150° to 100° East.

Wilkes, whose exploration was not confined to the Antarctic, did not finally return to an American port until June 1842. Instead of the welcome due to a great explorer he found himself facing a court martial. Some of the charges, e.g. wearing a uniform to which he was not entitled,

appear ridiculous, and it seems that they originated in the unfortunate hostility existing between Wilkes and his subordinate officers. Wilkes was a tough skipper and an uncompromising man. He was acquitted of all serious charges, but the American government was not to launch another major Antarctic expedition until after the First World War. Wilkes' subsequent career was also controversial. He was the captain of the U.S. warship that stopped the British mail-steamer *Trent* in 1861 in order to remove two Confederate emissaries on their way to Europe. This action was subsequently disavowed by the government, leading to Wilkes' quarrel with Naval Secretary Gideon Welles and another court martial. Nevertheless, he made Rear-Admiral (on the retired list) before his death at the age of seventy-nine in 1877.

The third Antarctic expedition of this period was British. It was commanded by James Clark Ross, a veteran of seventeen summers and eight winters in the Arctic, and it was largely staffed by men with Arctic experience. It was in every way better equipped than the expeditions of Dumont d'Urville and Wilkes, and it is not surprising that it achieved greater results.

The character of Ross, who was born in London of a Scottish family, emerges from the historical record with less distinctive individuality than Parry's or Franklin's. Comparatively little is known of his early life; in joining the navy (at the age of twelve) he was following a family tradition; and his early experience was under his uncle, John Ross, who commanded the expedition during which James Ross discovered the north magnetic pole. All books about Antarctic explorers mention that the younger Ross was 'the handsomest man in the navy', and although a certain Byronic glamour is apparent, his portraits suggest that it must have been charm of manner rather than classical features that accounted for this reputation.

The Barrier – Ross's name for the great ice shelf barring the route south in the sea he discovered. The cliffs, rising high above the masts and stretching for immeasurable miles, inspired feelings of awe and a curious kind of admiration mixed with the pride of discovery, in spite of Ross's annoyance at being thwarted in his object – to reach the South Magnetic Pole.

Although the main purpose of the voyage was scientific–in particular, 'to determine the position of the magnetic pole'–no scientists as such were appointed. Ross himself could be described as an expert on terrestrial magnetism and the ship's surgeons were civilians temporarily commissioned because of their scientific interests. Among them was Joseph Hooker who, like his father, was to become the most notable botanist of his generation. Ross's two ships were the *Erebus* and the *Terror*, both under 400 tons, reinforced, shallow-draughted bombs, whose tendency to roll was an advantage in pack ice although not otherwise an attractive characteristic.

After stopping at various points to set up observatories, Ross's ships arrived in Tasmania in August 1840. The governor of that colony was none other than Sir John Franklin, whose admiring inspection of Ross's ships is one of history's most ironic scenes. He would one day command them himself in the most disastrous of all British polar expeditions. The crew were well entertained by Franklin and his attractive second wife, Jane, but news of the exploits of Dumont d'Urville and Wilkes put the chauvinistic Ross in an angry temper. Determined not to follow in anyone's footsteps, certainly not a foreigner's, Ross took advantage of the flexibility of his orders to begin his exploration of Antarctica farther east than originally intended. Ross had the reputation of being a 'lucky' captain, an enviable one for a navigator and one that poor Franklin would never share, and certainly this decision, made from pique as much as anything, had some fortunate results, for it led him into what is now called the Ross Sea.

On the last day of the year a giant petrel appeared high above the masts, and soon the 'blink' on the horizon gave warning of the presence of the ice pack. It lay thick ahead, the barrier from which all previous ships had retreated. But not *Erebus* and *Terror*. On 5 January 1841 the blunt-prowed vessels forged into the ice. They were biffed and bumped, banged and battered, but after an hour's nerve-racking sailing they thrust through the heavy rim of the pack and found themselves among a network of channels. Picking their way carefully, they followed the leads towards the south and soon lost sight of the open sea behind them. Flocks of unwary penguins followed them, and what appeared to be a great mountain looming up before them vanished in mist as they passed straight through it. Five days later, at close on 70° South, they were sailing in open sea. They were the first ships to breach the Antarctic ice pack.

The behaviour of his compasses told Ross that the magnetic pole was not far away, and the discovery of land ahead was therefore something of a disappointment as it threatened to bar him from his objective. Mountains appeared, and high cliffs, black against the snowy summits behind them. Ross named the range of mountains beyond Cape Adare the Admiralty Range and graced each individual peak with the name of one of the Lords of the Admiralty. The mainland was inaccessible; but Ross and Crozier, Captain of the *Terror*, landed on Possession Island and claimed the region, which they named Victoria Land, for Great Britain. The penguins provided a numerous if uncomprehending audience for the ceremony. After weathering a storm, the ships pressed on to the south with the shore three or four miles off the starboard bow. Passing Weddell's farthest south, they made a landing on Franklin Island, where Joseph Hooker barely escaped being cut off before his eminent career had begun when he fell into the water and was nearly crushed by the boat. The latitude was about 76° South and from this point they saw that most impressive of Antarctic sights, the lofty eminence of a volcano, belching black smoke, to which Ross gave the name of his ship–Erebus. The slightly lower mountain next to it naturally became Mount Terror.

They had now passed south of the magnetic pole and were over 200 miles east of it. Ahead their way was manifestly blocked by sheer cliffs of ice, and Ross elected to follow the Barrier (his name for the ice shelf) to the east. The impression that the Barrier made upon the English seamen was recorded by the blacksmith of the *Erebus* in lines of which McGonagall would not have been ashamed:

Awful and sublime, magnificent and rare,
No other Earthly object with the Barrier can
*   compare.*

In mid-February, Ross decided he had done enough for one season, and having followed the Barrier for over 200 miles, reaching a 'farthest south' of 78°4′, he turned back to look for winter quarters. Had he ventured deeper into McMurdo Sound he would have discovered there a suitable winter anchorage, as Scott was to do, but finding nowhere to land, he reluctantly turned back to Tasmania for the winter. He reached it in the first week of April 1841.

Although he had not reached the magnetic pole, Ross's first venture into the Antarctic had been a great success. In the following year he was less fortunate. Intent on exploring the Barrier to its end he started still farther east and thus found himself among the much heavier pack ice from what is now known as Marie Byrd Land. Navigation was also complicated by fog.

The ships made very slow progress, though boredom was temporarily relieved by some juvenile entertainments, including a snowball fight in which Ross and Crozier joined, enacted on the ice as part of the celebration of the New Year. Drifting with the pack, the ships were often driven in a contrary direction, and yet the pack was loose enough to make conditions extremely hazardous in a storm. On 18 January 'the wind suddenly freshened to a violent gale. . . . The sea quickly rising to a fearful height, breaking over the loftiest bergs, we were unable any longer to hold our ground, but were driven into the heavy pack under our lee. Soon after midnight our ships were involved in an ocean of rolling fragments of ice, hard as floating rocks of granite, which were dashed against them by the waves with so much violence that their masts quivered as if they would fall at every successive blow; and the destruction of the ships seemed inevitable. . . . The loud crashing noise of the straining and working of the timbers and decks, as she was driven against some of the heavier pieces . . . was sufficient to fill the stoutest heart that was not supported by trust in Him who controls all events, with dismay. . . .' Severe damage was caused, the *Terror* losing her rudder, but two days of fairer weather allowed the necessary repairs to be made. After forging through the pack for 800 miles, the ships were still only about thirty miles farther south than Cook in the same region and the Barrier was not sighted until the end of February, when it was getting late in the season for venturing farther south.

Few opportunities were lost for scientific research, in which Ross himself played a capable part, and zoological specimens were sometimes obtained in a fortuitous manner. It was so cold that a fish thrown against the bows of the *Terror* was immediately frozen there and soon encased by a protecting block of ice. It was rescued by the ship's surgeon, who removed the surrounding ice and put it on one side for later examination. Unfortunately the ship's cat got wind of its presence, and science was baulked of a possible advance.

Towards the end of February Ross broke his own record for farthest south by some five miles (his record was to stand for sixty years) and following the ice shelf to north-east, saw an

Seals enjoy the sunshine on pancake ice in the Antarctic. The distinctive appearance of pancake ice is caused by the softening floes continually bumping into each other. A photograph by Herbert G. Ponting.

'appearance of land' but he could not be positive about it. (He was right, but his hesitancy compares favourably with the tendency of other explorers to record land where none existed.)

The worst experience of the whole expedition came when the ships were on their way to the Falkland Islands, where they were instructed to call, some 250 miles north of the Antarctic Circle. In the evening, a strong wind got up, bringing snow with it which together with the gathering darkness severely reduced visibility. The two ships were proceeding on a roughly parallel course with the *Erebus* leading when suddenly a vast iceberg appeared out of the gloom directly ahead. Ross immediately bore away to port but in so doing crossed the bows of the *Terror*, which could not avoid a collision except by sailing smack into the iceberg.

'The concussion when she struck us,' wrote Ross, 'was such as to throw almost everyone off his feet; our bowsprit, fore-topmast, and other smaller spars, were carried away; and the ships hanging together, entangled in their rigging, [were dashed] against each other with fearful violence. . . . Sometimes she rose high above us, almost exposing her keel to view, and again descended as we in our turn rose to the top of the wave, threatening to bury her beneath us whilst the crashing of the breaking upperworks and boats increased the horror of the scene.' Fortunately the ships parted, but the iceberg was by then right on top of the *Terror*. A dark space appeared and Crozier steered for it. The cartographer on the *Terror*, J. E. Davis, described what happened. 'We were immediately rushing past an enormous berg, the ship being perfectly covered with the foam caused by the sea breaking against it. Every moment we were expecting the

ship to strike ice right ahead. "Hard-a-port!" was screamed out from forward (then indeed hope died within us) . . . "Shiver the main topsail!", cried the Captain as if he were steering into any harbour. The men flew to the ropes. . . . She came round, and passed through an opening between two bergs not twice the breadth of the ship. . . .'

The *Erebus*, damaged in the collision, drifted right on to the iceberg, her yards striking its face. Ross gave the order to go astern–'an expedient,' he remarked, 'that perhaps had never before been resorted to by seamen in such weather'. It worked, and the half-crippled ship scraped her way through the providential space between the two icebergs. The sailors were able to patch up the damage and the two ships reached the Falklands a month later.

In his third Antarctic summer, Ross planned to penetrate the Weddell Sea. It was not a good idea, although he could not know that Weddell had encountered freakishly favourable conditions, nor that the Ross Sea is invariably a better approach to the South Pole for ships. When Dumont d'Urville was in this region, he had begun to wonder if Weddell's claims were fraudulent, and although Ross found the pack seventy-five miles farther south than it was when d'Urville encountered it, he could not make much progress. After a week's determined charging at the pack, he was farther north than when he had started. Trying again towards the east he reached 71°30′ South, but failed to sight Princess Martha Coast though within thirty miles of it. He returned via Cape Town to England which he reached in September 1843 after an absence of four and a half years, having completed the most successful Antarctic expedition before Scott.

The Franklin Saga

On his return from the Antarctic James Clark Ross, perhaps aware that at forty-three his days as the navy's handsomest man were numbered if not over, got married, and to please his wife announced his retirement from polar exploration. Thus it was that the Admiralty gave the command of a new expedition in search of the Northwest Passage to Sir John Franklin, who had recently returned from Tasmania under something of a cloud. Those who knew the whole story did not hold Franklin to blame for his political difficulties but the Admiralty was not surprisingly a little reluctant to appoint a man of Franklin's age to command a voyage of Arctic exploration. 'I might find a good excuse for not letting you go, Sir John, in the rumour that tells me you are sixty years of age,' said the First Lord. 'No, no, My Lord,' Franklin responded as if thoroughly disposing of this objection, 'I am only fifty-nine.'

Others were consulted. The First Lord summoned Parry. 'Do you think we ought to let [Franklin] go?' he asked. 'He is a fitter man to go than any I know,' Parry said, 'and if you don't let him go the man will die of disappointment.'

The Northwest Passage had been out of favour at the Admiralty since Parry's third voyage, but the combined pressure of the Royal Geographical Society and Sir John Barrow, one of its founders, had finally resulted in the decision to make a final effort which would complete the charting of the passage.

Franklin's ships were the *Erebus* and *Terror*, the latter again commanded by Captain Crozier. Ross's old ships were newly equipped with steam engines and propeller screws; they carried supplies for three years, and Franklin himself advised that no one should start worrying about him if nothing was heard after two years.

They departed in June 1845. 'Sir John is a *new man* since we left,' wrote a young officer on the *Erebus*. 'He . . . looks ten years younger and takes part in everything that goes on with as much interest as if he had not grown older since his last Expedition. We are all delighted to find how *decided* he is in all that he resolves on, and he has such experience and judgement that we all look on his decisions with the greatest respect. I never felt that the Captain was so much my *companion* with anyone I have sailed with before. He has certainly made a *friend* of every person on board and I believe not a thing he has said or done has given rise to the slightest complaint. . . .'

This letter was one of a batch sent back from off the coast of Greenland. The officers advised their friends to address any future correspondence to Petropavlovsk, Kamchatka.

By late July they were in Baffin Bay, where a whaler saw them preparing to cross to Lancaster Sound. The expedition appears to have begun well, but ice obstructed Barrow Strait so Franklin took advantage of a suggestion in his instructions to explore Wellington Channel, to the north. By the time he had circumnavigated Cornwallis Island winter was approaching, and he established winter headquarters on Beechey Island, a small islet south-west of Devon Island.

In the following season conditions were still bad in Barrow Strait, and Franklin elected to sail down Peel Sound, the passage between Prince of Wales Island and Somerset Island. He kept to the eastern side of Peel Sound until he approached King William Island. James Clark Ross had reached this island from Boothia Peninsula without realizing that he had crossed a strait between them; Franklin's map therefore showed that King William Island was joined to the mainland in the east, and he naturally turned towards the west (Victoria Strait). Never was there a more disastrous wrong turning. Victoria Strait is a virtual cul-de-sac for the Arctic ice pack, which accumulates there in dense, piled masses.

In September the *Erebus* and *Terror* were imprisoned in the ice about twelve miles off King William Island, then known as King William Land. At first their situation seemed not dangerous and perhaps even hopeful, as the ice was drifting slowly westward. However, the ice pack did not make ideal winter quarters, and the discovery that some of the tinned supplies had gone bad could only increase the uneasiness of the crew.

In the spring parties from the ships explored the neighbouring coasts and discovered – too

late – that a passable strait existed between King William Island and Boothia Peninsula.

In June Franklin died, probably from natural causes and still unaware that he had led his men into a deadly trap. But August passed and the ships were still frozen in. During the second winter in the ice food became scarce; the first men died, scurvy made its dread appearance, and Captain Crozier realized that to remain where they were would mean certain death for all on board. When spring came he decided to attempt an escape overland to the Great Fish River.

Towing heavily laden boats behind them, 105 men (out of the 129 who had left England) set out on their desperate march. At Cape Felix, where James Ross had built a cairn to mark his passage, they left their last message. It was written in the margins of an Admiralty report form which had been left there a year earlier, reporting 'all well', by one of the exploring parties from the ships. It read:

'April 25, 1848. HM Ships Terror and Erebus were deserted on the 22nd April, 5 leagues NNW of this, having been beset since 12 September, 1846. The officers and crew consisting of 105 souls under command of Captain F. R. M. Crozier, landed here.

Sir John Franklin died on the 11th June, 1847 and the total loss by deaths in the expedition has been to this date 9 officers and 15 men.
F. R. M. Crozier
Captain and Senior Officer
James Fitzjames
Captain HMS Erebus
and start on tomorrow 26th for Back's Fish River.'

The long and hopeless march began. Between Cape Felix and the Great Fish estuary they left their terrible trail: items thrown away to lighten their load, graves and finally bodies lying where they fell. Cold, disease and starvation picked them off relentlessly. Strung out over an ever-increasing distance, their number dwindled daily. Here lay a cooking stove, there a tent, here a shovel, then a whole boat abandoned when it could be dragged no farther. Not a man survived.

Nothing of this disaster was known in England. When *Erebus* and *Terror* faded into the mist in Baffin Bay all sight or sound of them was lost.

It has been said, by Sir Clements Markham among others, that the Admiralty was to blame for not sending a relief expedition after Franklin more quickly. But Franklin himself had warned that he expected to be out of touch for at least two years, and 1847 was really the earliest time for making plans to aid him. The Admiralty did launch a massive search in 1848 and even if it had been at once successful it would probably not have been in time to save a single life. It was only later that the Admiralty persisted in searching what many people correctly considered to be the least likely areas.

The search for Franklin opened a new era in Arctic exploration. Sir John Richardson, Frank-

lin's old comrade, lists some forty expeditions of one kind or another that set out at least partly with the object of searching for Franklin in the decade beginning in 1848. The result of all this activity, which was not confined to Britain, was not only the discovery of the fate of the Franklin expedition but also a rapid and large advance in the exploration of the Canadian Arctic.

With no clue to Franklin's movements, the first major search was launched from all three of the possible approaches. Sir James Ross approached from the east, through Lancaster Sound; ice prevented him advancing beyond Barrow Strait. Two ships went via South America to Bering Strait in case Franklin had got through the Northwest Passage; they found no sign of him but charted many miles of unknown waters. The overland expedition from the south was led by Richardson himself and John Rae; it covered the coast between the Coppermine and Mackenzie Rivers.

The search reached a peak in 1850, when no less than fourteen ships were in Arctic waters engaged upon the search for Franklin. They included a naval squadron under Captain Horatio Austin, via Lancaster Sound; Ross's old ships *Enterprise* and *Investigator*, under Collinson and McClure, which approached from Bering Strait; and two ships under US naval command fitted out by Henry Grinnell of New York, who was inspired, like many others, by the courageous determination of Lady Franklin to discover the truth about her husband's expedition. She herself paid for the expedition of the *Prince Albert* under Captain Forsyth in 1850, and the Hudson's Bay Company backed a schooner commanded by none other than Sir John Ross, then in his seventy-third year.

Of all these expeditions, the most important are those commanded by Austin and Collinson. Franklin's first winter headquarters on Beechey Island were soon found (Lieutenant De Haven of the US Navy was there first), but they yielded no clue as to Franklin's direction from there. Austin's ships wintered in the pack off the south of Cornwallis Island, and Leopold McClintock of the *Assistance* lost no time preparing for the sledge journeys planned for the following spring. He was already an experienced sledger, having beaten Wrangel's record for the longest sledging journey with James Ross in 1848–49. In the autumn, McClintock established depots to supply his sledges in the spring. This was one of many minor innovations he made which together added up to the greatest advance in Arctic exploration since Parry's first expedition.

When spring approached, the sledging parties set off in various directions, with McClintock taking the longest route–to Melville Island. He was away for eighty days, during which he averaged ten miles a day, advancing along the south coast of Melville Island and into Liddon Gulf. He found many traces of Parry's sojourn at Winter Harbour, and the friendliness of an

Arctic hare that had set up its home near Parry's commemorative rock suggested that no man had been there since.

The expedition failed to find any further traces of Franklin, though it did rule out some areas that he had obviously not visited. In other respects it was a notable step forward in Arctic exploration, and in the words of Sir Clements Markham, then a midshipman on the *Assistance*, it was a 'happy and jolly' expedition, with very few casualties.

The voyages of the *Enterprise* and the *Investigator* were more dramatic. The two ships were supposed to proceed together, but they became separated off Cape Horn and thereafter pursued independent courses. This was unfortunate, because the only Eskimo interpreter was on the *Investigator* with McClure; he would have been invaluable on the *Enterprise*.

Finding no trace of the lost expedition on the north Alaskan coast, McClure turned north on the theory that Franklin had passed through Wellington Channel. Thus he entered unknown waters. He rounded the south of Banks Island (seen and named from the north by Parry) and, enjoying temporarily good weather, sailed north through Prince of Wales Strait. This hitherto unknown strait, heading north-east towards Barrow Strait, convinced McClure that he had found the Northwest Passage. He was forced to

winter in the ice, but by sledge he established the link with Barrow Strait. Other sledging parties explored the coasts of Banks Island and Prince Albert Peninsula.

McClure was confident that he would complete the Northwest Passage in the following summer, and when the ice failed to clear sufficiently, he retraced his route and sailed up the western side of Banks Island—an extremely tricky journey accomplished with many narrow escapes. He found a winter refuge in the Bay of Mercy on the north coast of Banks Island, almost opposite Parry's farthest west: he was still feeling confident of achieving the passage to Lancaster Sound. But the *Investigator* was never to leave Mercy Bay.

Collinson, with more attention to orders and less ambition for fame, spent most of the first season searching for the *Investigator*. Failing to find her he retired to the more amiable climate of Hong Kong for the winter. The *Enterprise* thus began her equally remarkable voyage a year after the *Investigator*.

To begin with, Collinson followed McClure's route with uncanny exactness. He sailed up Prince of Wales Strait and, finding a message from McClure in which he claimed to have discovered the Northwest Passage, sailed down again, round Banks Island, and up its western coast. He turned back when almost within sight

The squadron commanded by Captain Austin putting to sea in 1850 on the search for Franklin. The *Resolute* in the centre.

of the Bay of Mercy where his missing partner was immured.

Collinson wintered in a bay on the south coast of Prince Albert Peninsula and as the days lengthened again sent out sledging parties to search for traces of Franklin. He was not able to escape from his winter quarters until August 1852, whereupon he sailed up Prince Albert Sound, proving that it was not a strait, then picked his way carefully to the east, through Dolphin and Union Strait, Coronation Gulf, and Dease Strait (along the south coast of Victoria Island). He spent his second winter in Cambridge Bay, at the eastern end of Dease Strait.

If McClure had not disappeared with the only interpreter Collinson would, almost without doubt, have discovered the remains of the Franklin expedition. The Eskimos he met near Cambridge Bay had items from the *Erebus* in their possession, but Collinson could not understand their explanation of where the relics came from. In the spring sledging parties explored the western coast of Victoria Strait as far north as McClintock Channel, where they found a note from the energetic John Rae explaining that he had already scouted this region. It is possible that, in clear weather, Collinson's men would have been in sight of the wrecks of *Erebus* and *Terror*, then still showing above the ice.

Collinson had hoped in the following year to reach Lancaster Sound via Victoria Strait, but his coal was running short and he was compelled to retreat to the west. Another winter passed before he reached Bering Strait and the *Enterprise* finally entered English waters in the autumn of 1855, over five years after she had left.

In that period much had happened. John Rae, preceding Collinson in Victoria Strait, had found traces of the Franklin expedition–enough to gain him half of the £20,000 reward offered by the Admiralty. Among the relics he obtained from the Eskimos was a silver plate engraved with Franklin's name. The Frenchman Lieutenant Bellot, sailing as a volunteer in the *Prince Albert*, had discovered the strait that bears his name between Somerset Island and Boothia Peninsula, which John Ross had mistaken for a bay. In 1852 the Admiralty had mounted another expedition of no less than five ships.

The command of this enterprise was given, for some extraordinary reason, to Captain Sir Edward Belcher, who was elderly, inexperienced, pompous and nervous. The only good result of his appointment was that Belcher's inadequacy threw into high relief the contrastingly high quality of the leadership of other Arctic expeditions in this period. The expedition was an expensive failure, although Belcher cannot be blamed for the fact that his instructions directed the search into unlikely areas.

However, the Belcher expedition contained a number of experienced Arctic officers and as it was divided into two divisions, McClintock and others in the western division were able to carry

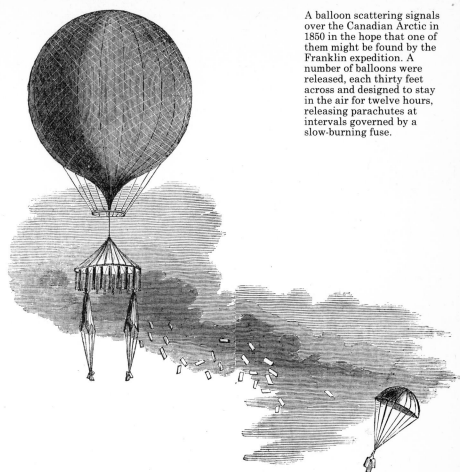

A balloon scattering signals over the Canadian Arctic in 1850 in the hope that one of them might be found by the Franklin expedition. A number of balloons were released, each thirty feet across and designed to stay in the air for twelve hours, releasing parachutes at intervals governed by a slow-burning fuse.

out some interesting and instructive work under Captain Kellett.

Franklin's expedition was not the only missing party. When the Belcher expedition set out nothing had been heard of the *Enterprise* and the *Investigator*; fear was growing that they too were in trouble.

The expedition made its headquarters on Beechey Island. Belcher in the *Assistance* together with Sherard Osborn in the *Pioneer* went north, up Wellington Channel, while Kellett and McClintock in the *Resolution* and *Intrepid* sailed on towards the west, and found winter quarters off the south coast of Melville Island.

In the autumn, sledging depots were laid down in McClintock's now customary manner, and during one of these sorties Lieutenant Mecham, whose reputation as a sledger might rival McClintock's had he not died before the age of thirty, visited Parry's commemorative rock where he found a note from McClure, dated six months earlier (April 1852) and describing his position in the Bay of Mercy. The sledging parties set out in the spring, Mecham to the west, McClintock to the north-west, Vesey Hamilton to the north, while a fourth party under Lieutenant Pim crossed McClure Strait to Mercy Bay.

By this time the crew of the icebound *Investigator* were in a desperate plight. McClure had hoped to be able to break away in the summer of 1852, but the ice did not disperse. His supplies had deteriorated and some of his men were far from fit. Although the ship was still sound, to remain in Mercy Bay seemed likely to result in the death of all, as relief was extremely unlikely

(Mecham's discovery of McClure's note at Winter Harbour was a fortunate chance).

During the winter of 1852–53 the first man died and McClure decided in the spring to make a rather despairing trek overland in the hope of reaching Port Leopold, over 500 miles to the east. 'Like doomed men quitting their cells for the last walk to the gallows', they prepared the sledges for the hopeless journey. They were on the point of leaving when they saw a figure in the distance approaching rapidly. They assumed that he was one of the crew being pursued by a bear; about 200 yards away he began shouting, only the wind distorted his words into a meaningless shriek. As he drew nearer they saw, with the utmost astonishment, that he was a stranger. 'I'm Lieutenant Pim of the *Resolute*. Captain Kellett is in her at Dealy Island.'

McClure was still reluctant to abandon his ship altogether, but when Kellett saw the condition of the first arrivals from the *Investigator* he ordered McClure, whom he outranked, to bring his whole crew out. Thus McClure and his surviving men were the first to complete the Northwest Passage, though not in the same ship and with a long sledge journey in between.

Meanwhile, the three chief sledging parties were discovering new ground. McClintock crossed the strait between Melville Island and Prince Patrick Island, which he named, reached the northern tip of this new land and, bar a few miles' interval, connected with Mecham's journey up the west coast of Prince Patrick Island from the south. The ordeals that McClintock and his men suffered may be judged by one of their place-names – Torture Cove. McClintock regained his ship on 18 July after an absence of 105 days during which his sledge covered well over a thousand miles: in Sir Clement Markham's view (1909) this was 'the greatest Arctic effort that ever was made and ever will be made'. Three of McClintock's party died on the journey and several others never completely recovered.

Mecham's record was no less remarkable: in ninety-one days he too travelled over a thousand miles. Vesey Hamilton passed the north of Melville Island and reached Markham Island (77° North).

The ships were unable to retreat far that summer and wintered south-west of Bathurst Island. Vesey Hamilton connected a telegraph between them. In the spring of 1854 they re-established contact with the *Assistance* and *Pioneer*, which had wintered in Wellington Channel. During the summer Sherard Osborn had explored part of Bathurst Island by sledge, and had also quarrelled with his difficult commander who placed him under arrest. Later, Osborn was swiftly promoted by the Admiralty as a deliberate snub to Belcher. By 1854 Captain Belcher had had enough of the Arctic, and to the astonishment and anger of Captain Kellett he ordered the abandonment of the *Resolute* and *Intrepid* rather than risk another winter. He had already decided to abandon his own ships.

Meanwhile, Mecham carried out the greatest sledging trip yet, which carried him south of Prince of Wales Strait. He returned in seventy days after travelling 1,300 miles – an average of nearly 20 per day.

Sir Edward himself had made a journey across the ice – of eight miles. He sat in his boat which was dragged on a sledge by ten men, and was accompanied by his medical adviser. He complained bitterly of discomfort.

Owing to Belcher's extraordinary order only one ship was left to carry the crews of five others – plus McClure's men – back to England, but fortunately Captain Inglefield, who had himself made two previous voyages to the north-west in search of Franklin, arrived at a timely moment with two ships to make the homeward voyage less intolerable.

The *Resolute* subsequently drifted east with the ice and was discovered in the summer of 1855, a thousand miles away from where she had been abandoned, by an American whaler who sailed her to a United States port. She was purchased by a generous group of Americans and presented to Queen Victoria. When she was finally scrapped, Victoria returned the compliment by having a fine desk made from her timbers which she presented to the American President. It was said to be John F. Kennedy's favourite desk in the White House.

By the time that the Belcher expedition returned the Admiralty had not unnaturally decided that the long and costly search for the Franklin expedition could no longer be continued. Franklin and his men were declared officially dead on the strength of the findings of Dr Rae. Lady Franklin, who had become something of an international heroine, would not accept the Admiralty's decision to call off the search. She symbolically discarded her mourning clothes, and in pinks and yellows she demanded that the quest should go on. Already she had spent a large part of her own fortune in sending out ships which, moreover, were directed to a more likely area than that curiously favoured by the Admiralty and its advisers. In 1856 she purchased the steam yacht *Fox*, to follow up the discoveries made by John Rae.

This splendid little vessel, of only 177 tons, was captained by McClintock and officered by volunteers released for the purpose, reluctantly in some cases, by the Royal Navy. In the first year this expedition was dogged by astonishingly bad luck which might have been enough to discourage further effort. The year 1857 turned out to be a particularly bad one in Baffin Bay, and the *Fox* could not even reach Lancaster Sound. Less than thirty miles from its open water she was imprisoned by the ice and not released for 242 days, during which she drifted nearly 1,400 miles south and east. The storm that finally broke her free almost broke her up as well – 'eighteen hours of such battering as I hope not to see again', said the always restrained McClintock.

In 1858 conditions were easier and the *Fox* reached Lancaster Sound without serious difficulty. After stopping at Beechey Island, McClintock sailed down Peel Sound, but on being checked by ice reversed his course and attempted

the alternative passage down Prince Regent's Inlet. Though held up for over a month by ice, the *Fox*, with her sharp, reinforced prow, forced a way through Bellot Strait – the first ship to do so – but she was inexorably driven back again and winter quarters were established at the eastern end of the strait.

McClintock led the first sledge trip in mid-February 1859. This early start marks another small advance in the technique of Arctic travel. McClintock had also learned from experience that the sledges must be loaded less heavily. He used dogs as auxiliaries, but the main haulage was done by his seamen.

On the coast of Boothia Peninsula he met a party of Eskimos who had many relics from Franklin's ships and told him how they had seen one ship crushed and sunk by the ice. In April

The Arctic Council, formed to plan the rescue of Franklin. At the left Parry makes a point to George Back, observed by the Byronic figure of James Clark Ross (fourth from the left). The portraits on the wall are of Sir John Barrow and Franklin himself, both dead although Franklin was not known to be so. In fact the Arctic Council seldom if ever met as a body, and the Admiralty's plans for the search were strikingly foolish.

McClintock set off again, leading one of three sledging parties. He began his search down the east side of King William Island, which gives him some claim to be the discoverer of the final link in the Northwest Passage. Having reached Montreal Island in the estuary of the Great Fish River, he returned northwards along the western coast of King William Island. He was then pursuing, in the opposite direction, the route taken by Franklin's men from their icebound ships.

On 25 May he found a human skeleton lying face down in the snow. What was left of the dead man's uniform showed him to have been a steward; he was still carrying a small clothes brush. The position of the skeleton confirmed the words of the Eskimos, 'they fell down and died as they walked along'.

Meanwhile, at Cape Felix in the north of the

List of the Medicines &c.

opposite
Relics of the *Erebus* and *Terror* brought back by McClintock in the *Fox*. They include a dipping needle (at right), a pair of snow goggles (left foreground), a gun, medicine-chest, prayer-book, etc. The spears in the background are Eskimo weapons.

left
Leopold McClintock, from the portrait by Stephen Pearce in the National Portrait Gallery.

below
The *Prince Albert*, equipped by Lady Franklin and her supporters to search for the missing explorer in 1850, off the coast of Greenland, surrounded by some rather Gothic icebergs.

bottom
The death of Franklin, from a painting by Thomas Smith of 1895. The disaster to Franklin's expedition caught the imagination of the public, who responded to pictures like this. But it is wholly a work of imagination – Franklin died before the expedition's ships were abandoned.

"PRINCE ALBERT" SURROUNDED BY ICEBERGS IN MELVILLE BAY.

The famous Franklin note, containing two messages. The first, written around the margin in 1847, reports that all is well. The second, added a year later, tells a grim story of death and disaster.

island, another party from the *Fox* had discovered the cairn containing the last written record of the Franklin expedition, signed by Crozier and Fitzjames. The melancholy fate of the men on the *Erebus* and *Terror* was known at last. Advancing northward rapidly (for he was running short of food) McClintock found further traces of the long march to nowhere: a ship's boat on a heavy oak sledge contained cutlery, tools and toilet articles, and in McClintock's estimate weighed 1,400 lb. So far had Arctic exploration advanced during the preceding twelve years that the experienced McClintock was amazed at the naïvety of men taking such strange and unnecessary objects on their journey. According to a dubious story, McClintock was once discovered in his cabin before a sledging trip carefully weighing his pocket handkerchief before deciding whether he could afford to add it to the load.

Not only had McClintock's expedition in the *Fox* discovered the fate of the Franklin expedition (more was discovered later and, of course, some questions will never be answered) it had also revealed about 800 miles of hitherto unknown coast and established a new standard for speedy sledging.

As both the engineers on the *Fox* had unfortunately died, it was the versatile Captain himself who got her engines going; by the end of September he was back in London, where his report caused a sensation. A letter to Lady Franklin from her generous American supporter Henry Grinnell summed up the public mood in North America: 'The news', he wrote, 'has caused intense interest and excitement in this country, perhaps quite as much as in old England; it is the general subject of conversation, the political affairs of Europe and this country are insignificant in comparison. I can truly say I thank the Great Disposer of events for the result attained by *your expedition* under the command of that most able and excellent officer, McClintock. He has acquired a just fame for himself, which the pages of history will never allow to be obliterated.'

A question remains. Who discovered the Northwest Passage? For by 1859 it was known, although no ship was to pass through from Lancaster Sound to Bering Strait until Amundsen in the *Gjøa* (1903–05). The map of course shows a number of routes. McClure felt that he had some claim to be the discoverer of the passage; McClintock had filled in the last gaps on the route that Amundsen was to follow successfully; Collinson had navigated the little-known western section. But after all it is perhaps to Franklin's men that the credit should be given. Had *Erebus* and *Terror* passed to the east of King William Island instead of the west they might have made the passage. After the ships became icebound they discovered that the vital eastern strait did exist. As Franklin's old friend Richardson put it. Franklin's men 'forged the last link of the North-West Passage with their lives'.

opposite, top
McClintock's discoveries did not end the search for Franklin's remains. Charles Francis Hall hoped to find survivors. Lieutenant Frederick Schwatka, backed by the *New York Herald*, led an expedition in 1878 which brought back a few more pathetic items. The Schwatka expedition pauses for a midday break in the shelter of its heavily loaded sledges.

opposite, bottom
The final word from *Erebus* and *Terror*. The original message, reporting 'all well', was deposited in May 1847 by Lieutenant Gore. The later message was written round the edge by James Fitzjames, captain of the *Erebus* after Franklin's death, and countersigned by Captain Crozier, in overall command, who added under his signature 'and start on tomorrow 26th for Back's Fish River'.

left
Lieutenant Hobson and his party from the *Fox* at Cape Victory on the north-west coast of King William Island, breaking down the cairn containing the last record of the Franklin expedition. Articles thrown aside by the men of *Erebus* and *Terror* lie scattered round about.

left, below
The remains of Fort Hope, erected near Repulse Bay in 1846 by that remarkable employee of the Hudson's Bay Company, Dr John Rae. Rae and his ten companions, exploring northward from Rae Isthmus, hoped to link up with Sir John Franklin, then embarked on his quest for the Northwest Passage. Wintering for two seasons at Fort Hope, Rae explored almost the whole unknown coast of Committee Bay south of Felix Harbour in the west and Fury and Hecla Strait in the east. As Franklin had passed through Peel Sound rather than Prince Regent Inlet, Rae saw no sign of him, but in 1853 he was to discover the first evidence of the fate of the Franklin expedition on the west coast of Boothia Peninsula.

The Americans in the North

The years of the Franklin search form a watershed in Arctic history. The long, narrow line of almost exclusively British explorers, which stretches from Frobisher to Franklin himself, suddenly becomes a scurry of expeditions; and the British naval tradition peters out amid the multiplying journeys of other men and other nations. With the exception of the Nares expedition (1875–76), the British played only a minor role in the Arctic after McClintock. The initiative passed to the Americans and the Scandinavians.

As Henry Grinnell said in his letter to Lady Franklin, the search for her husband's remains had aroused as much public interest in the United States as it had in England. Grinnell himself was the foremost advocate of Arctic exploration in America and the chief financial support for most American polar enterprise in the 1850s and 1860s, while the fascinating character and fluent pen of Elisha Kent Kane, historian of the first two Grinnell expeditions, kept public interest high.

Surveying the wide range of human activities and the people who become involved in them, it is something tempting to postulate a new law of human behaviour to the effect that people tend to adopt professions for which they are ill-suited by nature. Polar exploration provides many examples in support of this hypothesis, not least Elisha Kent Kane. That attractive and intrepid young man, whose unusual love life provided subject-matter as popular with American readers as his extraordinary travels, was physically rather a frail specimen. Yet he seems to have counted as time wasted any year in which he was not in danger of being buried in a volcano, frozen in ice, spitted on a lance, lost in a bog, or of being carried off by one of various tropical diseases that he narrowly survived in the course of his travels around the most inhospitable regions of the earth. It's a wonder that his heart, long known to be in a precarious condition, lasted until he was thirty-seven before it finally gave out.

Kane served as surgeon on the De Haven expedition in search of Franklin in 1850–51 and the experience of being frozen into Baffin Bay throughout one winter only served to increase his desire to return to the Arctic. Two years later, with Grinnell's support, he was back, with sixteen men and one tiny ship, the *Advance*. He was to search for Franklin and to get as near the pole as possible. The second object figured larger in Kane's mind.

Like subsequent American expeditions, the route of the Kane expedition lay north through Smith Sound. Although Baffin had noted the presence of this northern exit from Baffin Bay, it had been neglected during the search for the Northwest Passage until Captain Inglefield entered it in 1852. The *Advance* pushed a few miles north of the point where Inglefield had turned back the year before and found a winter harbour in what is now known as Kane Basin. The death of the expedition's dogs restricted Kane's movements in the following spring, but various parties carried out a number of short journeys into unexplored regions, one group crossing over to Ellesmere Island, another travelling north of the Humboldt Glacier, which Kane discovered and named. None of this would have been possible without the help of the Eskimos, in particular Hans Hendrik, who was to be an invaluable aid to many later expeditions in north-west Greenland. Many years later Hans Hendrik wrote his memoirs, and that is why more is known of his invaluable service to explorers than that of many other Eskimos who saved the lives of Europeans in the Arctic. Later in the year the Eskimos living around Etah provided food without which Kane and his men, having been unable to free their ship from the ice during the summer, would almost certainly have died.

In the spring of 1855 Kane and his fourteen surviving companions decided to abandon the *Advance*. After a long and distressing trek in small boats along half the length of Greenland, they reached the nearest Danish settlement at Upnarvik in August. Five years later, one of Kane's companions on this expedition, Isaac Hayes, returned to Smith Sound in the *United States*, but the early death of the expedition's chief scientist and Hayes' inability to make accurate observations without him reduced the effectiveness of the Hayes expedition practically to nil.

In the same year (1860) the first expedition of America's most famous Arctic explorer before Peary set out from New London, Connecticut, with the aim of discovering more about the fate of Franklin. Anything less like the expedition mounted by the British Admiralty for that purpose a few years earlier could hardly be imagined. Here was no squadron of specially equipped warships. Here were no officers carefully selected for their Arctic experience: no long lists of supplies and equipment, no printing presses, hand organs or other diversions for the amusement of the crew. The expedition did not have even one ship, just a boat the size of a ship's dinghy. Its total equipment could have been transported in two wheelbarrows, and its total expenses were $980.

Nor did the personnel of the expedition inspire much confidence. Personnel is the wrong word, for the expedition consisted of one man. He was a beady-eyed, plump-faced, middle-aged publisher of a small Cincinnati newspaper, who was hitching a lift north on a Yankee whaler.

Charles Francis Hall was very slightly mad. Perhaps anyone who voluntarily goes to live in the Arctic for years at a time must be a little crazy, and Hall's oddness was not a handicap, rather an advantage on occasions. Not much is known of his origins. He seems to have been a drifter, vaguely unsatisfied with life, who drifted out west, as far as Cincinnati, drifted into the printing business and in his desire to broadcast his opinions—which were strongly held, on whatever subject—to a wider audience than his wife and few friends, set up as proprietor of a local newspaper, at which he became reasonably successful. The aimlessness of his early life may suggest a weak personality, an unenterprising,

perhaps pessimistic man; in fact Hall was the reverse. In an age of individualism he was an individualist of extreme type. The force of his will might have stemmed Niagara. His optimism overrode all obstacles. The news of McClintock's findings hardly checked for a moment his eagerness in the Franklin search; the American Civil War was a minor nuisance hampering the organization of his second expedition.

He had the faults that often go with a dynamic character. He could be excessively unreasonable, and he was subject to feelings of persecution that made him quarrelsome.

Except for the all-important factor of determination, he was ill-qualified as a polar explorer. He was not a scientist, like Elisha Kent Kane. He had no experience of living in difficult country and had probably never been farther north than Vermont. He was sensible enough to recognize these deficiencies and to make some attempt to overcome them. He took lessons in mathematics and astronomy while he was in New York preparing for his first journey. As his maps were later to be commended for their accuracy, his lessons seem to have been successful, but his attempts to practise Arctic living were perhaps less valuable. 'He took to camping on a hill behind Cincinnati's observatory. He pitched a tent, carried up a Spartan supply of food and water, and spent several cool autumn nights in what passed for the wilds', says his latest biographer, Chauncey Loomis. The experiment came to an end when a pair of drunken Irishmen stumbled upon him and, disappointed at learning that he had no whisky, opened up with a shot gun and sent him galloping half-naked across the hillside.

Nobody knows why Hall decided to go to the Arctic. A religious man, he believed that he had a divine mission, and he certainly pursued it with the vigour of St Paul himself. Not that Hall saw himself as a Christian missionary. His willingness, in spite of his considerable self-esteem, to learn from others made him at first an earnest advocate of the Eskimo way of life and it was only after he had suffered some unpleasant experiences of the rougher aspects of Eskimo society that he began to intone in his journal, 'Christianize! Civilize!'

With the moral and financial support of Henry Grinnell, Hall embarked himself and his supplies on the *Henry George* at New London in May 1860. A severe bout of seasickness quelled his ardour only briefly; the sight of his first iceberg sent him into ecstasy. 'Nearing the goal of my fondest wishes. Everything in the Arctic is deeply interesting to me. . . . I am on a mission of love. I feel to be in performance of a duty I owe to mankind, myself, God. Thus feeling, I am strong at heart, full of faith, ready to do or die in the cause I have espoused.'

Hall's plan was to leave the whaler at Cumberland Sound and, having hired Eskimo helpers, to cut across Baffin Island, via Fury and Hecla Strait and Prince Regent Inlet to King William Island. For some reason, however, Captain Budington of the *Henry George* decided to head for Frobisher Bay instead.

Frobisher Bay was not then so called. No one knew for certain that this was the object of Frobisher's expeditions nearly 300 years before,

and no one knew that the bay was a bay. Hall was content to go there because he believed it was a strait which would lead him into Foxe Basin. It was the chief accomplishment of his first expedition that the facts about Frobisher and his bay were established.

Having made friends with the Eskimos of the region, Hall soon learned that Frobisher's Bay was indeed landlocked and he explored it himself the following year. He also discovered, amazingly enough, that Frobisher's activities still formed part of Eskimo oral tradition. He was told of 'a very heavy stone' and 'something red', which Hall understood to be iron and bricks, that the *kadloonas* (whites) had left. Later he found actual relics of the Frobisher expedition in the form of seacoal, iron, fragments of tile and glass and the ruins of three stone houses. He was able to identify the places named in contemporary accounts of Frobisher's expedition, and brought many relics back with him.

By misadventure, the *Henry George* was imprisoned in the ice for a second winter, and Hall's first expedition lasted a year longer than he had intended. Although he had not travelled farther than the southern part of Baffin Island, his discovery of the Frobisher relics was a major success. Still more important, he had acquired experience of the Arctic.

Although his sense of mission was as strong as ever, he had found that the Arctic was no Garden of Eden. His attitude towards the Eskimos, though still admiring, was a good deal less romantic. There had been times when he

Hall with Eskimo companions, crossing the ice of Frobisher Bay during his first trip to the north. His sledging technique has apparently not been perfected, for there are marked signs of indiscipline on the flanks.

thought them devils and savages. Hall's determination to learn from the Eskimos is admirable but often comic. On the whole his efforts to suppress the prejudices of conventional, puritanical, Victorian morality, though less than wholly successful, were surprisingly effective. 'I must learn to live as Esquimeaux do!' he wrote in his journal, and underlined it. It was not easy. Eskimo eating habits were very different from those of respectable Cincinnati society. Hot seal's blood, for instance: '. . . I screwed up my courage to try it, and finally, when the dish came again to those by my side, I asked Koojesse, "Pe-e-uke?" (Is it good?) "Armelarng, armelarng" (Yes, yes) was the reply. All eyes were fixed upon me as I prepared to join with them in drinking some of their favorite soup.' Contrary to expectations he found it excellent.

More disturbing to this fundamental Christian were Eskimo superstitions and their subservience to shamans, although he later submitted politically to shaman treatment for a minor physical ailment. He was shocked too by their custom of leaving an old person to die alone, especially when they bricked up an igloo before the occupant was actually dead. On one occasion he broke in and sat holding the hand of the old woman inside for twelve hours—in extreme cold—until she died.

Hall arrived in New York in September 1862 to find the Civil War in progress. Not unnaturally, the government proved unwilling to support the large Arctic expedition to King William Island that Hall wished to lead, and although a perhaps surprising amount of public interest was shown in Hall's exploits, he was forced to mount his second expedition in circumstances little more propitious than those of 1860. Nothing could daunt Hall's enthusiasm, however, and in dealing with hard-headed businessmen and civil servants he must have modified his mystical longings and suppressed the near-hysterical effusions that sometimes appear in his journal. For example, on the occasion when Henry Grinnell told him he was prepared, 'if need be', to contribute $10,000 to a second Franklin search expedition: 'This was like an electrical heartshock to me. Even as my loved friend ceased utterance to these words, I was in his arms—my hands clasping his—my lips to his noble brow—& *we mingled our tears together* Never—*never* in my life was I happier!'

Plenty of setbacks and difficulties occurred to diminish Hall's euphoria in subsequent months but in early July he embarked on the *Monticello* at New London, bound for Hudson Bay, with the Eskimo couple who had appeared at his lectures. This couple were, as Hall's biographer says, probably the closest friends he ever had; they remained with him for the rest of his life.

On his second expedition Hall was to spend five years in the Arctic. Things started badly when the Captain of the *Monticello*, apparently through error, put Hall ashore forty miles south

BEAR KILLING WALRUS.

of his objective, with the result that he was not able to reach Repulse Bay before winter closed in and thus lost a year almost before he had started. Living with the Eskimos, he heard many stories that appeared to relate to the Franklin expedition, and began to have hopes of finding some survivors. Hall well knew by this time that the Eskimos, in spite of their formidable memories, were hazy about time, but he was eager to hear hopeful news and they were eager to tell him what he wanted to hear. Stories of an officer who had apparently survived the disaster, whom Hall believed must be Crozier, eventually turned out to concern John Rae, who had been in the area some years before. When he did reach King William Island in 1869 (he had made earlier forays westward from Repulse Bay without actually reaching the island) Hall found many relics of the Franklin expedition. He was able to fill in some of the blanks remaining in the story; for instance, Crozier and his men had been unable to get food from the Eskimos because the Eskimos had none to spare; also, documents left behind at various places had been thrown away by the rummaging Eskimos for whom they had no value. After nearly five years, the results were depressing. 'For a week,' writes Chauncey Loomis, 'Hall wandered the dreary southeast coast of King William Island, a forlorn and discouraged man. At several places where the Eskimos said they had seen relics or bodies, he held ceremonies and built little monuments on the deep snow. It was all he could do. This was the conclusion of the great quest to which he had dedicated ten years of his life—a caretaking for the unfound dead.' In August Hall, accompanied

'The natives tell many most interesting anecdotes of the bear. . . . He has a very ingenious way of killing the walrus, which is represented in the accompanying engraving.' From Charles Francis Hall, *Life with the Esquimeaux.*

above
The *Alert* towing the
Discovery past Disco Island
during the Nares expedition.

right
Sir George Nares, 1831–1915,
who led the British Arctic
expedition of 1875–76, the
last major effort in the
British naval tradition
established by Ross and
Parry and, for all its
successes, by then out of
date.

again by his Eskimo friends, sailed for home.

The third and last expedition of Charles Francis Hall was more substantial and more ambitious than his previous two. It was a government-backed expedition under the aegis of the US Navy, with a naval ship and crew, a scientific staff, and a plan for reaching the North Pole. It was also a total disaster.

The fault was not Hall's; perhaps it was nobody's. Certainly Hall's personality does not seem ideal for the leadership of an arduous exploration, though the evidence suggests that he was more tolerant and more sensible than might have been expected. As he grew older he grew more stable, though his enthusiasm for the Arctic burned as bright as ever. With one or two exceptions, the officers of the expedition seem to have been a poor lot–not the type of men that Hall deserved. The ship's captain, Budington, was an old friend; his gossip against Hall among the crew and his secret drinking were unexpected. The chief scientist, Emil Bessels, was previously unknown to Hall, who was warned, however, that Bessels was very 'sensitive'. He may have been something much worse.

The *Polaris*, a converted steam tug of 387 tons, left Brooklyn at the beginning of July 1871. After calls in Greenland, she carried thirty-three people (including Hall's Eskimo friends and their adopted child and Hans Hendrick with his family) to Smith Sound. Personality conflicts had already arisen and at Disco Captain Davenport of the *Polaris*'s supply ship had come aboard at Hall's request to read the riot act to the dissident scientific staff. Nevertheless, during the summer the expedition made good progress. The *Polaris* steamed past Kane's harbour before the end of August and reached a farthest north of 82°11′. The Lincoln Sea, however, was choked with ice and Hall's hopes, shared by many others, of finding an open polar sea–or, if not, land stretching to the pole–were dashed. Soon afterwards the ship was caught by the ice and driven southwards. After four days she broke free and found a bay on the Greenland coast, named Thank-God Harbour by Hall, that Captain Budington thought would do as a winter refuge.

During the autumn, short exploratory journeys were made. Hall returned from a two-week trip on 24 October and on entering his cabin called for a cup of coffee. Shortly after drinking it he complained of feeling ill. In a few days he was delirious. After a week, he seemed to be getting better, and he began to give instructions again, spending most of the day out of his bunk. Just as it seemed he was fully recovered, he had a sudden relapse. In the early hours of 8 November he died. He was fifty years old.

After Hall's death, command was divided between Bessels, chief scientific officer, and Budington, ship's captain. Neither of them seem to have been up to the job and morale among the crew that winter sank to an abysmal level. In the summer there was slight improvement, and a few half-hearted scientific forays were conducted by Bessels. No one was anxious to continue to press

The party led by Markham on their way to establish a new 'farthest-north' record, in fact less than 100 miles north of their anchorage. The journey was agonizing and on some days they covered only a mile.

Amateur theatricals on board the *Alert*. Not the least problem of large-scale naval expeditions was the boredom of the crew. The tradition of staging plays begun by Parry was enthusiastically followed, and the costumes and footlights here suggest that great pains were taken with these productions.

on to the north and in August the *Polaris* forced her way out of Thank-God Harbour and headed south. The ship had already suffered damage from an iceberg, and in the second week of October she was sharply nipped by ice. Budington ordered the supplies and equipment to be unloaded on to the ice in case the ship sank. In the middle of this operation a sudden gust took hold of the *Polaris* and swept her with appalling rapidity away to sea. Nineteen people, including the Eskimo families, were left stranded on an ice floe about four miles in circumference.

The experiences of the castaways, one of the great survival stories of polar history, were to be related by Captain Tyson, the senior officer among the group and apparently one of the more efficient members of the *Polaris* expedition. He was in a difficult position because the sailors, not surprisingly, would not accept discipline and Tyson, without a gun until one of the Eskimos got hold of a pistol for him, felt on more than one occasion that his life was in danger from his fellow creatures as well as the elements. Needless to say, the party would not have survived long without the Eskimo men, who always managed to kill a seal just as starvation seemed inevitable. It was in the spring that death came nearest. As they drifted south and the temperature rose, the ice began to break up and dissipate. When their ice floe was down to forty yards they had to move to another, and by the end of April they were desperately hopping from floe to floe. In their one small boat, the chances of reaching land were almost nil. They could not have lasted much longer when the steamer *Tigress* picked them up on 30 April 1873, after a drift of nearly 1,500 miles lasting more than six months.

Meanwhile, the *Polaris* had gone to the bottom,

but not until the fourteen men left on board her had reached land near Etah, where the Eskimos saw them through the winter in relative comfort.

A board of inquiry was set up to inquire into the disastrous *Polaris* expedition. It took evidence from almost all the survivors and eventually decided that no action should be taken against anyone. But a number of mysteries remained, and the chief query concerned the death of Captain Hall.

It was the opinion of Dr Bessels that Hall suffered a stroke and this was the cause of death. The Surgeons-General of the army and the navy, having listened to Bessels' account, agreed. Nobody ever said in so many words that he thought Hall had been murdered but there is strong evidence that he was, and if he was, Bessels himself is the likeliest suspect. Bessels did not get on with Hall, and in his delirium Hall accused the German doctor of trying to kill him. Hall was, however, a slightly paranoid type and made the same accusation against other officers. He did at one time refuse treatment from Bessels, and his relapse occurred after Bessel's treatment had resumed. There are other scraps of evidence pointing towards Bessels, although perhaps most of them would not seem suspicious were not suspicion already present.

At the instigation of Chauncey Loomis, Hall's grave was opened in 1968. In the cold climate of northern Greenland the body had not completely decomposed, although nearly a hundred years had passed since Hall's death. A fingernail was sent for chemical analysis, and the result proved that in the last two weeks of his life Hall had taken in a deadly quantity of arsenic. In the 19th century arsenic was used for a variety of medicinal purposes, and it is possible that Hall had

been dosing himself fatally with patent medicines. The verdict of Chauncey Loomis, who has
investigated the matter as thoroughly as anyone
possibly could, is that Hall's death cannot be
definitely ascribed to murder. The mystery
lives on.

Five years after Hall's death on the bleak
shores of Greenland a bronze plaque, carefully
engraved, was erected over his grave. It had been
made in England and was placed in position by
members of the Nares expedition of 1875–76.

The Nares expedition, the last British naval
assault upon the Arctic during the 19th century,
was inspired partly by John Murray's *Challenger*,
then engaged upon her great oceanographical
expedition which proved, among other interesting facts, that Antarctica was definitely a large
land mass. George Nares himself had been Captain of the *Challenger*, but was recalled by the
Admiralty in order to command the *Alert* and the
Discovery on the Arctic expedition of 1875. A
second motive for the expedition was the desire
to restore to Britain the 'farthest north' record,
Parry's limit having been surpassed by Hall in
1871. In this the Nares expedition was successful
– successful in spite of the antiquated techniques
of travel employed, which were hardly different
from those of Parry. 'It would almost seem', as
Jeanette Mirsky wrote, 'as though the British
naval mind were incapable of learning the lessons
that the Arctic had been, over generations, ex-
pounding.' The success of this expedition, like
others before it, was due to the high quality of
British seamanship and the gritty determination
of the younger officers, in particular Albert
Markham.

Nares encountered bad conditions along the
Greenland coast, where Hall had enjoyed fairly
plain sailing. With great skill he pushed on
through Smith Sound and the strait that, on
British maps, is named after him, established
winter quarters for the *Discovery* in a bay of
Ellesmere Island and, in the *Alert*, threaded his
way through to the Lincoln Sea. With a matter of
hours to spare, he got the ship settled in a north-
ward-facing bay before the whole area froze
solid.

It was clear to Nares that any hope of reaching
the North Pole must be abandoned. The tortured pack, with ridges thirty feet high, sudden
cracks, twists, and writhing forms, stretched
endlessly before him. The Polar Sea was not
open, and his heavy sledges, pulled by men,
would not be able to advance far across the ice.
There was some hope that the land to the west or
east of them might stretch farther north, but this
hope too soon died as, in the spring, sledging
parties advanced along the northern coasts of
Ellesmere Island, charting its northernmost
point at Cape Constitution, and Greenland.

The sledging parties suffered frightful priva-
tions. They often had to travel six miles to gain
one, chiefly because the whole party was needed
to move a single sledge. They went down with
scurvy, an affliction that Hall had avoided by
living on an Eskimo diet, and suffered from snow-
blindess. Markham's party reached a new 'farthest north' of 83°20′, but he had to abandon one of
his boats and regained the ship with half his
party unable to walk. A second party, exploring
the Ellesmere coast, was in even worse state. A
group from the *Discovery* explored the Greenland coast and covered some of the distance on
all fours, to such a state were they reduced by
scurvy, cold and exhaustion. Knud Rasmussen,
who followed their track in 1912, confessed that

The horrid scene that greeted the rescuers of Greely on 22 June 1884. 'We cut a hole in the canvas to give us room, and commenced to feed them, serving them all round gradually, not letting them have as much as they wanted.'

how they managed to make the journey at all in their condition was 'a perfect riddle'.

Extricating the *Alert* from the bay, a procedure that required luck as well as Nares' outstanding navigational skill, the expedition made a safe return to England, though some of the men must have suffered for the rest of their lives from the ordeals they had undergone. Against the odds, the Nares expedition had been a success, and it had opened the way for Peary's journey to the pole thirty-three years later.

In 1875 Karl Weyprecht, the discoverer of Franz Josef Land, addressed a meeting of the German Scientific Association on the subject of polar exploration. There was, said Weyprecht, far too much emphasis on spectacular deeds of exploration, of ambitious nationalistic efforts to be first to the pole. What was required was team-work, objectivity, disinterested research. Weyprecht's views were obviously right, although that did not necessarily make them popular. Nevertheless, his suggestions did eventually bear fruit in the International Polar Year of 1882–83 (Weyprecht himself died a few months earlier). The various countries involved in polar exploration undertook to maintain research stations at points in the Arctic and the Antarctic, so that some comparative studies could be made and polar research would be established as a respectable, international study. Ironically, the most notable result of this programme of international research concerned the American expedition to Ellesmere Island, which was perhaps the most unabashed attempt at national one-upmanship so far.

This expedition was a military enterprise,

staffed by officers and men of the US Army under the command of Major A. W. Greely. It was charged with making meteorological observations and gathering scientific data, but the main ambition of its commander was to exceed the 'farthest north' of Lieutenant Albert Markham. The base was established where Nares' *Discovery* had wintered, named by the Americans Fort Conger. Thanks to Lieutenant James B. Lockwood, probably the most capable member of the expedition, Markham's 'farthest north' record was broken by about four miles in the early summer of 1882. In other respects, too, the expedition began well. Greely himself made a trip along northern Ellesmere Island in June, finding butterflies and bumblebees flitting among the poppies.

Thereafter, deterioration set in rapidly. The rest of the story of the Greely expedition is, in the words of L. P. Kirwan (*The White Road*), tragic and discreditable: 'At home, indecision, incompetence and corruption . . . in the field, great courage, starvation, madness, death.'

Disciplinary problems began early. Greely ordered the arrest of an officer, and later one of the soldiers was shot for stealing food. But far worse was the failure of the United States government to fulfil its obligations. This disgraceful dereliction appears to have been due to a combination of inefficiency, corruption and ill-will on the part of a high government official as well as serving officers. Greely had been told to expect a relief ship in 1882 and another the following year. If they were unable to reach his base they would, in 1882, deposit stores as near as they could and, in 1883, land a party to make contact with Fort Conger over the ice.

When no ship appeared in the first year, Greely was not worried. Their situation was reasonably comfortable and they had enough supplies, augmented by seals shot by their two Eskimo hunters, to see them through another winter. When no ship appeared in 1883, things began to look more serious. Greely decided to retreat to Cape Sabine, some 200 miles south, where supplies were to have been cached. Packing up their records and instruments, the men piled into their steam launch and set out.

They had a very rough trip, battered by gales and ice, and were finally frozen up some miles short of their destination. As they trekked across the ice a blizzard struck; it took them three weeks to accomplish the last stage of the journey which, when they began it, was less than twenty miles. At Cape Sabine their troubles increased. The stores left there were quite insufficient and the only shelter they had was a hut consisting mainly of an upturned boat. By the New Year, 1884, they were in a desperate state.

The rescue ship *Thetis* reached them on 22 June. Of the original party consisting of four officers, twenty men, and two Eskimos, one officer (Greely) and six of the men were still alive.

The Arctic Drift

While the Americans were gradually extending knowledge of the Arctic in Ellesmere Island and north-west Greenland, even greater feats were being recorded by the Scandinavians, so that the late 19th century has sometimes been called a second Viking age. In the persons of Nordenskjold and Nansen, Scandinavia produced the most capable explorers of the age.

By this time Arctic exploration was advancing rapidly every year, and inevitably the less dramatic expeditions get overlooked in a brief survey. The record of human progress in any field tends to become a series of mountain peaks while the broad plains between them are forgotten or ignored. It is important to remember, therefore, that Nordenskjold's forging of the Northeast Passage or Nansen's first crossing of the Greenland ice-cap were merely the outstanding achievements of a time when many people and many countries were involved in Arctic research. The story of the exploration of Greenland, since the Danish missionary Hans Egede aroused the world's interest in the early 18th century, is a saga worth a book of its own. The work was carried out chiefly by the Danes, but among other notable expeditions was that of the German Karl Koldewey in 1869–70, in which the crew of the *Hansa* camped on an ice floe for almost six months, anticipating the ordeal of the *Polaris* survivors. Despite the inexperience of his men, Koldewey explored 150 miles of the frightening north-east Greenland coast.

A prominent member of the Koldewey expedition was Lieutenant Julius Payer who, a year later, teamed up with Karl Weyprecht in the expedition which, by pure chance, was to fill in one of the last pieces in the Arctic jigsaw.

This memorable journey originated in the theory propounded by a German geographer that a branch of the warm Gulf Stream current might carry a ship near to the pole north of Siberia. The shade of Barents must have boggled at this notion but it happened that in 1871, when Weyprecht and Payer made a trial cruise north of Novaya Zemlya, they encountered less ice than expected. It was an unusually good season, the same year that a Norwegian whaler discovered the Barents relics.

The following year they set out in earnest. Their ship, the *Tegetthoff*, a 220-ton steamer with auxiliary sails, was equipped for three years, and they established an additional supply depot on Novaya Zemlya. They were soon in trouble, the *Tegetthoff* being trapped by the ice only a few miles north of Novaya Zemlya. The ship began to drift slowly northward with the ice. The twenty-three men on board were at first expectant and hopeful that the ice would break up and the *Tegetthoff* resume her cruise in clear water but, as Payer put it, 'the hour of deliverance never came'. Haphazardly, sometimes reversing its direction, sometimes almost stopping, the ice carried her on, and as winter approached it became obvious that there would be no escape that year. In February 1873, after many weeks of drifting eastward, the ship began to move north and then west, until they were back in 60° East longitude. Attempts to cut the ship out of the ice floe in which she was imprisoned revealed that it was over six feet thick. As August, the most ice-free month, drew towards its end the men were feeling extremely despondent, when, to their astonishment land appeared, just south of 80° North. 'At first we all stood transfixed, hardly believing what we saw. Then carried away by the reality of our good fortune we burst into shouts of joy.' The land they had sighted was the southernmost island of Franz Josef Land, which they named Wilczek Island after their chief patron.

The new land, while a blessed relief after the shifting ice, did not offer much material comfort, the only vegetation being lichens. Weyprecht knew they would have to make an effort to return in the following summer, and therefore the time available for exploration was confined to a few months in the spring of 1874. Between March and May, Payer led a number of sledging trips, organized in the McClintock manner, and covered a total of some 500 miles. His mapping was, of course, incomplete and in some respects inaccurate, as he was misled by mirages which suggested non-existent lands; his map was later to puzzle Nansen. The work of mapping Franz Josef Land thoroughly was continued by Leigh Smith in his yacht *Eira* (1880–81), by Frederick

Baron Nordenskjold (1832–1901), the first great scientist-explorer of the Arctic. Although remembered best for his voyage through the Northeast Passage, he was a veteran of many expeditions in Spitsbergen and Greenland and had tried to reach the pole with sledges drawn by reindeer.

plishments of a James Ross, who made himself an outstanding authority on terrestrial magnetism and other subjects, ought not to be underrated; nevertheless, Ross was a naval officer first. The keen curiosity and unquenchable will of Charles Francis Hall was worth any amount of academic qualifications; but Hall himself was aware that his lack of scientific background was a handicap. The British *Challenger* expedition showed what could be done by a purely scientific expedition, and Weyprecht himself, who though a naval man was also a trained scientist, called for greater emphasis on scientific research in polar exploration.

In N. A. E. Nordenskjold (later Baron Nordenskjold), the Arctic found a man who besides possessing the necessary physical and mental attributes of a polar explorer was a trained

Jackson of the Harmsworth-Jackson expedition (1894–91), and by the Duke of the Abruzzi (1899–1900), one of whose officers, Umberto Cagni, gained the 'farthest north' record for Italy for a short period.

In May 1894 the *Tegetthoff* was abandoned (she had disappeared by the time Leigh Smith reached the area six years later), and her crew set out for Novaya Zemlya with sledges and three boats. They made such slow going over rough ice with a contrary wind, averaging less than a mile a day, that they decided to camp and wait for warmer weather to clear a passage for their boats. There followed weeks of extreme tedium in which, as Payer said, it was a happy event to discover a hole in one's clothing because the task of darning it occupied one's attention for a time. When August came without the ice clearing tension mounted, but by the middle of the month they were able to launch their boats in open water and begin the 200-mile voyage to Novaya Zemlya. They made quick progress and by the end of the month they were near the southern end of the islands, just in time to catch a Russian fishing boat. They had enjoyed plenty of good luck, particularly in discovering important lands that they were not really looking for, but they had also shown great spirit and skill in completing, without casualties, an extremely dangerous and frightening journey that for some time seemed likely to end in their deaths.

One reason why more substantial results were often obtained by European as distinct from British and American explorers is that the former were more often trained scientists. The accom-

chemist and geologist. Of Swedish ancestry, he was born in Finland in 1832, but in his early twenties some unguarded remarks aroused the disapproval of the Russian authorities, and in 1858 he was forbidden to hold a teaching post in Finland. Thereupon he removed himself to the land of his forefathers and became a professor at the Swedish state university. He took part in several expeditions to Spitsbergen and in 1867 he reached the farthest north yet achieved in that region (81°42′) in the steamship *Sofia*. By that time he had been gripped by the Arctic passion.

Three years later, Nordenskjold visited Greenland. He arrived soon after the departure of Henry Rink, the Danish government official whose writings did so much to arouse scientific interest in the Greenland ice-cap. Besides scientific curiosity, Nordenskjold was also inspired by the idea of crossing the ice-cap from coast to coast. Accompanied by a Swedish botanist and two Eskimos, he embarked upon this endeavour in July 1870. The going proved rough; the Eskimos rapidly lost interest and returned to their homes. Nordenskjold and his companion penetrated the interior for some forty miles from Godthaab and found not a featureless white sheet but a maze of ridges, cliffs and running rivers, and a surface pitted with holes. Nordenskjold still had some hopes that fertile valleys might exist somewhere in the interior of the great island and, thirteen years later, he was to make another effort to cross to the east coast. During that journey he found no trace of green pastures and wooded slopes but again he was unable to complete the crossing, which was to be first

Leigh Smith and his crew say good-bye to their steam yacht *Eira*, sunk off Franz Josef Land in 1881. She was not properly equipped for ice and only skilful seamanship had extracted her from peril the previous year. Smith and his men wintered without mishap and in the following spring made their way to Novaya Zemlya, where they were rescued.

119

achieved fifteen years later by his disciple, Nansen.

Meanwhile, Nordenskjold returned to the east. On another expedition to Spitsbergen he led an attempt to reach the pole using sledges drawn by reindeers. As draught animals, reindeers had not improved since Parry had experimented with them, while Nordenskjold's sledges proved too frail for the rough ice he encountered. He had to turn back while some way short of his own 'farthest north'.

At that time Nordenskjold was already considering another Arctic project, a plan whose fulfilment was to put his name among the greatest of Arctic explorers.

The early history of polar exploration was largely concerned with the search for northern sea routes from Europe to the Far East. The Northwest Passage, if it existed, would be virtually useless for commercial purposes; this had been obvious long before Franklin's ill-fated expedition of 1845. Within another ten years its existence was *known*, and occasional efforts were made to force a ship through it—for instance, by Allen Young in 1875. The splendid efforts of the Great Northern Expedition had similarly shown that the existence of a Northeast Passage was probable, and Cook and Wrangel had finally proved it, while again suggesting that the difficulties of actually sailing it made it practically useless. Subsequently, the Northeast Passage had, for a variety of reasons, fallen even further from governmental favour than the Northwest Passage. With the building of the transcontinental American railroads and the projected building of the Suez and Panama canals, a sea route to the Pacific had in any case become less urgent. However, the vast natural resources of Siberia were virtually untapped and were likely to remain out of reach of western Europe (notably Scandinavia) as long as communications remained so poor. Nordenskjold, like all great innovators, had a gift for spotting the significant factor in a problem which, once stated, becomes blindingly obvious to all. He pointed out that the north Siberian coast had been explored almost exclusively by small boats; no one had ever tried to sail along it in a powerful, ocean-going ship. With the support of his loyal patron, Oscar Dickson, Nordenskjold planned to do just that.

The voyage of the *Vega* is one of the great landmarks of polar exploration, comparable with Cook's circumnavigation of Antarctica and Parry's voyage to Melville Island. It was equally successful and equally free from accident, but as most of its course had been explored before—though in dribs and drabs—it was perhaps less dramatic. Thanks to Nordenskjold's planning and Captain Palander's skill it was, indeed, almost easy.

The 300-ton *Vega* had steam engines and sails, and carried supplies for two years. She was supported during the first part of the journey by Russian merchant ships and her last consort left her at the mouth of the Lena, which she reached on 28 August 1878, only six weeks after setting out from Tromsö. Ice presented few problems as the coastal channel remained clear, though persistent fog made navigation difficult. East of the Lena the expedition encountered the Chukchi tribes, whose way of life had hardly changed

A powerful Russian icebreaker in Arctic waters in the early 20th century. Unlike the Northwest Passage, the Northeast Passage has become a well-travelled waterway, at least during the summer months.

Nansen at about the time of
his crossing of the
Greenland ice-cap.

since the time of Bering. Nordenskjold was interested to find that although there were no signs of contact with Europe from the west, there was a well-established barter trade between Siberia and Alaska. He also noted ruefully that prices had gone up since the first Russians had penetrated the region. He could not afford to buy a fox fur which he craved: a valuable cooking pot was the price demanded for that single skin.

In September conditions began to deteriorate. Fog and snow frequently reduced visibility to almost nil, and in the uncharted Siberian coastal waters navigation became increasingly awkward. A launch had to be sent ahead of the *Vega* to take depth soundings. Beyond North Cape lay a belt of heavy pack ice. The *Vega* could not force a way through and Nordenskjold had to resign himself to a winter in Siberia when he was only 120 miles short of Cape Dezhnev and the Bering Strait. Additionally irritating was the knowledge that if the ship had stuck to the coast along the whole length of her journey and not made a couple of exploratory diversions towards the New Siberian Islands, the voyage could have been completed in one season.

The long winter passed slowly while Nordenskjold and his multi-national crew, Swedish, Norwegian, Danish, Russian and Italian continued their programme of scientific research and suppressed their fastidious habits hobnobbing with the earthy Chukchi. They had to wait almost ten months to complete the final stage of their voyage, which took them less than two days' steaming. As they passed Cape Dezhnev and felt the deep swell of the Pacific they ran up

below
Nansen and Sverdrup (holding gun) and their party before the crossing of Greenland. Note the lightweight sledge, Eskimo snow-shoes as well as Norwegian skis. Dietrichsen and Kristiansen stand behind, flanked by the two Lapps, Balto and Ravna.

The Polar Night, 24
November 1893. A
watercolour sketch by
Nansen.

every available flag and startled the walruses with the celebratory popping of their one small cannon.

Nordenskjold had shown that the Northeast Passage could be made, given luck and a good ship, in a two-month voyage. However, it was not exactly a straightforward route and no immediate commercial advantages accrued. In fact the passage was not attempted again until 1913–15 when a Russian ice-breaker navigated it in the opposite direction, i.e. from east to west, in the course of hydrographical research. More recently, Nordenskjold's hopes for the Northeast Passage have been fulfilled. The construction of ports and meteorological stations and improvements in communications generally have made the channel along the north Siberian coast into a regular Russian shipping route.

Nordenskjold returned to Sweden to public acclaim and the reward of a barony. For the remaining twelve years of his life he was generally acknowledged as the foremost expert on Arctic conditions. He made his second trip to Greenland in 1883 and later encouraged the young Nansen to undertake his successful trans-Greenland journey. By the publication of two remarkable works on medieval and Renaissance cartography and navigation, another field in which Nansen was to follow him, he established his reputation as an outstanding scholar in the field of historical geography.

For all the proliferation of exploratory expeditions, the Arctic Ocean remained an enigma in the late 19th century. A number of hoary old notions were still current, including the medieval theory, dear to Elisha Kent Kane, that the area in the vicinity of the North Pole was an open sea. Other theories were put forward, criticized, jealously defended and reluctantly discarded. Weyprecht had believed in a northward-flowing warm current that approached the pole, and his discovery of Franz Josef Land had given extra weight to another idea – that there was a large land mass in the far north corresponding with Antarctica in the south. Both these notions lay behind the attempt of George Washington De Long to reach the pole in 1879.

A lieutenant in the United States Navy, De Long was an adventurer rather than a scientist, and his expedition was backed by that sensation-seeking publisher, James Gordon Bennett of the *New York Herald*, who had also equipped H. M. Stanley's East African expedition in search of Livingstone. But De Long was not without

Arctic experience, having taken part in the *Polaris* search, and he seems to have been an excellent commander, who in conditions that could not have been worse kept morale among his crew fairly high: there is no record of dissension such as troubled nearly every other major American polar expedition in the 19th century. He also had a sense of humour, not a common characteristic among polar pioneers.

De Long's ship, named the *Jeannette*, was in fact the *Pandora* in which Sir Allen Young had attempted the Northwest Passage in 1875; she was purchased for the polar expedition by Bennett. She sailed from San Francisco and after picking up dogs in Alaska headed north through Bering Strait, hoping to drift with the Japanese Current and find a large land mass above 'Wrangel Land' (Wrangel Island). She was soon caught in the ice and, like the *Tegetthoff* before her she was destined, contrary to the hopeful

expectations of her captain, never to be released. Wrangel Island appeared not long afterwards as the ship drifted west, and proved to be a relatively small place after all. During the winter of 1879–80, throughout the following summer and the winter after that, the *Jeannette* was held prisoner; she must have been a tough little ship to withstand the pressure so long. What made the situation of De Long and his men especially depressing was that they were clearly not getting anywhere. Understandably he felt aggrieved that other ships in their situation had usually drifted to land sooner or later. They did discover new islands–Jeannette and Henriette islands–but they were mere specks of rock among the ice in the East Siberian Sea. De Long and Bennett islands, discovered after they had left the ship, were little larger.

By the summer of 1881 the *Jeannette* was in her last throes. The men took to the ice as water

A pressure ridge advanced steadily upon the icebound *Fram* in January 1895 (*above*), giving the crew some anxious moments as the ship creaked and crunched in the winter darkness. *opposite* With Windmill mounted amidships, the *Fram* pursues her slow drift with the Arctic current. Members of Nansen's crew were able to carry out programmes of observation and research over a long period, adding to man's knowledge of environmental conditions in the Arctic.

125

poured through the growing rents in her hull, and a few hours later, watched her sink. After a hellish, six-week trek across the ice they reached the bleak shelter of Bennett Island, where they rested a few days before attempting to sail to the Siberian mainland. They had food for a few weeks only and, although it was August, ice still lay thick in the sea they would have to cross. They made very slow progress, and the gale that blew up eventually to scatter the ice also scattered the boats. One of the three was never seen again and probably sank in the storm. The second, commanded by Lieutenant Melville, reached the Lena Delta and found shelter in a village farther inland. The boat commanded by De Long himself reached land also, but in a particularly inhospitable region of the great delta. The food was practically finished and the men were so weak that they could hardly lift their feet and shuffled along like old men. There was no settlement near, and by the time that two of the fitter members of the party, sent by De Long to fetch help, reached the village where Melville was recuperating, winter was too far advanced for rescue. The following spring Melville covered several hundred miles by sledge in searching for his commander. Inevitably, he found only bodies. The brave De Long, who probably could have saved his own life if he had not insisted on staying with the members of his party too ill to move, had watched his comrades die before he died himself on about 1 November 1881.

Three years after the sailing of the *Jeannette*, various articles apparently from the ship were discovered on the south-west coast of Greenland. A Norwegian professor wrote an article saying that if these were relics from the *Jeannette* then they must have drifted on the ice right across the Arctic Ocean. His article was read by a young Norwegian scientist, Fridtjof Nansen, and began a train of thought that was to end in the voyage of the *Fram*.

Sir Leopold McClintock once called Nansen a 'true Viking' and the description was so apt that it has been repeated by everyone describing Nansen ever since. He was six feet tall and strongly built, an athlete and hunter, who chose to study zoology at university partly because it would allow him to live an active, outdoor life. Tall and vigorous, with bright blue eyes and blond hair, he certainly looked like the popular image of a Viking, but although Nansen fitted the image of an intrepid man of action he was much else besides. The Viking adventurer was also an intellectual; the outdoor man was also a scholar who gained his doctorate with a paper on 'The Structure and Combination of Histological Elements of the Central Nervous System' which the professors at Bergen hardly understood and therefore almost rejected (it was later seen to be a remarkable breakthrough in histology). The zoologist and oceanographer was also an artist, a poet, a mystic even, who sought in the far north something more profound than fame or scientific data. On the icy Arctic plains Nansen found self-knowledge and spiritual replenishment.

Nansen would be remembered today even if he had never set foot north of the Arctic Circle, yet as an explorer alone he is perhaps the outstanding figure in the distinguished line of men from Frobisher to Admiral Byrd. He was one of those rare people who combine intellectual perception with practical application. He learned lessons from the experience of others that no one else grasped, and he applied his knowledge in conceiving plans that struck more conventional minds as wild and outrageous. Fortunately, he had considerable confidence in himself and was not diverted from his conclusions by near-universal criticism. His imagination was always active, but always controlled by his scholar's brain with its sharp analytical powers and tireless attention to detail. It was typical of Nansen that he learned the Eskimo language before his Greenland trip. His sheer inventiveness was extraordinary and, except perhaps for Parry, no previous explorer had a greater impact on the course of polar exploration.

When planning his crossing of Greenland, a journey that no one had succeeded in completing, Nansen elected to cross from east to west: as there were virtually no settlements on the east coast he would be unable to turn back to seek shelter but would have to press on. It was equally characteristic that the expedition was planned down to the smallest detail—and that it accomplished its object.

But not without difficulty. Nansen and his four companions (including Otto Sverdrup) were dropped two miles off Greenland's ice-clogged east coast by a Norwegian sealer in mid-July 1888. It took them a month to reach their starting point as their little boats were caught in the ice; by the time they gained the shore they had drifted 200 miles south and had to make their way north before starting the crossing. The first part of the journey was the worst, as they had to haul their sledges uphill and the weather was extremely cold (up to 70 °F below freezing) with heavy snowfalls. But at times they were able to tie the sledges together and rig up a sail, whizzing across the hardened snow surface before the wind. They climbed to an altitude nearly 9,000 feet above sea-level before the ground began to slope downhill and they were able to make faster progress on skis. They were tortured by thirst, carrying bottles next to the skin to prevent it freezing (eating snow does not assuage thirst),

and their food was insufficient (a common error on polar expeditions, corrected by Nansen during his trans-Arctic expedition but committed by subsequent explorers, including Scott). There were near-disasters too. On one occasion, while 'sailing' the sledges along at a rapid pace in the gathering gloom, Nansen saw a dark patch appear in front of him and swung the sledge round into the wind on the very edge of a broad crevasse.

Before the end of the month they had reached the coast, and after an extremely hazardous cruise down the fjord in a boat made of willow sticks and sail cloth, they reached the settlement of Godthaab. They spent the winter there and thus their feat was not known until the following spring when they returned to Norway. It was pleasant to find that instead of the scorn, mockery and doubt that had greeted the announcement of Nansen's plans, he and Sverdrup were treated to a welcome fit for heroes.

Not long after his return from Greenland, Nansen addressed the geographical society in his home town of Christiania (Oslo) on his plans for a polar expedition. He reviewed recent expeditions and their methods, and suggested that their lack of success called for a different approach. The finding of the *Jeannette* relics pointed to the existence of a current flowing from near the Siberian coast across (or in the vicinity of) the North Pole and out towards the Greenland Sea. There was other evidence of such a current, some of it collected by Nansen himself, in the shape of driftwood and mud of Siberian origin found on the coasts of southern

The Northeast Passage. The route taken by Nordenskjold during his successful voyage in the *Vega*.

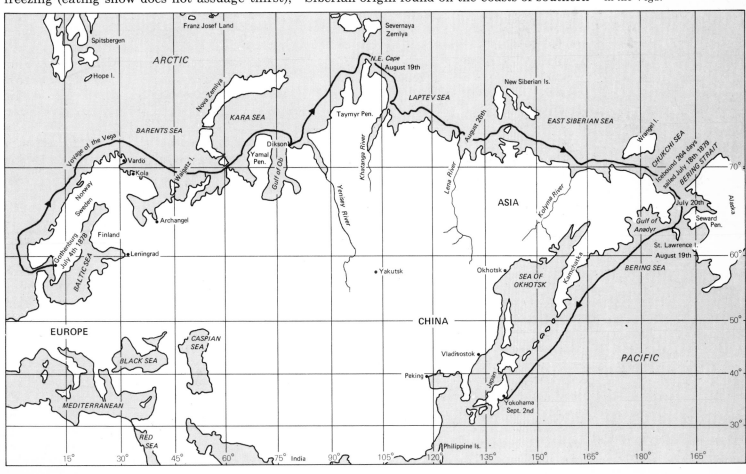

127

Greenland. Nansen proposed to take advantage of this Arctic phenomenon, which had destroyed the *Tegetthoff* and the *Jeannette*, by building a boat that would not be crushed by the ice but would ride above it. He would sail it to the New Siberian Islands, push as far north as he could get and then allow the drifting ice to carry the ship onward, eventually emerging, after two or three years, north of Spitsbergen. Nansen admitted that there was a strong chance that the ship would not pass directly over the pole but between the pole and Franz Josef Land. But he added that this was not important. 'It is not to seek for the exact mathematical point that forms the northern extremity of the world's axis that we set out, for to reach this point is intrinsically of small moment. Our object is to investigate the great unknown region that surrounds the Pole. . . .' Although Nansen was not immune to the lure of the North Pole (as subsequent events showed), he always remained a scientist first.

Nansen's plan was well received in Norway, where the government and Norwegian private interests were eventually to put up virtually all the money for the expedition (it was not enormously expensive – approximately £25,000). Elsewhere, the project encountered doubt, if not ridicule. In London Nansen presented his idea to the Royal Geographical Society in 1892. Although he was still only thirty-one years old, his successful crossing of Greenland had made his name well known. He confronted an audience of Arctic veterans who clearly regarded his project with grave doubts. Sir Leopold McClintock paid tribute to Nansen's great qualities and pronounced his plan 'the most adventurous programme ever brought under the notice of the Royal Geographical Society'. He agreed that Nansen's theories were well supported by facts, but he could not believe that any ship that gave herself up to the grip of the ice would ever be seen again. Sir George Nares was even less hopeful: 'The adopted Arctic axioms for successfully navigating an icy region are that it is absolutely necessary to keep close to a coast line. . . .' He did not believe in Nansen's theory of polar drift. Sir Allen Young raised another objection, the likelihood of land near the pole where the ship would be immovably halted; nor did he think it possible to build a ship that could resist the pressure of the ice for an indefinite period. With a few exceptions, such as Sir Edward Inglefield, the great names in British Arctic exploration were lined up against Nansen, while in America General Greely wrote, 'it strikes me as almost incredible that the plan here advanced by Dr Nansen should receive encouragement or support. It seems to me to be based on fallacious ideas as to physical conditions within the polar regions, and to foreshadow, if attempted, barren results, apart from the suffering and death among its members.'

These objections, though hardly encouraging,

Nansen took in his stride. The *Fram* rapidly took shape under the supervision of the Scottish shipbuilder, Colin Archer, to whom Nansen made generous acknowledgement in his account of the expedition. 'Plan after plan did Archer make of the projected ship; one model after another was prepared and abandoned. Fresh improvements were constantly being suggested. The form we finally adhered to may seem to many people by no means beautiful; but that it is well adapted to the ends in view I think our expedition has fully proved.' The shape of the hull was designed so that the pressure of the ice would tend to push it up rather than squeeze it in; thus the sides were rounded, the bottom flat and the ship one-third as broad as she was long. In open seas she sailed with the smooth aplomb of an old barrel, but in the ice she performed splendidly. Her hull was actually of three layers, making a total thickness of over two feet of matured oak and greenheart, and was so braced

that 'the hold looks like a cobweb of balks, stanchions, and braces'. Bow and stern were rounded off to give no holds for the ice.

The pessimists said that the *Fram* (the name means 'onward') would never reach the starting point of her drift near the New Siberian Islands and, indeed, this was one of the most anxious periods during the long voyage. She met ice sooner than expected and had a difficult time getting through the Kara Sea. But once the danger point of Cape Chelyuskin was passed the conditions improved and Nansen's fear that he would have to spend the first winter on the Siberian coast receded. The *Fram* steamed across the Laptev Sea and turned north towards the ice. By 25 September 1893 she was frozen in just north of 78° latitude, almost exactly where Nansen had reckoned.

The Norwegians prepared for their long, involuntary journey. The engine was dismantled, oiled and stored away; screw and rudder were raised. 'We cleared up the hold to make room for a joiner's workshop... our mechanical workshop we had in the engine-room. The smithy was at first on deck, and afterwards on the ice; tin-smith's work was done chiefly in the chart room, shoemaker's and sailmaker's, and various odd sorts of work, in the saloon.... There was nothing, from the most delicate instruments down to wooden shoes and axe-handles, that could not be made on board the *Fram*.' A windmill was erected on deck to drive a dynamo, which gave sporadic electric light during the long Arctic night. Nansen had thought of practically everything, and if something was lacking he could often invent a means of supplying it – hence the famous 'Nansen cooker'.

Nansen's journal contains many almost guilty remarks about the comfortable situation of the thirteen men on board the *Fram*. Except for boredom they were not undergoing the ordeals that the public had come to associate with Arctic exploration. It was perhaps Nansen himself for whom the tedium was most trying, especially during the long periods when they made no progress or, worse, drifted steadily south; then Nansen wondered if his theory was going to collapse 'like a house of cards'. Writing was the chief outlet for his pent-up energy and anxiety. He was, it seems hardly necessary to say, an excellent writer. No one has made a better attempt than Nansen at describing, for instance, the indescribable aurora:

'... the aurora borealis shakes over the vault of heaven its veil of glittering silver – changing now to yellow, now to green, now to red. It spreads, it contracts again, in restless change, next it breaks into waving, many-folded bands of shining silver, over which shoot billows of glittering rays; and then the glory vanishes. Presently it shimmers in tongues of flame over the very zenith; and then again it shoots a bright ray up from the horizon, until the whole melts away in the moonlight, and it is as though one heard the sigh of a departing spirit. Here and there are left a few waving streamers of light, vague as a foreboding – they are the dust from the aurora's glittering cloak. But now it is growing again; new lightnings shoot up; and the endless game begins afresh. And all the time this utter stillness, impressive as the symphony of infinitude.' Nansen's account is full of such passages in which the observation of the scientist and the imagination of the poet are nicely blended.

By the New Year (1894), when the *Fram* had advanced less than one degree of latitude towards the pole, Nansen was already contemplating a sledge trip. 'The longer I wander about and see this sort of [flat] ice in all directions, the more strongly does a plan take hold of me that I have long had in my mind. It would be possible to get with dogs [there were thirty Siberian dogs on the *Fram*] and sledges over this ice to the Pole, if one left the ship for good and made one's way back in the direction of Franz Josef Land,

Nansen. From a photograph taken by Frederick Jackson on the day of their dramatic meeting in Franz Josef Land. Jackson noted that the great Norwegian had grown rather fat on his diet of bear meat.

85°, Nansen was thinking more seriously of his sledge trip. He consulted Otto Sverdrup, who would command the expedition in his absence, and Sverdrup was encouraging. Nansen's spirits rose at the prospect. 'What joy! When I look out over the ice now, it is as if my muscles quivered with longing to be striding off over it in real earnest – fatigue and privation will then be a delight. It may seem foolish that I should be determined to go off on this expedition, when, perhaps, I might do more important work quietly here on board. But the daily observations will be carried on exactly the same.'

In January 1895 the *Fram* was subjected to the fiercest pressure she had yet encountered. A pressure ridge built up and advanced inexorably on the ship, rising above the rail and threatening to overwhelm her. It was like the movement of a great wave advancing on the ship and crashing over the side except that it happened over several days instead of a few seconds. The *Fram* creaked and shifted amid the crunch and crack of the ice, but she survived undamaged, and Nansen decided that in February he and another member of the crew, Hjalmar Johansen, would leave the ship and try to reach the pole with sledges and dogs.

Damage to the sledges and various other necessary adjustments resulted in two false starts, and it was not until mid-March that they left the ship for the last time. Nansen planned to travel north for fifty days when it would be necessary to turn back, whether they had reached the pole or not, because food for the dogs would not last longer. They travelled with three sledges, one carrying their kayaks which they would need on the way south, and made slower progress than Nansen had hoped. The ice was extremely rough, with frequent ridges across which the sledges had to be exhaustingly manhandled.

Their method of travel with the dogs was to kill off one of the weaker animals every few days and feed it to the remainder, a method that Amundsen was to employ with great efficiency. Nansen himself acknowledged that their treatment of the dogs was barbaric. 'It was undeniable cruelty to the poor animals from first to last, and one must often look back on it with horror. It makes me shudder even now when I think of how we beat them with thick ash sticks when, hardly able to move, they stopped from sheer exhaustion. It made one's heart bleed to see them, but we turned our eyes away and hardened ourselves. It was necessary; forwards we must go, and to this end everything must give place. It is the sad part of expeditions of this kind that one systematically kills all better feelings, until only hard-hearted egoism remains.'

There is no room for sentiment on polar expeditions, and the least attractive aspect of Nansen's perhaps misleadingly cheerful account of the *Fram* expedition is his graphic description of the slaughter of Arctic fauna, from polar bears to herring gulls. They killed, of course, for meat

Spitzbergen, or the west coast of Greenland. It might almost be called an easy expedition for two men.' By Nansen it might; no one else would have called such a trip 'almost easy'. A month later he noted; 'Oh! at times this inactivity crushes one's very soul; one's life seems as dark as the winter night outside. . . . I feel I *must* break through this deadness, this inertia, and find some outlet for my energies.' Six weeks later he gave himself a reprimand: 'I am staring myself blind at one single point – am thinking solely of reaching the Pole and forcing our way through to the Atlantic Ocean. And all the time our real task is to explore the unknown polar regions. Are we doing nothing in the service of science? It will be a goodly collection of observations that we shall take home with us from this region, with which we are now rather too well acquainted. The rest is, and remains, a mere matter of vanity. "Love truth more, and victory less".'

By September, when it was clear that the *Fram* was not likely to drift much farther north than

and in self-defence. Polar bears in the far north, unaccustomed to man and his weapons, are unfortunately immune to intimidation and must sometimes be killed simply to make them go away.

By the second week of April they were making only a mile or two a day and Nansen decided to turn back. They were in latitude 86°13′, 160 miles farther nòrth than any man had been before. Ironically, the moment they turned south the going suddenly improved. Nevertheless, the journey back was longer and harder than Nansen had calculated. Their watches had stopped at one point and as a result they could not be sure exactly where they were (it turned out that their estimate of longitude was 6° out) and the land, when they eventually reached it at the end of July, did not correspond with Payer's map of Franz Josef Land. Payer had been misled into marking land where none existed. Nevertheless, they were exalted to reach land – any land – after three years on the ocean.

Nansen had hoped to reach Spitsbergen and a home-bound whaler before the winter, but that was now out of the question. They had to resign themselves to a third winter in the Arctic, and this time without the comforts of the *Fram*. They built a stone hut and laid in a supply of walrus blubber and bear meat. Although they still had food left from the supplies they had brought from the ship they existed throughout the winter on a diet of bear meat. They were not affected by scurvy and when he was able to weigh himself Nansen discovered he had put on 22 lb since leaving the *Fram*.

As spring approached they began to think about the last lap of their journey – the long and hazardous voyage to Spitsbergen in their kayaks. First they had to travel to the south coast of Franz Josef Land. Fatal accidents were twice narrowly avoided; once when an angry walrus attacked Nansen's kayak and neatly holed it with his tusks, and then when both kayaks, tied together to form a sailboat, broke from their moorings and drifted towards the open sea with

all their equipment. There was nothing to do but swim after it. Nansen threw off his outer clothes and plunged in after them. He just managed to reach them before he was overcome by cold and exhaustion, and somehow hauled himself aboard. Almost rigid with cold he began to paddle back. On the way he saw two auks. They were very low in food at the time and Nansen, in this moment of extreme physical distress, managed to get his gun out and control his frozen hands sufficiently to shoot the birds. Johansen, anxiously watching Nansen from the floe, thought he must have gone out of his mind.

On 13 June Nansen was up preparing breakfast when he heard a highly unexpected sound – a dog barking. He was just beginning to think he must have been mistaken when he heard it again. Dogs meant men, but on Franz Josef Land? It had been visited only twice before, by Payer and the men of the *Tegetthoff* and by Leigh Smith a few years later. It was true that there had been some talk of an English expedition to be led by Frederick Jackson at the time the *Fram* was preparing for her voyage.

Nansen gobbled his breakfast and hurried off. He found tracks, too big for a fox. Soon he heard more barks. 'It was with a strange mixture of feelings that I made my way in towards land among the numerous hummocks. . . . Suddenly I thought I heard a shout from a human voice, a strange voice, the first for three years. Now my heart beat, and the blood rushed to my brain, as I ran up on to a hummock, and hallooed with all the strength of my lungs. . . . Soon I heard another shout, and saw . . . a dark form moving among the hummocks farther in. Who was it? . . . We approached one another quickly; I waved my hat: he did the same. I heard him speak to the dog and I listened. It was English, and as I drew nearer I thought I recognised Mr Jackson, whom I remembered once to have seen.'

The two men – the wild, oily, ragged and hairy Norwegian and the pink-skinned, check-suited Englishman – advanced, raised their hats, and greeted each other. At first, Jackson did not realise the significance of this strange human apparition from the ice. 'Suddenly he stopped, looked me full in the face, and said quickly:
'"Aren't you Nansen?"'
'"Yes, I am."'
'"By Jove! I am glad to see you!"'
'And he seized my hand and shook it again, while his whole face become one smile of welcome. . . .'

The ordeal of Nansen and Johansen was over. They travelled back to Norway in delightful comfort on Jackson's ship, the *Windward*.

On the same day that the famous meeting between Nansen and Jackson took place in Franz Josef Land, the splendid little *Fram* burst triumphantly from the ice north of Spitsbergen after her drift of thirty-five months across the Arctic Ocean. At Tromsö, in joyful, welcoming Norway, the whole company was reunited. The most brilliantly conceived and courageously executed expedition in Arctic history was at an end.

Nansen's services to the Arctic were not over. His *In Northern Mists* (1911) is still perhaps the best general history of Arctic exploration up to the Renaissance, while his account of the *Fram* expedition, *Farthest North* (1897), though it leaves much unsaid, is one of the most exciting of all explorers' stories. He made several more expeditions concerned with scientific research in the Arctic. He contemplated an Antarctic expedition in the *Fram* but never carried it out, and instead lent his beloved vessel to Amundsen for an Arctic expedition. Nansen was as surprised as everyone else when Amundsen sailed her to the Antarctic instead.

Nansen's career as a statesman lies outside the scope of this book. His liberal conscience, profound intelligence and universally acknowledged integrity had lasting effects on Norway and on Europe. A powerful supporter of the League of Nations, he was appointed commissioner responsible for repatriation of prisoners of war after the First World War. The Russians would not recognize the League, but they *would* recognize Nansen, so he set up a private organization which repatriated about half a million men in a very short time. He was later in charge of famine relief in Russia, Greece and Armenia. No man better deserved the Nobel Peace Prize, which he was awarded in 1922. With his wide-brimmed hat (he had worn a similar model in the Arctic), mane of white hair and luxuriant Viking moustache, he remained in his later years a figure of immense panache at meetings of international organizations. He died in May 1930 at the beginning of a decade in which he would have found little comfort.

The Pace Quickens

As the *Fram* steamed south on her way home in 1896 she called at Spitsbergen to witness the preparations of Salomon Andrée, a Swedish engineer, for his attempt to reach the North Pole by balloon. Extraordinary as it may seem, the idea of ballooning over the pole was not regarded as impractical, nor was it novel. De Long had seriously considered using a balloon instead of the *Jeannette*. Nansen had remarked in 1890 that the time was coming when balloon flights would undoubtedly be made over the pole, and Andrée's plan had received enthusiastic support from Baron Nordenskjold.

Andrée himself appears to have been rather less confident. Having postponed the attempt in 1896 owing to the lack of a favourable wind, he reluctantly agreed to make a start the next year because his comrades insisted. The *Ornen* ('eagle') began shakily. As the restraining ropes were cut away she rose into the air then began to dip towards the water. Ballast was thrown out. She rose again, faltered, then floated up and away, soaring high into the sky. In a few minutes she had disappeared. Unfortunately she had broken several of her guide ropes, by which Andrée was able to control her course to some degree.

The quixotic Andrée aimed to keep the world informed of his progress by homing pigeons and one of these birds, released two days after the *Ornen*'s ascent, was shot by a whaler and picked up. Its message reported all well, at latitude 82°.

And that was the end of it. Nothing more was heard from Andrée and his two companions for many years. Then in 1930 a Norwegian scientific expedition touching at White Island, between Spitsbergen and Franz Josef Land, found their remains, including Andrée's cheerful, humorous diary and photographs which were successfully developed after thirty-three years in the ice. The *Ornen* had been enveloped in dense fog, and Andrée was unable to gain enough height to prevent the basket banging about among the hummocks. On 14 July 1897 after three days' flight, they had landed just short of the 83rd parallel and begun the march back. They were not experienced Arctic travellers and their equipment was less than ideal. They miscalculated the Arctic drift and thus missed their

Salomon August Andrée (1854–97), a capable engineer, he planned his flight meticulously. But he and his companions were less well prepared to survive in the Arctic once they were forced to land.

objective–Franz Josef Land, where Frederick Jackson had left a well-stocked depot for Andrée's use. All three men died in October, perhaps of carbon-monoxide poisoning from their leaky cooker as at that time they had both food and shelter.

In the year that Andrée set out for the North Pole the *Fram*, with the tireless Otto Sverdrup again in command, was preparing for a new Arctic voyage. Nansen himself had been approached, but Nansen had a wife and baby daughter and, not surprisingly, he was unwilling to leave them again for a long journey in the ice. The region which Sverdrup and the *Fram* were originally intended to explore was northern Greenland, but here they were confronted by heavy ice and by the hostility of Robert E. Peary, who had come to regard that region as his private preserve and was highly sceptical of the Norwegians' claim that research was their sole object. Peary feared that Sverdrup might make a dash for the pole, thus ruining his own plans.

Sverdrup gave up the idea of circumnavigating Greenland and shifted his attention westward. In the course of three years (1899–1902) he and his colleagues, notably Gunnar Isachsen, explored and mapped with devoted accuracy the western coast of Ellesmere Island and discovered the unknown islands to the west of it, sometimes known as the Sverdrup Islands (Axel Heiberg, Amund Ringnes, Isachsen and Ellef Ringnes islands). Sverdrup returned to Norway in 1902; he was then forty-seven years old and had spent eight of the previous ten years in the Arctic.

The following year another great Norwegian explorer entered Lancaster Sound from Baffin Bay in the 150-ton cutter *Gjøa*. This was the first polar expedition that Roald Amundsen had commanded, though he had previously served as a midshipman on the *Belgica*, with de Gerlache's Antarctic expedition.

Amundsen was only thirty years old when he embarked on his attempt to sail the Northwest Passage. A physician by training, he gave up his medical career for the sake of polar exploration. It was really a case of exchanging careers, for Amundsen's approach to exploration was essentially professional. He was not, like Nordenskjold or Nansen, a scientist engaged in research. He was not, like Parry or Ross, or even Scott, an officer seconded to exploratory expeditions in the course of his service. He was not, like Hall or Andrée, an inspired amateur. He was a clever, thorough man who set out seriously and methodically to make himself an expert in all the techniques of travel and survival in the polar regions. Like Peary, Amundsen represented a new breed

The oceanographical research carried out on the *Challenger* expedition helped to stimulate interest in geographical exploration generally and especially in Antarctica. The ship is seen here made fast to St Paul's Rocks in the South Atlantic.

of polar explorer, dedicated and even ruthless, immensely capable, tough, shrewd, patient and determined. It was not chance that made Peary and Amundsen the conquerors of the poles.

The one persistent handicap that Amundsen laboured under was shortage of money; in order to buy the herring-boat that he named *Gjøa* and mount his north-west expedition, he had to leave as quietly as possible, at midnight, so it is said, to escape his creditors.

Though it ran out in the end, Amundsen possessed a good share of that essential commodity, explorer's luck. Thus in 1903, having crossed Baffin Bay and penetrated Lancaster Sound without difficulty, he turned south down Peel Sound and found the ice comparatively light. In 1875 Allen Young in the *Pandora* had been stopped north of Bellot Strait. As the *Gjøa* approached the spot, Amundsen walked the deck anxiously. 'As I walked, I felt something like an irregular lurching motion. . . . There it was again. . . ! I could not be mistaken, there was a slight irregular motion in the ship. . . . It was a swell under the boat–a message from the open sea. The water to the south was open.'

North of King William Island, Amundsen diverged from Franklin's route and took the passage east of the island. His ship was soon among dangerous shoals, and a storm blew up to drive the *Gjøa* aground on a reef. Next day the tide failed to float her off. In the middle of the night, in a north wind near gale force, Amundsen decided to raise the sails. All superfluous cargo was jettisoned, and somehow the *Gjøa* bumped and banged her way across the reef into clear

water. All the way to the south of the island Amundsen and his men had a very rough passage, but in Rae Strait the water was deeper, and in September they found secure winter quarters in a harbour opposite the estuary of the Fish River.

They remained in Gjøahavn for two winters. Wiik, the young geologist who was to die before the *Gjøa* reached the Pacific, was able to carry out a prolonged study of terrestrial magnetism, while Amundsen, living cheek by jowl with the Eskimos, learned their techniques of travel and survival, knowledge which laid the basis for his successful journey to the South Pole seven years later.

The *Gjøa* resumed her voyage in August 1905. In thick fog, she zigzagged cautiously through the narrow channel in Simpson Strait and Queen Maud Gulf. After an anxious week she reached the vicinity of Cambridge Bay and Amundsen knew that success was in sight, for Collinson had reached this point in a much larger ship from the west. The compass was working again as the magnetic pole was left behind, and with the aid of Collinson's charts the expedition had a fairly swift and easy voyage through Dease Strait, Coronation Gulf, and Dolphin and Union Strait into the gulf now named after Amundsen. Soon after, they met an American whaler, which supplied them with charts of the coast as well as some welcome California vegetables. But they were unable to finish the voyage that year. Off the mouth of the Mackenzie River they again encountered dense fog, the ice closed in, and they were forced to spend a third winter in the Arctic. There were many Eskimos in the area and several whalers wintering not far off, so the season passed comfortably enough. The following summer the *Gjøa* completed the last stage of the Northwest Passage. By the beginning of September she was at anchor in Nome harbour.

The Northwest Passage, unlike the Northeast, has not so far proved of much commercial interest. Amundsen did not seriously suppose that it would: his purpose was not to open a new route, as Nordenskjold's was, but to establish a record. He hoped to be first to the North Pole as well. The passage has on rare occasions been traversed since, notably overland by Knud Rasmussen in 1923, and by the vast American tanker, *Manhattan*, in 1968. This 1,000-foot long monster (the *Gjøa* was seventy-two feet long), which pounded her way through in both directions, was intended to pioneer a new route for Alaskan oil. In spite of the congratulatory reports, it appears that the *Manhattan* had an even tougher time than expected, and in the aftermath of her voyage the controversial trans-Alaska oil pipeline began to appear a less impractical project than many people had thought (or hoped).

Another notable Norwegian explorer who had appeared on the polar scene before the end of the 19th century was Carstens Borchgrevink, who in 1894 joined the Bull-Kristensen expedition in which man first set foot on the mainland of the Antarctic continent. This expedition, largely backed by Svend Foyn, inventor of the harpoon gun and, as far as exploration was concerned, something of a Norwegian Enderby, marked the beginning of a renewal of interest in Antarctica which in less than twenty years was to culminate in the conquest of the South Pole.

After the triumphs of James Clark Ross in Antarctica, the interest of the British had been diverted northwards by the Franklin fiasco and its aftermath. The Americans were discouraged by the echoing recriminations of the Wilkes expedition. The French failed to follow up Dumont d'Urville's discoveries and took no further part in Antarctic exploration until the 20th century. As in the Arctic, it was the Norwegians who were in the van of the renewed interest in the Antarctic.

For more than half a century Antarctica, it would seem, was almost forgotten. But not quite. Just as the work of such famous scholars as Alexander Humboldt and Johann Gauss had helped to create the climate in which Dumont d'Urville, Wilkes and Ross were dispatched to the far south, so in the second half of the 19th century there were one or two prominent oceanographers (the American M. F. Maury, the German Georg von Neumayer, and the British-Canadian John Murray) whose persistent propaganda on behalf of Antarctic research eventually bore fruit. Murray was one of the scientists on the *Challenger*, which made 'a momentary swoop' into Antarctic waters in 1874. The work carried out by the *Challenger* proved indisputably that Antarctica was a continent, in spite of the fact that she never came within sight of its coasts. In fact Murray was able to sketch a remarkably accurate map of Antarctica on the basis of the information gained from rocks dredged from the bottom of the ocean, where they had been deposited by icebergs.

Whalers also visited Antarctic waters in the late 19th century, among them the Norwegian Captain C. A. Larsen, whose interest in polar exploration had been sparked by a voyage to Greenland carrying Fridtjof Nansen to complete his famous crossing. Larsen made a number of discoveries in the region of Graham Land in his ship the *Jason* (later, renamed *Stella Polare*, to carry the Duke of the Abruzzi to Spitsbergen).

The Bull-Kristensen expedition returned to Melbourne in March 1894. Borchgrevink brought back lichens he had found growing where the landing had been made on the Antarctic mainland, at Cape Adare, but the commercial purpose of the voyage of the *Antarctica*, to locate the 'right' whales that James Ross had reported (erroneously), was a failure, and Borchgrevink had to look elsewhere for a chance to pursue his eager interest in the Antarctic.

The next expedition to Antarctica also sailed in a stout Norwegian whaler, and many of the crew were Norwegians. The ship was named, however, the *Belgica*, and the commander of the expedition was a Belgian naval officer, Adrien de Gerlache. Among others on board the *Belgica* were several whose names were to become more familiar later. Roald Amundsen, on his first polar expedition, sailed as mate. The ship's doctor was an American named Frederick Cook; he had been with Peary in Greenland and joined the *Belgica* at Rio de Janeiro after the originally chosen doctor had pulled out at the last minute.

The *Belgica* arrived in the Antarctic rather late in the season of 1897–98: the South Shetland Islands were not sighted until 20 January. A number of landings were made in Graham Land during the next three or four weeks and de Gerlache's multi-national staff collected many samples of Antarctic rocks, lichens, mosses and even insects. The geologist on board was to complain that he was not given enough time for his studies, but the de Gerlache expedition did more work than any of its predecessors, and subsequent events suggested that the scientists were allowed too much time, for in March the *Belgica* was frozen into the ice in the Bellingshausen Sea. There or thereabouts she remained for just over a year.

De Gerlache and his fellows were not prepared for a winter in the Antarctic and they had an exceedingly unpleasant time. The trouble seems to have been as much psychological as physical, for the dreaded polar night that most polar explorers (to say nothing of the Eskimos) have found to be not very dreadful did have dire effects on members of the de Gerlache expedition. They suffered from poor circulation, from

signs of heart trouble, and bad digestion. Food was not scarce but possibly lacking in certain vitamins, and fresh penguin meat did not go down well. It was, Dr Cook said, a 'hellish' existence. However, only one man died and some scientific work was continued when the weather permitted.

Summer came again, but the floe in which the *Belgica* was caught showed no signs of breaking up. In January the crew set to work with saws, axes and explosives and eventually blasted their way into open water. It took another month to escape from the pack. In November they reached Belgium and received a rapturous welcome.

In the same month that de Gerlache was anxiously seeking a way out of the ice in Antarctica, Borchgrevink, on the other side of the continent, was happily settling himself in.

Having served in a subordinate capacity on the Bull-Kristensen expedition, Borchgrevink returned to Europe determined to gain support for another expedition to the Antarctic. He had no particularly outstanding qualifications for leadership of such an expedition except his own enthusiasm and energy, and efforts to promote a commercial expedition failed. Official institutions looked on him askance. The body of opinion represented by Sir Clements Markham, President of the Royal Geographical Society, treated him as a meddlesome interloper threatening to upset

Captain Adrien de Gerlache of the Belgian Antarctic expedition.

Roald Amundsen (1872–1928), the most successful of all polar explorers, who forsook the medical profession for fame and adventure. He registered a remarkable series of 'firsts': first to winter in the Antarctic, first to sail the Northwest Passage, first to reach the South Pole, and first to make the Spitsbergen–Alaska crossing – in the airship *Norge*.

plans for the *Discovery* expedition (which Scott was to lead in 1901). However, Borchgrevink found an influential patron in the person of a rich publisher, Sir George Newnes, who was prepared to back a scientific expedition and purchased a Norwegian whaler, renamed the *Southern Cross*, for the purpose.

The *Southern Cross* left London in 1898, called at Hobart, and approached Antarctica in late December. She had a great deal of trouble breaching the pack and did not pass through until the second week of February. She anchored near Cape Adare and winter headquarters were built just in time to allow the ship to withdraw for the winter to New Zealand. No very extensive exploration could then be undertaken, and Borchgrevink had only nine men with him, including two Lapps to handle the dogs. Meteorological and magnetic observations were taken and some valuable work was done by Nicolai Hanson, a zoologist from the British National History Museum.

The Antarctic winter proved even grimmer than expected. More dangerous than the blizzards that howled around their wooden hut was the low morale of the men, although the peculiar physical ailments from which the men of the *Belgica* had suffered did not afflict Borchgrevink and his companions. The one exception was the brilliant young zoologist, Hanson, who went down apparently with some intestinal disease just as winter was ending. He died in mid-October as the first penguins were returning from the north.

It made a strange scene, that first burial in Antarctica. The grave was blasted open with explosive to receive the rigid corpse. A forlorn group of men stood around in the pale light, the ice crunching under their feet. One hand moved automatically towards a hat and was quickly withdrawn as the icy air breathed a warning. In the distance the penguins squeaked and chattered to each other, flapping their rudimentary wings as if shrugging their shoulders, while the black cliffs loomed above the glacier and the two Lapps, tears frozen on their leathery cheeks, sang a strange northern dirge on the Southern Continent.

When the *Southern Cross* returned in January 1900 Borchgrevink was able to extend his explorations farther. He landed on the Ross Ice Shelf and made a short sledging journey with William Colbeck, a British naval officer, in the course of which they established a 'farthest south' record of 78°50′ and opened the way for Scott.

On 19 February the *Southern Cross* turned north. This time she encountered almost no pack ice though the reason for this pleasant surprise—high winds—was itself unpleasant. Back in England, Borchgrevink's success had not made him any more popular with his critics, and his somewhat racy accounts in the popular magazines owned by Sir George Newnes provoked acid comments in more academic circles. Nevertheless, his expedition was on the whole a remarkable success, and Colbeck's charts of the Ross Sea region were to prove extremely valuable to the successors of Borchgrevink, who by now were almost queueing up to get into the Antarctic.

For Science or Glory

In the sudden burst of polar exploration that began in the last decade of the 19th century there were two main motives at work: scientific curiosity and individual, or nationalistic, rivalry. Sometimes the two were mingled, perhaps disastrously on Scott's second expedition. Sometimes scientific research was the sole object, as it was for Charcot; less often the aim was primarily competitive. There was never much doubt that Peary, Shackleton and Amundsen were driven, almost exclusively, by the desire to establish a record that would never be broken—first man to the pole—and that scientific research was for them an incidental activity. But most expeditions at least included geologists, botanists and zoologists among their number, whatever the ambition of their leaders.

Antarctic expeditions were expensive, and the aims of an expedition had to be tailored to the interests of those who were putting up the money. These were often scientific institutions, which were usually interested in research rather than heroic achievements. On the other hand, polar exploration had become popular; there seems to have been a need for heroes and the explorer, engaged in a relentless battle with the mighty forces of nature, fitted the public's bill. Earlier generations had applauded the career of a Livingstone or a General Gordon, but by the turn of the century imperialism was already turning slightly sour. The British found themselves fighting a white-skinned people in South Africa and began to have doubts. In the polar regions, the struggle was simpler; the seals and the penguins had no territorial rights.

Similar influences were at work in other countries. The Norwegian national holiday, 17 May, was always celebrated with great festivity by Nansen and his comrades in the Arctic, and rising Norwegian nationalism eventually led to the crisis of 1906 and the dissolution of the union with Sweden, in which, incidentally, Nansen himself played a prominent part. Although it would be difficult to describe precisely the connection between the movement which ended in an independent Norway (for the first time since the Middle Ages) and the contemporary predominance of the new Norsemen in

polar exploration, obviously an ancient nation in the process of reasserting its identity felt a need for national heroes.

Nowadays, heroes are not so fashionable, and most people would agree that the change is for the better. We tend to prefer the devoted researcher with his painstaking collection of samples, his careful classification, his tentative hypotheses and his vast unreadable publications, to the glamorous adventurer with his tales of derring-do. In fact the explorer's role is often underrated. Just as trade follows the flag (or the other way about), so, in the polar regions, science follows the sledge. It is evident that man ought to know as much as possible about the planet he lives on, and he will not find out unless he visits all parts. There were those who pointed out, quite correctly, that the *Challenger* expedition discovered more about Antarctica without visiting it than any previous expedition, except perhaps that of James Clark Ross; just as there are those who say, no doubt equally correctly, that it is not necessary to send men into space to find out about the universe. But without practical experience, hypotheses remained unproven, while the challenge of unperformed physical feats tempted men to undertake them.

There is something undignified, to say the least, about the intense competition between nations and individuals to reach the poles, although the individuals involved behaved, on the whole, with commendable restraint. The most unseemly chauvinism was displayed not by the explorers but by those who stayed at home.

In Britain, the clash of interests between the scientists and the explorers delayed the renewal of officially sponsored Antarctic exploration. As early as 1893, John Murray of the *Challenger* expedition called for further investigation of the Antarctic at a meeting of the Royal Geographical Society. His suggestion was enthusiastically embraced by Sir Clements Markham, President of the Society and an ardent devotee of the naval tradition of British polar exploration. Markham was a very influential man, every bit the equal of Sir John Barrow in the early 19th century. He was not interested in an international expedition of scientific research such as Murray had in mind. He endeavoured to enlist the support of the Admiralty for an expedition of the type that he himself had taken part in, over forty years before, during the search for Franklin, and when the Admiralty proved reluctant, he turned his formidable persuasive powers upon the Society over which he presided in a highly authoritarian fashion. The Society agreed, but its resources were insufficient to pay for the massive, two-ship expedition that was contemplated. The rest of the funds would have to be raised by public appeal.

Meanwhile, the Belgian expedition had sailed and, far worse in Markham's eyes, Borchgrevink had succeeded (thanks to Sir George Newnes) in raising the money for his 1898 expedition. In the same year, however, the prospects for a national British expedition brightened considerably at a meeting of the Royal Society, the major society of British scientists, where Markham received keen support. Two wealthy members of the Royal Geographical Society then offered large donations, and on the strength of that, in 1899, Markham was able to enlist government backing.

Serious differences soon arose between Markham, representing the Royal Geographical Society, and Murray, representing the Royal Society. Murray did not rule out geographical exploration, but what he wanted was 'a steady, continuous, laborious, and systematic exploration of the whole southern region'. In other words, no mad dashes for the pole, no British heroics. Markham wanted a naval expedition; Murray favoured civilian scientists. Murray wanted to wait until enough money had been collected to equip two ships; Markham believed a start should be made as soon as possible, even if only one ship could be equipped. The eventual result was a compromise, but a compromise in Markham's favour. The expedition sailed in a single vessel, the *Discovery*, specially designed for Antarctic waters, and it was commanded by a naval officer of Markham's choice, Robert F. Scott, with three other naval officers and two officers of the merchant marine, Shackleton being one of them. The chief scientific officer resigned when he found he was not to be in charge of land exploration; but despite that naval victory the scientific staff of the *Discovery* expedition was of high calibre.

The year 1901 was designated 'Antarctic Year' by an international geographical congress in 1900. It witnessed the dispatch of three expeditions, the other two being German (Drygalski) and Swedish (Otto Nordenskjold).

Erich von Drygalski, a professor of geography at Berlin, had previously taken part in an expedition to Greenland. He owed his appointment to Neumayer, who was more than any other individual responsible for the minor though by no means negligible German participation in polar exploration during the late 19th and early 20th centuries. The Drygalski expedition concentrated on the unknown region south of Kerguelen, where a base was established. Its ship, the *Gauss*, was specially built and owed much to the design of the *Fram*.

In February, the coast was sighted and named by von Drygalski Kaiser Wilhelm II Land. Soon afterwards the *Gauss* was imprisoned by the ice and, as the land could not be reached, snow-built observatories were set up on an ice floe. Drygalski ascended in a captive balloon, such as Scott also used, and surveyed the scene from 1,500 feet. Extensive sledging journeys were carried out in the spring, but only for the purpose of gathering scientific data, and as summer approached thoughts turned to freeing the ship from the ice. The floe was up to twenty feet thick and resisted blasting but the Germans cleverly induced a fault in the floe, along which it eventually cracked, by laying a path of cinders which absorbed heat from the sun and melted a channel six feet deep. Even so, it took two more months for the *Gauss* to escape from the pack and proceed to Cape Town.

The Swedish expedition was also led by a scientist and was exclusively scientific in purpose. Otto Nordenskjold, a nephew of the first man to complete the Northeast Passage, was a geologist whose work in Tierra del Fuego had suggested to him that the tip of South America was geologically linked with Graham Land. His ship was the *Antarctic* of Kristensen and his captain was that experienced Norwegian skipper, C. A. Larsen. The expedition reached the South Shetlands in January 1902, and after failing to penetrate the Weddell Sea, established a winter base at Snow Hill Island, just south of James Ross Island (Graham Land). For most of the winter the scientists were confined by bad weather to their hut but they undertook a number of sledging trips in autumn and spring and greatly improved existing maps of the peninsula.

During the summer of 1902–03, the *Antarctic* failed to appear to evacuate the expedition. She had in fact been nipped by the ice in January and sunk; two men who tried to reach the camp over the ice were forced to winter alone, surviving mainly on seals, until Nordenskjold met them while on a sledging trip the following October.

Nothing having been heard of the *Antarctic* by the spring of 1903, the Argentine Navy sent a ship to investigate. By a lucky chance, the Argentinians arrived at the Snow Hill camp on the very same day that the shipwrecked Captain Larsen and his men staggered in. The Swedish expedition thus survived thanks to the arrival of the Argentine Navy at a time as incredibly opportune as the cavalry in a B-feature Western.

Scott's *Discovery* expedition was in every way the most accomplished and best-equipped Antarctic expedition to date. Scott himself proved an excellent leader and, although plucked almost at random from the ranks of young naval officers by Sir Clements Markham, he became a dedicated Antarctic man whose very name im-

mediately summons an image of man's struggle with the ice.

The object of the *Discovery* expedition was to follow up the discoveries of James Clark Ross, to explore that part of Antarctica which could be reached, and to carry out various scientific programmes. The ship passed through the Antarctic ice pack in the first week of January 1902, and steamed south along the coast of Victoria Land until the Barrier was reached. A landing was made on Ross Island where Shackleton, 'seeing some green stuff at the foot of a boulder', called to Koettlitz, one of the scientific staff, to come and look at it. 'He went down on his knees then jumped up, crying out, "Moss!! Moss!! I have found moss!!!" I said, "Go on! I found it." He took it quite seriously, and said, "Never mind, it's moss; I am so glad."'

The *Discovery* sailed eastward along Ross's famous Barrier until, finding an inlet where she could safely anchor, Scott went up in a captive balloon to get his first look at the interior of the Antarctic continent. The land stretched away grey and cold, into the limitless distance. Below, the first sledging party on the ice shelf appeared as black specks slowly moving across the surface. With some relief (it was his first ascent) Scott relinquished his place in the basket to an eager, camera-toting Shackleton, who photographed Antarctica from 800 feet up. East of them lay the mountains of what Scott called King Edward VII Land, which Ross thought he had seen, though not closely enough to be certain.

The *Discovery* then returned to the west and, following the recommendation of H. R. Mill, entered McMurdo Sound to find secure winter quarters south of Ross Island. Scott planned to winter on board, but observatories were set up on the shore and preparations made to abandon the

ship should it become necessary. In the short interval before winter set in and the sun disappeared Scott, who maintained fairly tight naval discipline although this was a civilian expedition, had his men out practising the techniques of polar travel. An obvious weakness of the expedition was that although Armitage, the second in command, and Dr Koettlitz had been with Jackson in Franz Josef Land and one or two of the sailors had made polar voyages previously, no one was an experienced Antarctic explorer. Scott had consulted Nansen and his equipment was based closely on Nansen's experience. But one does not become an expert dog-driver or skier in a few weeks.

The camp site of the *Discovery* expedition, 1901–04, at McMurdo Sound.

The winter passed fairly comfortably. The ship's company, segregated into offices and men, appears to have got on well. On occasions when voices were raised, the warning 'Girls! girls!' was often enough to break the tension. Shackleton edited the inevitable *South Polar Times* which is said by those who have courageously plodded through a large proportion of numerous similar publications to have been one of the best explorers' newspapers.

In the spring, Scott prepared for a major journey south. He decided to take with him Dr Edward Wilson, who besides his medical qualifications was an artist of more than ordinary talent and a loyal and lovable man, and Ernest Shackleton, the young, cheerful and energetic Anglo-Irishman picked by Markham for his experience with sail, who had arrived in Antarctica without the least interest in polar exploration except as a way to make a fortune – an object Shackleton had been pursuing without much success since his schooldays at Dulwich College.

They set out across the Ross Ice Shelf on 2 November 1902. Depots had previously been laid down along their route so that they would not have to carry supplies for the whole journey. They took three sledges with nineteen dogs. On good days they managed fifteen miles or more, but on other days, struggling through deep snow or over rough ice, they advanced only five. As the dogs weakened, they could only move one sledge at a time, so that each stage of the journey was covered three times. Occasionally, a blizzard held them stationary for as long as two days. All three men suffered from snow-blindness, and once they crossed a thin snow bridge over a crevasse without realizing it until they were

safely on the other side. They were also constantly hungry.

On Christmas Day, which was fine and comparatively warm, they advanced ten miles and treated themselves to a feast. To the delight of his companions, Shackleton produced a Christmas pudding, which he had been hiding in a pair of clean socks. By this time they had already given up hope of reaching the South Pole, and at the end of the year they turned back. They had reached 82°15′ South, over 200 miles beyond the previous 'farthest south'.

The return journey was grim. Food was extremely short, and they had barely enough to last until they reached a depot which they could not be certain of finding (they did find it – with two days' provisions left). The dogs were all dead and all three men were beginning to show symptoms of scurvy. By the middle of January, Shackleton's condition was making Scott and Wilson anxious. He developed a bad cough and was spitting blood. Scott forbade him to do any hauling, so that he and Wilson had to drag their last sledge between them. Shackleton kept on his feet mainly by effort of will. They arrived back at the ship in the first week of February and Shackleton noted in his diary with characteristic understatement that he was 'not up to the mark', so had a bath and turned in.

To Scott's delight, he found on his return that a relief ship, the *Morning*, had arrived, thanks to Sir Clements Markham's great effort in raising nearly £50,000 to buy her and fit her out. The *Discovery* was still frozen in, and the new supplies had to be sledged across the ice. As a result of the delays, the *Morning* made a rather late departure from the Ross Sea, but she managed to find a way out safely and reached New Zealand

Of all the extraordinary
happenings in the long
search for the Franklin
expedition none is more
remarkable than the story of
the men who sailed under
McClure in the *Investigator*,
whose epic voyage along
hundreds of miles of
unknown Arctic coast ended
in a remote bay off an
unexplored land. A stroke
of luck brought about their
rescue – and made them the
first to travel from Bering
Strait to Baffin Bay.

"STARS AND STRIPES NAILED TO THE NORTH POLE"

DR. FREDERICK A. COOK

APRIL 21
1908.

COMMANDER ROBERT E. PEARY

APRIL 6
1909.

TWO DAUNTLESS AMERICANS WHO REACHED THE GOAL OF A
THOUSAND YEARS AND PLANTED THE STARS AND STRIPES
UPON THE AXIS OF THE WORLD.

on 19 March. Among those who disembarked there was Ernest Shackleton.

Scott had decided that the state of Shackleton's health would not permit another winter in the Antarctic and, as kindly as possible, ordered him home. The patient's own diagnosis was that a month's rest would set him up again, and he was extremely reluctant to leave. It looked as though he had failed. He was determined to return and to obliterate the memory of his humiliation by a glorious march upon the pole. On the day that the *Morning* carried Shackleton away from Antarctica, the basis was laid for a great polar career.

During Scott's trek to the south with Wilson and Shackleton the other members of the expedition had not been idle. The most notable exploit was that of Armitage and Skelton in ascending a glacier south-west of Ross Island. They travelled 130 miles from the ship and reached an altitude of 9,000 feet in the Transantarctic Mountains, beyond which they could see the central Antarctic plateau stretching away toward the South Pole. In November of the following year (1903) Scott himself, with two seamen including Edgar Evans, trekked up one of the glaciers into the mountains and advanced farther west.

The news that the *Morning* had found the *Discovery* still locked in the ice in the summer of 1902–03 caused some anxiety in England, and the government insisted that the Admiralty should undertake the rescue of the Scott expedition. In January, Scott was surprised to see two ships (the *Morning* and the *Terra Nova*) arrive in the Ross Sea, and he was staggered to hear that his orders were to abandon his ship, beyond which the ice still extended for about ten miles. Scott was not the type of officer to abandon a ship with equanimity, but fortunately, as the laborious business of loading equipment on the relief ships went on, the ice began to thaw. With the aid of cutting and blasting, to which the crew of the relief ships readily lent a hand, the *Discovery* at last broke free, though as the Admiralty had not thought of sending coal for her boilers Scott was compelled to make a very slow voyage home.

The expedition had been a notable success. Scott and his men were popular heroes and Sir Clements Markham, basking in the glow of long-delayed success, felt able to relinquish the presidency of the Royal Geographical Society to a younger man (Markham was seventy-four). Scott had brought the South Pole in sight, and as it was never part of his instructions to reach the pole he had done better in this respect than might have been expected. However, the chief accomplishment of the *Discovery* expedition lay in the work of the scientific staff, and no one who has so much as glanced at the fat quarto volumes of scientific data, which take up more space on library shelves than the *Encyclopaedia Britannica*, can doubt the serious scientific purpose of the expedition.

One scientist who had been approached to serve on the *Discovery* expedition had refused because he was about to launch his own Antarctic voyage. He was W. S. Bruce, a Scot, and another veteran of the Jackson-Harmsworth expedition. Backed by a rich patron, Andrew Coats of Paisley, Bruce sailed for the Weddell Sea in the *Scotia*, a converted Norwegian whaler which H. R. Mill, the contemporary Antarctic historian, regarded as 'the most graceful and ship-shape of all the vessels which the beginning of the twentieth century sent out towards the South Pole'. In February 1903 the *Scotia* was caught in the ice not far south of 70° latitude but got free and returned to the base that Bruce had already established in the South Orkney Islands. There, a meteorological observatory was organized; whereupon the *Scotia* retreated to the Falkland Islands and Buenos Aires, where she received a hospitable welcome.

In the following summer, the Scots manning the South Orkneys observatory were replaced by Argentinians, and having made the exchange the *Scotia* began her second attack on the ice of the Weddell Sea. This time she reached 74° South, a few miles short of Weddell's record but farther east. Land was sighted, though it could not be reached, and Bruce named it Coats Land after his friend and supporter. Having charted a large stretch of ocean almost unvisited since Ross, some of whose figures Bruce corrected, the *Scotia* returned via Cape Town to the Clyde. When Bruce subsequently offered his stone-built observatory to the British government he was snubbed, so he gave it instead to the Argentinians who had been so co-operative. This was to give Argentina ammunition in her conflict with Great Britain over territorial rights in that part of the world.

France also returned to the Antarctic in the early years of the 20th century. The successor to Dumont d'Urville was a likeable and talented explorer-scientist, Jean-Baptiste Charcot. Like Amundsen, Charcot was a doctor by profession,

Shackleton's farthest south, on the plateau less than 100 miles from the pole, 19 June 1909.

opposite, top
Bowdoin Fjord and Glacier, off Inglefield Bay, north-west Greenland. The scene of Peary's winter in the Arctic.

opposite, bottom
A souvenir postcard of the conquest of the North Pole by – as it seemed – two Americans on separate expeditions within a year of each other. It is unlikely that the irate Peary sent any of these cards to his friends.

The polar party photographed on board the *Nimrod* soon after their return from their record-breaking journey. Left to right: Wild, Shackleton, Adams and Marshall.

and the son of the famous Paris neurologist who had great influence on the early work of Freud. The original motive for his 1903 expedition in the St Malo-built *Francais* was to look for and assist Nordenskjold, but before he reached his destination Charcot heard of the Swedish explorer's rescue by Captain Irizar of the Argentine Navy. He continued his voyage to Graham Land and began the work of charting the islands and bays of the Antarctic Peninsula which was to prove of inestimable value to sailors, map-makers and even politicians during the next thirty or forty years.

In his account of his second Antarctic expedition (1908–10), Charcot explained 'why I chose as my working-centre this inhospitable region, so unpromising at times and so distant from the actual pole'. He avoided the region of the Ross Ice Shelf because 'two expeditions of different nationality, with the best intentions in the world and with the best of hearts, could not have avoided coming into rivalry over the glorious prize of the Furthest South; and, great sporting interest as this rivalry would have had, it could not but have prejudiced completely the observations and perhaps the ultimate results'. Almost as the scientist Charcot wrote those words, the race he rightly disdained was taking place. He

had no intention of trying to reach the pole, but 'lest anyone should cry "Sour Grapes!" I must hasten to say that if I had had the chance of stumbling on a road by which I could realize the dream of all Polar explorers I should have made for the Pole enthusiastically, and should certainly have spared nothing to reach it'.

Charcot was nothing if not up to date, and his second expedition, in the endearingly named *Pourquoi Pas?*, was notable for its advanced gadgetry and hardware. The motor sledges (predecessors of the tank), which he had tested in company with Scott, proved of little use either to Charcot or to Scott (they were tested, as Charcot said, in conditions that hardly compared with Antarctica). The most useful innovations were the electric lamps, as recommended by the Marquis de Dion, run from an 8-h.p. motor and extended by cable to huts on shore; and a De Dion-Bouton motor boat, with rounded prow protected by iron plates. Clothing and personal equipment generally followed the Norwegian example, with certain modifications devised by Charcot himself or recommended by Scott. Yellow-glassed eye-goggles and masks with cross-shaped slits proved 100 per cent effective against snow-blindness. Charcot had a reputation for abstemiousness; but he thought alcohol

no more dangerous in the polar regions than anywhere else, while rum had medicinal uses; 'but from the start I have made a point of waging unrelenting war against the *apéritif*, the great curse of France'. The library was better stocked than the cellar on the *Pourquoi-Pas?*

Charcot was a humane man, who could be thoroughly upset by the plight of an orphaned seal cub, and to the displeasure of the 'sportsmen', he forbade 'killing for the mere pleasure of destruction'. Much of his work was done among whalers, whom he admired; but he also uttered a warning against overhunting and pointed out the difficulty of restoring the balance, once numbers have been seriously reduced, because the long gestation period of the whale means that two generations may be wiped out in one year.

In his first expedition, Charcot had explored the little-known west coast of the Antarctic Peninsula, wintering on board ship in the Biscoe Islands. The following season he explored Alexander Island. In the *Pourquoi-Pas?* he continued this work and among a number of minor discoveries named Charcot Land (later found to be an island) after his father. Not only was his charting more accurate and extensive than that of most comparable expeditions but a large

amount of scientific work was carried out by his colleagues in the fields of hydrography, geology, zoology, botany, etc.

In later years, Charcot and the *Pourquoi-Pas?* made many voyages of scientific research in Arctic waters. The gallant ship was wrecked off Iceland in 1936 and Charcot, together with most of the crew, was drowned.

That large and cheerful extrovert, Ernest Shackleton, had not abandoned his intention to return when he was invalided from the Antarctic in 1903, but before he was able to do so he passed through a bewildering succession of occupations as part of his endeavour to raise his social status (not that he was ever much concerned with the social position of other people) and increase his wealth (though he was rather inclined, when he did make some money, to give it away). Having been refused a permanent commission in the Royal Navy, he became a journalist. 'I never met a more exhilarating man,' said his boss, 'a more genial, a better companion, a racier raconteur', but 'his knowledge of the technical side of bringing out a magazine was *nil*.' Within a few months, Shackleton heard that the position of secretary to the Scottish Royal Geographical Society was vacant. He applied and got the job. Within a year he had married his fiancée, gained an heir, and

Men hired to advertise a lecture by Shackleton on his Antarctic experiences, December 1909. The name of the contractor who presumably provided the strange clothes as well as the sandwich-board was, interestingly, Scott.

151

Members of Charcot's team preparing the ground for their house.

become Liberal-Unionist parliamentary candidate for Dundee. He was a popular canvasser but, as he remarked, 'I got all the applause, and the other fellows got all the votes.' A friend, William Beardmore, gave him a job in his large engineering works in Glasgow, and so impressed was he by Shackleton's enthusiasm and determination that Beardmore volunteered, early in 1907, to guarantee most of the cost of an Antarctic expedition.

Shackleton's first expedition was really a bit of a shambles, although the lack of institutional support (if not of funds) had some advantages as well as drawbacks. But the tremendous success of the expedition was mainly due to the character of the man known as 'the Boss'—Shackleton himself. Shackleton missed being first man at the South Pole by the skin of his teeth; moreover, in spite of the Boss's decidedly cursory interest in pure research, the scientific work of the expedition was considerable.

The year 1907 was taken up with hectic fundraising and organizing and the fact that the expedition sailed in August with nearly everything and everyone in place suggests that Shackleton's notorious disregard for detail could be overcome when necessary. Lack of cash had prevented his buying a splendid new 700-ton polar ship which he had inspected and coveted in Norway. But the *Nimrod*, a sealer one-third the size and a veteran of forty years in the Arctic,

was to prove a satisfactory compromise.

Shackleton's original plan was to establish his headquarters where the *Discovery* had wintered in McMurdo Sound, while the *Nimrod* would withdraw to New Zealand for the winter. Three exploring parties were to be sent out, one to the east, towards Scott's King Edward VII Land, one over the mountains to the west to locate the magnetic pole, and one, led by Shackleton himself, to the South Pole. In the spring of 1908, however, these plans had to be revised. Scott himself, writing from Gibraltar where he was in command of a warship, informed Shackleton that he was contemplating a second expedition to the Antarctic, and would therefore be grateful if Shackleton would establish his base elsewhere.

Relations might have become rather prickly, but the personalities of both Scott and Shackleton ensured that no unpleasant wrangling took place. Shackleton, quite correctly, gave way to Scott's prior claim, and switched his destination to the Bay of Whales at the eastern end of the Ross Ice Shelf. But when the *Nimrod* arrived at the Bay of Whales late in January 1908 the inlet where Borchgrevink had landed and the *Discovery* had anchored while Scott made his balloon ascent no longer existed. No alternative safe harbour could be found and after two days of dithering, the *Nimrod* being in immediate peril from the ice, Shackleton decided to make

for McMurdo Sound after all. He did so only after deep heart-searching: 'I never, never knew what it was to make such a decision as the one I was forced to make last night', he wrote to his wife. Scott was angry when he heard but did not make his feelings public; he might have been less charitable if Shackleton had actually reached the pole from Ross Island.

While Shackleton organized winter quarters, a party led by the Australian Professor Edgeworth David, who was not far off fifty, climbed to the lip of the crater of Mount Erebus, over 13,000 feet. They 'stood on the edge of a vast abyss, and at first could see neither to the bottom nor across it on account of the huge mass of steam filling the crater. . . . After a continuous loud hissing sound, lasting for some minutes, there would come from below a big dull boom, and immediately great globular masses of steam would rush upwards. . . . Meanwhile, the air around us was extremely redolent of sulphur.'

Owing to his late arrival, Shackleton had not been able to lay down depots for his assault on the pole during the autumn. Even before the sun reappeared, he sent out parties to move supplies to the south. Most of the transporting was done by man-hauled sledges but Shackleton did have one form of transport that had never been used before in the polar regions—a motor car. It proved useless in snow, but did good work in moving heavy loads across the sea ice to Hut

Point. Shackleton did not attempt to use it on the permanent ice shelf and altogether the car was more significant as a portent than as a practical means of transport: many people had doubted that an internal combustion engine would work at all in sub-zero temperatures.

Both in picking his personnel and selecting his equipment, Shackleton was in general less conservative than Scott, but in one important respect he rejected the advice of the Norwegian 'progressives' (Nansen, Amundsen) whom he consulted, and opted for traditional British methods. This was the vexed question of dogs. Although he did purchase a few dogs in New Zealand–descendants of Borchgrevink's animals–he decided against using them for long journeys, preferring to rely on man-hauling and on the Siberian ponies that he brought with him. Modern writers usually dismiss the use of ponies as a weird aberration. Certainly they have obvious disadvantages. They require a relatively large quantity of food which must be carried as, unlike dogs, ponies cannot be fed to each other. Also, they have fairly heavy bodies and small feet, and thus sink into snow. Events also proved that even Siberian ponies do not stand up well to the rigours of the Antarctic climate. Nevertheless, ponies were not the total failure that they are often assumed to have been; their performance for Shackleton did not convince Scott that they were useless. Although they were

disappointing, they did travel a considerable distance across the ice shelf with Shackleton and with Scott. They were also–for men–tastier than dogs.

Shackleton began his polar journey on 29 October 1908. He had only four ponies left after the winter and therefore decided to restrict the party to four men; himself, Frank Wild (a seaman on the *Discovery*), Lieutenant J. B. Adams of the Royal Navy and Dr Eric Marshall. They left Hut Point on 3 November and two days later they were confined to their tent by a blizzard. Shackleton had estimated that they would have to average nearly twenty miles a day to get back before their provisions ran out and before the *Nimrod* was compelled to leave without them. It was not a promising start. However, conditions soon improved and Shackleton was able to record with satisfaction that they were well ahead of the *Discovery* party on the corresponding date. On 26 November they passed Scott's 'farthest south' nearly five weeks earlier than he. Ahead, mountains loomed. Though they had never been seen before, they were not unexpected. From Scott's journey into the mountains of Victoria Land, it had seemed likely that the chain stretched around to the south of the Ross Sea, barring the way to the pole.

A way into the mountains had to be found. They marched on, chewing pieces of uncooked frozen horsemeat as they went. It did not quell the pangs of hunger that all were feeling.

On 3 December Shackleton found his route to the pole–Beardmore Glacier. They began to climb its icy, treacherous slope. In near white-out conditions it was perilous going, and four days later they suffered a disaster when the last surviving pony fell into a crevasse. Fortunately it had snapped its trace so that the man leading it, Wild, and the sledge it was hauling were saved. But it meant a further diminution of the food supply.

As the glacier steepened, their progress was reduced and they had to resort to relaying the two sledges, walking three miles for each one gained. Each man had stepped into a crevasse at least once, though without harm, by the time they finally sighted the central Antarctic plateau on 17 December. Near the top of the glacier they made their final depot and continued with one sledge only. On Christmas Day they were 250 miles from the pole and Shackleton was still hopeful. The worst problem was insufficient food. Then the weather began to deteriorate; one day in a blizzard they advanced only four miles. High altitude and food deficiency steadily sapped their strength. Shackleton had been banking on an easy crossing of the plateau to the pole, but by the New Year he was beginning to realize that they would not make it–or rather, that they would never get back if they did. On 6 January he decided that they must turn back next day, but a blizzard arose and turned the plateau into biting, swirling blankness. For two days they did not move from their tent.

On 9 January they dragged themselves out at 4 a.m. for one last march to the south. They reached a point 88°23′ South, less than a hundred miles from the pole, where they planted the British flag, took photographs, and began the long journey back. Shackleton had left his decision to return dangerously late, but his luck held good, and after some near-escapes two exhausted men staggered in to Hut Point, at the south end of Ross Island. It was 28 February, and a note at Hut Point said that the *Nimrod* would remain only until 26 February. Fortunately, the *Nimrod* appeared next morning. Typically, Shackleton himself accompanied the party to bring in Adams and Marshall, who had been left in their tent a day's journey away when Marshall became too ill to travel farther.

Of all the advances towards the South Pole, from Cook's 71° South to Amundsen's 90°, Shackleton advanced the greatest distance beyond the previous record. During his absence, Edgeworth Davis had led another party, including his fellow Australian Douglas Mawson, to the south magnetic pole, travelling over 1,200 miles in the course of their successful journey. Valuable scientific work had been done, especially by the geologists, who included Raymond Priestley. Their work was to be continued by members of Scott's expedition. Shackleton concluded his account: '. . . the world was well pleased with our work, and it seemed as though nothing but happiness could ever enter life again'. He had every reason to feel satisfied.

The North Pole

If ever a man deserved to succeed in a self-appointed task, that man was Robert Edwin Peary. His attainment of the North Pole is the classic story of Arctic exploration; classic in the Greek sense too, for Peary's career, like Scott's had many of the ingredients of heroic drama.

'Bert' Peary was a Mama's boy. His father died when he was a baby and his mother at the age of thirty entered upon a career of devoted Victorian widowhood. Her every thought and feeling was centred on her only child: she was a loving but over-possessive mother who, when Peary won a scholarship to Bowdoin College, insisted on moving to Brunswick, Maine, so that she could be with him although it was not much more than twenty miles from their home in Portland.

Not surprisingly, Peary had been a difficult child, given to destructive jokes like tripping up his grandfather to see the old man tumble, and the difficulties created by his mother's protectiveness were increased by a lisp which he eventually overcame with the same grim determination that kept him striding across the ice after losing all his toes. He was a self-possessed, solitary youth, with a passion for natural history and considerable expertise in taxidermy. At college he blossomed somewhat, partly through the encouragement of his teacher in engineering and partly through his courtship of a girl whom he later jilted.

Given his background, it is not perhaps surprising that Peary became a tough guy. He was strongly built, with powerful chest and shoulders, and always kept himself fit; his concern with 'manliness' would today seem not far short of obsessive. Photographs show him confronting the camera with steely gaze, eyes slightly narrowed, jaw out-thrust; his weight rests on one leg, the other being set slightly forward at an angle, and although the stance may have been comfortable for a man with no toes, it is a pose familiar in Roman statues and portraits of Victorian generals. The image, however, was not phoney: Peary was as tough as he looked.

After a short spell with the United States Coast and Geodetic Survey Peary joined the navy as a civil engineer. He was to remain in the

Robert Edwin Peary (1856–1920), a man of powerful will and remarkable single-mindedness who when he at last achieved his lifelong goal may have felt, like Disraeli on becoming prime minister, that success had come too late.

navy until his retirement with the rank of Rear-Admiral but from the beginning he and the naval establishment were at odds: regular officers looked down on engineers, and unlike the majority of British explorers, Peary received reluctant, if any, assistance from the navy. Sometimes Peary's difficulties were of his own making; frank, not to say blunt, in his opinions, he had an unhappy facility for raising other people's hackles. He was also intensely ambitious, and hated to acknowledge any man as his superior. Some were impressed by his determination, others were put off by what they regarded as his cold selfishness and insensitivity.

In 1885 Peary spent three months in Nicaragua surveying the route for a proposed canal through the Central American isthmus (eventually built, of course, in Panama). Though the climate was highly unlike the Arctic, this was good training for an explorer. Peary was in charge of the field work, and had to force a way through swamps and jungles that few men had ever entered: he was constantly in water up to his knees or his waist or even his neck, cutting, lifting, pulling, pushing, swimming. His exploratory surveys cut several miles off the intended route and, according to Peary's latest biographer, J. E. Weems, would have saved the United States government $17,000,000 if the canal had actually been built.

In the following year, Peary took a six-month leave of absence and with $500 borrowed from his mother, took himself off to Greenland. At a settlement north of Disco he met a young Dane who volunteered to join him on a trip into the interior. They advanced across the ice-cap for about 100 miles, climbing to a height over 7,000 feet and narrowly avoiding an early death in a crevasse. No one had advanced so far across the interior before, and Peary's brief expedition caused a mild flutter.

This preliminary sortie was not the result of sudden inspiration, though it may have appeared so to all but Peary's closest friends. His interest in the Arctic dated from his schooldays, and a memorandum written by Peary to himself in 1885 on the subject of Arctic exploration shows that he had read widely and thought deeply about it. In fact, before he had seen even a small iceberg, Peary had formulated the ideas that were to lead him to the North Pole and had recognized with remarkable accuracy the inherent shortcomings of Arctic exploration as conducted, for instance, by the British. 'The new plan of a small party depending largely on native assistance . . . will put us far ahead in the race', he observed.

It is interesting to note that Peary speaks of 'the race'. His intention always was to be the first man at the pole, an achievement that would bring glory upon the United States and himself. Though a first-rate engineer and a keen naturalist, Peary was not much interested in scientific research. The North Pole was his objective, and anything less than that was of minor importance. At the same time it would be wrong to suppose that Peary had cold-bloodedly surveyed the alternative paths available to fame and fortune and settled on the route to the pole as the shortest. The Arctic attracted him, just as it had attracted another American of a solitary disposition – Charles Francis Hall. Peary became famous long before he finally reached the pole and as rich as he was ever likely – or wished – to be, but by that time it was the journey alone that mattered; resolutions to retire were regularly made at the end of each expedition and, after the novelties of civilization had again become customary, as regularly broken.

After a reluctantly embarked-on but highly successful marriage, and seven more months of invaluable experience in the Nicaraguan swamps, Peary began what is rather misleadingly called his first Greenland expedition in 1891. Since his previous visit the ice-cap had been

crossed by Fridtjof Nansen, to Peary's considerable annoyance. His plan was to explore Greenland 'from the *inside*', rather than round the difficult coast. 'It is like exploring an atoll around the margin of the placid central lagoon, instead of along the outer shore, through reefs and breakers.' He also hoped to prove that Greenland was an island. With difficulty he raised $10,000 from private sources and secured leave of absence from the navy.

He took six people with him. They included an amiable doctor, Frederick Cook, a Norwegian, Eivind Astrup, an ornithologist, Langdon Gibson, and a young adventurer named John Verhoeff who proved troublesome, disappeared while on a mineral-hunting trip, and was never seen again. Peary was also to quarrel later with Astrup, mildly, and with Cook, bitterly. The other two in the main party were Matthew Henson, Peary's black manservant, and Josephine, Peary's wife.

Peary had met Henson serving in a shop in Washington, hired him, and took him on his second survey in Nicaragua. Henson was to accompany him on all his future expeditions and to prove a man of courage and physical resource matching Peary, his senior by seven years; the Eskimos considered him their equal as hunter and dog-driver. The relationship between Peary and Henson seems, today, a particularly interesting one. Obviously they were close comrades, entirely dependent on each other in numerous situations of extreme danger. Henson was, however, sometimes the cause of minor dissension in larger parties, probably because other white members of Peary's expeditions resented Henson's status. Peary always insisted on subservience, and it seems strange that even after a

The dog teams set out, a photograph taken at the beginning of Peary's successful advance on the pole, an assault carried out with military precision.

quarter of a century of co-operative endeavour, Henson's letters to Peary still began, 'Dear Sir'.

Henson was the first man of African descent to winter in the far north; Josephine Peary was the first white woman. Peary's decision to take her with him was widely criticized, but she was eager to go and Peary was eager to have her. His view was that travel in the Arctic was hard enough anyway, and anything that made it more comfortable was highly desirable. Characteristically, Peary was more frank about the problem of sex than his predecessors. Its absence was a serious deprivation, and Peary did not make much effort to conceal the facts of his relationships with Eskimo women, something that most Arctic explorers, including some that came after Peary, tended to pass over in silence.

It has often been said that Peary was dogged by bad luck which he overcame by his unswerving determination. It is arguable that Peary could not have survived eight Antarctic journeys and reached the North Pole without considerable *good* luck; but it is true that he suffered many mishaps of an arbitrary kind which no one could have allowed for. Thus, on the voyage north in 1891, Peary walked to the stern of the ship at precisely the moment when a large piece of ice struck the rudder, spun the wheel out of the steersman's hands, swinging the tiller rapidly around – and breaking Peary's right leg. Among the objects unloaded at Whale Sound a few days later was a large board, to which the commander of the expedition was tightly strapped. He spent the next six weeks mainly on his back.

During the winter, Peary attracted Eskimos to his camp, and learned from them how to drive a dog team and how to make loose-fitting fur clothes. His journey across the ice-cap in the

following spring established the basic methods he was to use to reach the pole. He travelled on skis with Eskimo dogs drawing light sledges and gradually cut down the size of his party as he advanced. By the end of May he and Astrup were alone. At the beginning of July they reached what Peary called Independence Bay. He believed that it marked the north-eastern extremity of Greenland, a mistake that his numerous and inveterate opponents were to seize upon with delight. After feasting on the raw flesh of musk oxen, Peary and Astrup began the long and wearying journey back to base, which they reached early in August. By the end of the month the expedition was on its way home, to receive a warm welcome and many congratulations including a generous letter from Nansen that possibly, though it is not very likely, induced self-reproach in the man who had privately written scornfully of his Norwegian rival.

Although Peary aroused much resentment among many people during his lifetime, he always had a few highly influential supporters, notably Theodore Roosevelt. One of these was able to persuade the increasingly reluctant navy to give him three years' leave of absence to continue his work in Greenland. Peary threw himself unsparingly into the task of raising money: in a period of 103 days he gave 105 lectures (enhanced by a fur-clad Henson with Arctic equipment and six huskies) and earned $20,000.

Apart from Astrup and Henson the personnel were new (Dr Cook had been invited but declined). Josephine Peary also sailed, this time accompanied by a nurse as she was pregnant – evoking more howls of protest from those who believed that the Arctic was no place for a white woman.

Peary's famous photograph of his Eskimo companions cheering their achievement of the North Pole. The controversy that later broke out over who had reached the pole first resulted in Peary's account being doubted as well as Cook's, and the authenticity of this photograph was questioned by Peary's critics.

On his 1893–95 expedition Peary planned to repeat and extend his exploration of 1892, with a larger party. But for once Peary, perhaps misled by the comparative smoothness of his 1892 journey, had over-extended himself. The expedition was dogged by bad luck and failed to accomplish its chief objectives. An iceberg calving into Whale Sound caused a wave that swamped the fuel supplies, the occasion for Peary's remark, living up to his tragic-hero image, that 'the fates and all hell are against me, but I'll conquer yet'; the dogs sickened, the mules and homing pigeons (experiments that Peary did not repeat) proved useless; the journey to Independence Bay (Fjord) had to be abandoned after a series of icy blizzards. When the ship returned in August only one man, Hugh Lee, agreed to stay on for another year with Peary and Henson. Josephine Peary and her baby daughter also left with the ship, and Peary spent a gloomy winter.

The following season was little better. Unexpectedly severe blizzards had covered the depots laid down in the previous summer, and Peary took a severe risk in persevering with the 500-mile journey to Independence Fjord. The three men arrived with their food virtually exhausted, and if they had not soon found a herd of musk oxen would have starved. As it was the return journey was one long gamble with death. At one point, Lee begged the other two to go on and leave him in the snow. It seemed better to die than to struggle farther. Only one of the dogs made it back.

Though Peary felt he had failed again, the expedition had established valuable facts, and had raised doubts about the suitability of Greenland as a starting point for a North Pole expedition. It had made one interesting discovery, which was later to involve Peary's reputation in another controversy. Guided, it would seem reluctantly, by local Eskimos, Peary had found three meteorites, the largest weighing over 1,000 lb. from which the Eskimos had made iron tools. All three were removed by Peary (the largest, after considerable trouble, two years later) and were eventually sold by his widow to the American Museum of Natural History. It was perhaps presumptuous of Peary to deprive the Eskimos of these remarkable and valuable objects, although the argument that he was taking away their only supply of metal hardly stands up; after Peary the Eskimos were no longer cut off from manufactured tools.

For Peary, failure was a spur to further endeavours; but now he changed his strategy. He decided that the dash to the pole would have to begin from the northern tip of either Greenland or Ellesmere Island, though this meant that in addition to the usual difficulties to be overcome before an Arctic expedition could be mounted, he would need a ship powerful enough to break through to the Lincoln Sea. The attitude of the navy was increasingly hostile but fortunately Peary was again able to pull the right string at

the right time and was granted a five-year leave of absence. Financial support was also forthcoming, from a group of geographically minded businessmen who formed what became known as the Peary Arctic Club. The British Press baron, Lord Northcliffe, provided a steam yacht, the *Windward*, which however was underpowered for Peary's purpose. She advanced no farther than Kane Basin before the ice gripped and held her.

Peary's 1898–1902 expedition displayed his ambition more grimly determined than ever. As the ship could take him no farther than Kane Basin, he resolved to establish a forward base at Fort Conger, nearly 250 miles north along the perilous ice foot of Ellesmere Island, in the darkness of winter. Together with Matt Henson, Dr Dedrick and a party of Eskimos, he found his way to the hut that had not been visited since Greely evacuated it, arriving at midnight in pitch blackness. It was a good illustration of his finely developed navigational sense.

But Peary himself paid dearly for this effort. At Fort Conger, he found that the toes on both feet were badly frozen. Dr Dedrick performed a primitive operation, amputating parts of seven toes, but it was clear that another operation would be necessary. Eventually Peary was to lose all his toes. But would he be able to walk without them? Dr Dedrick said no. Needless to say, Peary thought differently.

After six weeks of idleness and agony Peary decided to return to the ship, although it meant that he had to be dragged along strapped to a sledge. It was a nightmare journey (although Peary insists it was comparatively easy for him) but it was completed in the rapid time of ten days in a temperature that frequently dropped below −60 °F. On the ship another operation was carried out and all but two of Peary's toes removed. Later, a surgeon in Philadelphia was to amputate these last survivors and, by drawing forward the tendons on the bottom of the feet, give some protection to the toeless stumps. But Peary was to make two of the toughest Arctic treks yet on his wounded feet.

In August 1899 the *Windward* finally escaped from the ice and retired to Etah, where a relief ship dispatched by the Peary Arctic Club brought letters from Josephine Peary relating the death of their second daughter and sadly remarking that while Peary was hidden away in the Arctic, life was slipping past. It was a frequent refrain, especially poignant in view of Peary's later absences and comparatively early death.

No major journeys were undertaken that summer, and Peary busied himself arranging for the conveyance of more supplies to Fort Conger. The Eskimo hunters there had shot many musk oxen, causing Peary to make some characteristically tactless remarks about Greely's rapid abandonment of the fort. Peary himself was in Fort Conger in March 1900 and the following month began a remarkable journey along the coast of northern Greenland to the cape named after the president of the Peary Arctic Club, Cape Morris Jessup, and beyond, to the northernmost point of Greenland which, to Peary's joy, had not been seen by Lockwood on his 'farthest north' trip from Fort Conger. The prospects for an assault on the pole, however, were far from good. He made three northward marches, suffering agony as his feet bumped the rough ice, before deciding to leave his major effort until the following year. In June he was back in Fort Conger, having established beyond reasonable doubt that Greenland was an island.

Peary wintered at Fort Conger in conditions of some comfort: 'I have no interruptions, have my place entirely to myself, and can work as I please'—for Peary, bliss. At the same time the *Windward*, with Josephine Peary and their first child, the 'snow baby', on board, was frozen in at Etah, unable to communicate with him. Contact was not established until the following May, when Peary had returned from an abortive trip to the Lincoln Sea. Peary thus spent most of the summer with his neglected family at Etah, postponing his last attack on the pole for another year. In August a relief ship arrived bringing news of the death of Peary's mother. He took it hard; he had been intensely devoted to that sometimes exasperating woman. Like many dedicated Arctic men, Peary was not without a streak of mysticism in his make-up, and he believed that on several occasions when he had narrowly escaped death it was because his mother was watching over him. Or so he wrote to her.

Conditions north of Greenland had convinced Peary that Ellesmere Island would be a better starting point, and thus in April 1902, accompanied by Henson and four Eskimos, he struck north from Cape Hecla. The going was very rough, with tumbled ice ridges and deep snow through which the dogs could hardly stumble. After three exhausting weeks, a storm arose, whipping the snow across the ice and opening great rifts ahead. Peary knew his goal was unreachable. He turned back at 84°16', well south of Nansen's record. 'My dream of sixteen years is ended. I close the book and turn to others less interesting, but better suited for my years.' Peary was now forty-six years old. He retired, as he thought for the last time, to his camp at Cape Sabine where, in August, the *Windward* came to take him home.

Peary photographed on board ship, with the Eskimo dogs and clothes he sensibly employed, after his journey to the pole. The mask of impervious confidence so evident in most pictures of Peary seems to have momentarily slipped.

But after a few months at home, Peary was talking of going north again. The encouragement of the Peary Arctic Club and the presence of a fellow he-man in the White House, together with Peary's now well-established reputation, made organization easier. His experiences in 1900 and 1902 had convinced Peary of the need for a more powerful ship which would push through to the Arctic Ocean, so that the men and dogs could start across the ice while fresh, and not half-exhausted from the preliminary journey to their jump-off point. The *Roosevelt*, named after the President, fitted the bill. She was designed chiefly by Peary himself, a tough, stubby, wooden-hulled steamer with auxiliary sails, retractable rudder and screw, and a steam-driven capstan for warping her through the ice. Her captain was a British Canadian, Bob Bartlett, who was to establish a reputation in the next ten years as the best Arctic skipper since Sverdrup.

In August 1905 the *Roosevelt* thrust her way through Smith Sound. By early September she was at Cape Sheridan on the north-east coast of Ellesmere Island, moored at an inlet in the coastal ice. She had achieved the highest altitude ever accomplished by a ship under way; the *Fram* of course had gone farther north but by drifting with the ice. Apart from an unfortunate outbreak of food-poisoning that killed eighty of Peary's irreplaceable dogs, everything was going well as the winter cast its darkness over the scene and Peary planned his spring journey.

Peary planned all his journeys with military precision. He had by this time arrived at the system of dividing his party into groups proceeding at intervals. As the expedition advanced,

the support parties would turn back one by one until a single group remained for the final stage. Each group was commanded by a member of Peary's company, and consisted of two or three sledges with Eskimo drivers. But for all his experience, there was one Arctic problem that Peary had not so far solved – had, in fact, seriously underrated. Peary's early journeys had been overland. He had not seen enough of the Arctic Ocean to appreciate the significance of currents, nor to realize the frequency of leads. His careful plans of 1906 were ruined by these factors. He was unable to lay out the trail of depots he had banked on because they did not remain sufficiently stationary, and the different groups, leaving at intervals, all ended up within a few days parked on the edge of an open lead, waiting for it to close.

Peary decided to make a final dash for the pole with Henson. They established a new 'farthest north' of 87°6′ before he made the painful decision to give up. The return journey was perilous; Peary, by his own account, was for the first time worried that he would never make it while gingerly crossing the thin ice over a lead. He was also concerned that the drift eastwards might carry them right past Greenland so that they would find themselves walking into the Greenland Sea. However, the coast at last appeared, and shortly after some musk oxen, several of which were shot. The flesh was gobbled warm and raw by the near-starving men.

Having regained the *Roosevelt* at last, the perils of the expedition were not over. The ship had broken free from her winter harbour only to be caught again and with a seriously damaged rudder, she drifted stern-first with the ice. It was late in August before Bob Bartlett could work her free, and she had a very tricky passage south towards Baffin Bay before her escape was assured.

Peary had hoped to return to the Arctic the following year, but repairs to the *Roosevelt* forced him to postpone until 1908 what would surely be his last journey. He was now fifty-two years old, an extraordinarily advanced age for Arctic exploration. There were other reasons for haste. In 1907 Dr Frederick A. Cook had disappeared northward on what Peary described as 'a yachting cruise', but what some of Peary's friends suspected might be an attempt to pre-empt Peary's conquest of the pole.

Dr Cook had added to his reputation as an adventurer since serving on Peary's first Greenland expedition. He had taken part in the first wintering in Antarctica in 1898, and in 1906 he had claimed to have reached the summit of Mount McKinley, the highest mountain in North America and then a virgin peak. Some people, however, doubted that Dr Cook had really reached the top.

The 1909 assault on the North Pole was organized in what had by now become Peary's customary manner, with certain changes resulting

DR. COOK AT THE NORTH POLE.

REMARKABLE ACCOUNT BY THE EXPLORER.

WONDERFUL EXPLOITS.

30,000 SQUARE MILES OF NEW LAND DISCOVERED.

THREE DAYS AT POLE.

UNIQUE JOURNEYS IN RECORD TEMPERATURE.

HERDS OF GAME.

The news that Dr. Frederick Albert Cook, the American explorer, had succeeded in reaching the North Pole is now supplemented by a remarkable narrative of the journey, telegraphed by the explorer himself from Lerwick, Shetland, to the "New York Herald" (Paris edition), and published yesterday.

The explorer tells how he raised the Stars and Stripes "to the breezes of the North Pole" on April 21st, 1908, and exclaims: "What a cheerless spot to have aroused the ambition of man for so many ages!"

Apart from the discovery of the Pole, he says the results of his journey are as follows:—

30,000 square miles of new land discovered.

New highway explored.

Big game haunts located which "extend the Eskimo horizon."

The earth's northernmost land discovered.

His narrative (which we publish through the courtesy of the "New York Herald") is as follows:—

PART I.—THE START.

Propitious circumstances for the venture 700 miles from the Pole.—Plans for a new route.—The start at sunrise, February 19, 1908.—Game trails.—Oxen, bears and hares shot.—Into the Polar Sea, and across the circumpolar ice.—Long marches in cold and wind.

ON BOARD THE STEAMER HANS EGEDE,
LERWICK (Shetland),
Viâ LONDON, Wednesday.

After a prolonged fight against famine and frost we have at last succeeded in reaching the North Pole.

A new highway with an interesting strip of animated nature has been explored, big game haunts were located which will delight the sportsman and extend the Eskimo horizon.

Land has been discovered upon which rest the earth's northernmost rocks.

A triangle of 30,000 square miles has been cut out of the terrestrial unknown.

The expedition was the outcome of a summer cruise in Arctic seas. The yacht Bradley arrived at the limits of navigation in Smith's Sound late in August, 1907. Here conditions were found favourable to launch a venture for the Pole. Mr. John R. Bradley liberally supplied from the yacht suitable provisions for local use. My own equipment for emergencies served well for every purpose of Arctic travel.

Many Eskimos had gathered on the Greenland shores at Annootok for the winter bear hunt. Immense catches of meat had been gathered, and about the camp were plenty of strong dogs. The combination was lucky, for there was good material for an equipment, expert help, an efficient motor force, and all that was required, conveniently arranged at a point only 700 miles from the boreal centre.

A house and workshop was built of packing boxes, and the willing hands of this northernmost tribe of 250 people were set to the problem of devising a suitable outfit.

Before the end of the long winter night we were ready for the enterprise. Plans were matured to force a new route over Grinnell Land and northward along its west coast out on to the Polar Sea.

Soon after the Polar midnight the campaign opened. A few scouting parties were sent over to the American shores to explore a way and to seek game haunts. Their mission was only partly successful, because storms darkened the January noon.

Sunrise Start for the Pole.

At sunrise of 1908 (February 19th) the main expedition embarked for the Pole. Eleven men and 103 dogs, drawing eleven heavily-loaded sledges, left the Greenland shore and pushed westward over the troubled ice of Smith Sound.

The gloom of the long night was relieved by only a few hours of daylight. The chill of winter was felt at its worst as we crossed the heights of Ellesmere Sound to the Pacific slope. The temperature sank to −83deg. Cent. Several dogs were frozen, and the men suffered severely, but we soon found game trails, along which an easy way was forced through Mansen Sound to the Land's End.

In this march we secured 101 musk oxen, 7 bears, and 335 hares. We pushed out into the Polar Sea from the southern point of Heiberg Island on March 18th. Six Eskimos returned from here with four men and forty-six dogs, moving supplies for eighty days.

"Life a Torture."

The crossing of the circumpolar pack was begun three days later. Two other Eskimos, forming the last supporting party, returned, and the trials had now been reduced by the survival of the fittest. The and Ahwelsh, the two best men, and twenty-six dogs were picked for the final. There was before us an unknown line of 460 miles to our goal.

The first days provided long marches and encouraging progress. The big lead which separated the land ice from the central pack was crossed with little delay. The low temperature and persistent winds made life a torture, but couped in snow-houses, eating dried beef and tallow and drinking hot tea some animal comforts were occasionally to be gained.

PART II.—NEW LAND.

Into the unknown.—New land discovered.—Coast explored.—Last signs of solid earth.—Steady advance.—Beyond the life-range.—Camp in lat. 86 deg.—100 miles in nine days.—100 miles from the Pole.

For several days after sight of known land was lost the overcast sky prevented an accurate determination of positions.

On March 30th the horizon was partly cleared of its smoky agitation, and over the western mist was discovered a new land.

The observations gave our position latitude 84deg. 47min., longitude 86deg. 36min. The urgent need of rapid advance on our main mission did not permit a detour to explore the coast.

Here were seen the last signs of solid earth. Beyond nothing stable, and even on sealing nothing was noted to mark terrestrial Polar solidity. We

Dr. F. A. Cook. (Reproduced from "Northward over the Great Ice." By Robert E. Peary.)

advanced steadily over the monotony of a moving sea of ice. We now found ourselves beyond the range of all life—neither footprints of bears nor the blow-holes of seals were detected. Even the microscopic creatures of the deep were no longer under us.

A Maddening Desert of Frost.

The maddening influence of the shifting desert of frost became almost unendurable in the daily routine. The surface of the pack offered less and less trouble. The weather improved, but there still remained a light life-sapping wind which drove despair to its lowest recess. Under the lash of duty, however, interest was forced, while the merciless drive of extreme cold enforced physical action. Thus day after day the weary legs were spread over big distances.

The incidents and the positions were recorded, but the adventure was promptly forgotten in the mental bleach of the next day's effort.

The night of April 7th was made notable by the swing of the sun at midnight over the northern ice.

Sunburns and Frost Bites.

Sunburns and frostbites were now recorded on the same day, but the double days of glitter infused quite an incentive into one's life of shivers.

Observations on April 8th placed the camp at latitude 86deg. 36sec., longitude 94deg. 2sec. In spite of what seemed like long marches, we had advanced but little over 100 miles in nine days' march.

Much of our hard work was lost in circuitous twists around troublesome pressure lines and high irregular fields of very old ice. The drift, too, was driving eastward with sufficient force to give some anxiety.

Though still equal to about fifteen miles daily, the extended marches and the long hours of travelling with which fortune had favoured us earlier were no longer possible.

In the Heart of the Mystery.

We were now about 200 miles from the Pole. The sledgeloads were reduced. One dog after another had got into the stomach of his hungry survivors, until the teams were considerably reduced, but there seemed to remain a sufficient balance of man and brute to push along into the heart of the mystery to which we had set ourselves.

Beyond the 86th parallel the icefields became more extensive and heavier, the crevasses fewer and less troublesome, with little or no crushed ice thrown up as barriers. From the 87th to the 88th parallel much of the surprise was an indication of land ice.

For two days we travelled over ice which resembled a glacial surface. The usual sea ice lines of demarkation were absent, and there were no hummocked or deep cervasses. There was, however, no perceptible elevation and no positive sign of land or sea. Observations on the 14th gave latitude 88.21 longitude 95.52.

100 Miles from the Pole.

We were now less than one hundred miles from the Pole. The pack was here more active, but the temperature remained below 40deg., cementing together quickly the new crevasses. Young ice spread the narrow spaces of open water so rapidly that little delay was caused in crossing from one field to another.

PART III.—THE POLE!

Last efforts to reach Pole.—Land or Mirage?—Chronic fatigue.—Pole in sight.—Flag raised at Pole, April 21, 1908 (2 months 2 days after start).—Temperature 38 degrees.—Endless fields of purple snows.—No life, no land.—Left Pole, April 23.

The time had now arrived to muster energy for the last series of efforts. In the enforced effort every human strand was strained, and at camping time there was no longer sufficient energy to erect a snow shelter.

Though the temperature was still very low, the silk tent was pressed into service. The change proved agreeable. It encouraged a more careful scrutiny of the strange world into which fate had pressed us.

Magic of the Midnight Sun.

Signs of land were still seen every day, but they were deceptive illusions, or a mere verdict of fancy. It seemed that something must cross the horizon to mark the important [illegible] into which we were pushing.

When the sun was low the eye ran over the moving plains of colour to dancing horizons. The mirages turned things topsy-turvy, inverted mountains, and queer objects even rose and fell in shrouds of mystery. But all of this was due to the atmospheric magic of the midnight sun.

Slowly but surely we neared the turning point. Good astronomical observations were daily secured to fix advancing stages. They steadily improved, but still there was a depressing monotony of scene and life: no pleasures, no spiritual recreation, nothing to relieve the steady physical drag of chronic fatigue.

The Flag Raised at the Pole.

But there came an end to this as to all things. On April 21st the first corrected altitude of the sun gave 89deg. 59min. 46sec. The Pole, therefore, was in sight.

We advanced the 14sec., made supplementary observations and prepared to stop long enough to permit a double round of observations.

Etukishook and Ahwelsh were told that we had reached the big nail, and they sought to celebrate it by an advance of savagery.

At last we had pierced the boreal datir, and the flag had been raised to the coveted breezes of the North Pole. The day was April 21st, 1908. The sun indicated local noon, but time was a negative problem, for here all meridians meet. With a step it was possible to go from one part of the globe to the opposite side—from the hour of midnight to that of midday.

The latitude was 90deg., the temperature—38deg., the barometer 29.83 North, east and west had vanished. It was south in every direction.

A Dead World of Ice.

But the compass pointing to the Magnetic Pole was as useful as ever. Though overjoyed with the success of the conquest, our spirits began to descend. On the following day, after all the observations had been taken, with a careful study of the local conditions, a sense of intense loneliness came with the further scrutiny of the horizon.

What a cheerless spot to have aroused the ambition of man for so many ages! Endless fields of purple snows, no life, no land, no spot to relieve the monotony of frost. We were the only pulsating creatures in a dead world of ice.

PART IV.—THE RETURN.

The return march.—Fair weather, good ice.—Food giving out.—Battle for life with famine and frost.—Violent gales.—Desperate efforts.—Twenty days struggle through fog.—Food and ammunition exhausted.—Musk oxen and bears killed with bows and arrows at Cape Sparbo.—Greenland shores reached April 15, 1909, Upernivik May 21.

We turned our backs to the Pole on April 23rd, and began the long return march, counting on a continued easterly drift. The course was forced further west. With fair weather, good ice, and the inspiration of the home run, long distances were at first quickly covered.

Below the 87th parallel the character of the ice changed very much, and it became evident that the season was advancing rapidly. With a good deal of anxiety we watched the daily reduction of the food supply. It now became evident that the crucial stage of the campaign was to be transferred from the taking of the Pole to a final battle for life against famine and frost. The clear blue of the skies changed to a steady dismal grey, and several days of icy despair followed each other in rapid succession. There were some violent gales, but usually the wind did not rise to the full force of a storm.

Alternative to Starvation.

With starvation as the only alternative we could not wait for better weather. Some advance was made nearly every day, but the cost of the desperate effort pressed life to the verge of extinction. On May 24th the sky cleared long enough to give us a set of observations. We had reached the 84th parallel, near the 97th meridian. The ice was much broken and we drifted eastward, leaving many open spaces of water. There remained on our sleds scarcely enough food to reach our caches on Nansen Sound unless we averaged fifteen miles daily. With our reduced strength we were hardly equal to ten miles daily.

Trying to make the best of our hard lot a straight course was set for the musk-ox lands. Crossing the 83rd parallel we found ourselves to the west of a large tract extending southwards. The ice changed to small fields, the temperature rose to zero and a persistent mist obscured the heavens.

Days of Desperate Action.

The events of the following days were pressed into desperate action, with few lines on paper to register the life of suffering. The food for man and dog was reduced to a three-quarter ration, while the difficulties of ice travel rose to disheartening heights. At the end of a struggle of twenty days through a thick fog the sky cleared, and we found ourselves far down in Crown Prince Gustav sea, with open water and impossible small ice as a barrier between us and Heiberg Island.

In the next few days bears came along as life-savers. The empty stomachs were spread and the horizon for a time was cleared of trouble with the return to Annootok, rendered difficult by the unfortunate westerly drift.

We now sought to follow the ice movement south to Lancaster Sound, where we hoped to reach a Scottish whaler early in July. Further southward progress became impossible, and in quest of food we crossed Firth Devon into Jones Sound. The dogs were here given the freedom of their wolf propensities.

Underground Life—and Sunrise, 1909.

By folding boat and sledge we tried to reach Baffin's Bay. With but an occasional bird to eat and a long line of misfortune, we pushed eastward until the frost of early September stopped progress.

With neither food, fuel nor ammunition, we were forced to wrestle winter supplies from what seemed at first like a lifeless desert. Pressed by hunger, new implements were shaped. Cape Sparbo was picked up as a likely place to find life, and game was located.

With the bow and arrow, the line, the lance and the knife, the musk ox, bear and wolves yielded meat, skins and fat.

An underground den was prepared, and in it we remained until sunrise of 1909.

On February 18th the start was made for Annootok with a newly-prepared equipment. The Greenland shores were reached on April 15th. Here we were greeted by Mr. Harry Whitney, and an anxious group of Eskimo friends.

To facilitate an early return I moved southward to the Danish settlement, and reached Upernivik on May 21st, 1909.

RECEPTION OF THE NEWS.

SCIENTISTS' SCEPTICISM IN AMERICA AND FRANCE.

BARRIERS TO BELIEF.

"No one has any right to be sceptical," observes the man who has a greater right than most people to express an opinion on the claim that Dr. F. A. Cook reached the Pole on April 20th, 1908. The world is divided into two camps, one of which asks how it is possible that Dr. Cook should have done what many other better-equipped expeditions have failed to do; and the other of which asks why shouldn't he?

The principal barrier against belief is that, according to the published details of his own account, so far as it is possible to understand it, he accomplished the journey over the Polar ice at a rate of about twelve miles a day. That is a rate far beyond the speed which any previous Arctic explorer has compassed. On the other hand, again to quote a rather mysterious passage, he found land north of the part from which he started. If he found land then, as Lieutenant Shackleton observes, part of the mystery vanishes. A path might lie over land.

The difficulty of approach to the Pole has hitherto been that explorers have believed the path to lie over the terribly rough and broken surface of the frozen Polar ocean.

The "New York Herald," in publishing Dr. Cook's account, admits the credibility of the story in the absence of other civilised witnesses than Dr. Cook himself. The true Pole has undoubtedly been found, it says. The position of the sun in April, 1908, makes it possible to confirm Dr. Cook's story if his observations taken in the last dash correspond. Dr. Cook's reputation as an explorer stands very high in America, and the general opinion appears to be that he has succeeded in reaching the North Pole.

U.S. ADMIRAL SAYS REPORT IS A "FAKE."

With the publication of Dr. Cook's narrative, says Reuter's New York correspondent, a tendency is observable on the part of newspapers and individuals to accept the assertion, at least tentatively, and to congratulate the country that it was the Stars and Stripes flag which was first planted at the Pole.

Mr. Bradley, Dr. Cook's backer, in an interview, indicates that the amount expended in equipping the expedition was within £1,800.

"It is an event," says the Evening Post, "of which every American will be proud—this apparent victory over a hitherto, mysterious, unconquerable nature."

(Continued on page 10.)

THE NEW YORK HERALD.

NEW YORK, TUESDAY, SEPTEMBER 7, 1909.—TWENTY-FOUR PAGES.—

ROBERT E. PEARY, AFTER 23 YEARS SIEGE, REACHES NORTH POLE; ADDS "THE BIG NAIL" TO NEW YORK YACHT CLUB'S TROPHIES; DR. COOK TO SUBMIT RECORDS TO UNIVERSITY OF DENMARK

ROBERT E. PEARY AND MRS PEARY ON BOARD THE HERALD DESPATCH BOAT OWLET JUST BEFORE HIS DEPARTURE FOR THE NORTH.

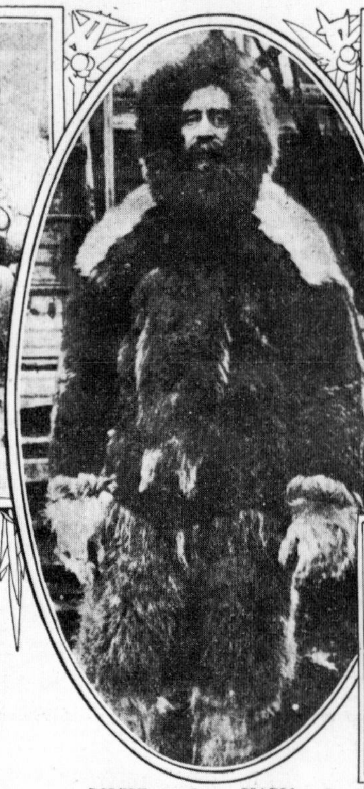

ROBERT E. PEARY FROM "NEAREST THE POLE" COPYRIGHT 1907 DOUBLEDAY PAGE & CO.

THE ROOSEVELT LEAVING NEW YORK HARBOR.

MISS MARIE A. PEARY, DAUGHTER OF ROBERT E. PEARY

ROBERT E. PEARY, JR. WITH THE ROOSEVELT'S MASCOT

CAPTAIN "BOB" BARTLETT OF THE ROOSEVELT

Discoverer of the Pole Joins in Cheering When Told Mr. Peary's Success

"If He Has Announced He Has Reached the Farthest North, He Has," Is the Physician's First Comment.

"THERE IS HONOR ENOUGH ON IT FOR BOTH OF US," HE ASSERTS TO ADMIRERS

Denmark's Foremost Scientists Thoroughly Familiar with Arctic Research Will Fully Investigate All the Facts and Instruments Brought Back by Dr. Cook.

EXPLORER CONFIDENT OF THE VERDICT

Declares He Knows He Is Right, but, While Retaining Highest Respect for Rivals in Polar Fields, He Will Not Engage in Any Controversy.

DR. COOK CONGRATULATES MR. PEARY

Copyright, 1909, by the New York Herald Company.
(Special Despatch to the Herald via Commercial Cable Company's System.)

Copenhagen, Monday.

To the Editor of the New York Herald:—

Kindly convey to Mr. Peary my hearty congratulations upon his success.

The victory is now surely all American. I am glad he has won, as two records are better than one.

His work over a new route has an added value. It will clear another large unknown space and add one epoch making contribution to the annals of polar explorations. FREDERICK A. COOK.

The HERALD has forwarded Dr. Cook's cablegram to Mr. Peary.

Copyright, 1909, by the New York Herald Company.
(Special Despatch to the Herald via Commercial Cable Company's System.)

Copenhagen, Monday.

To the Editor of the Herald:—

I have promised to submit my facts, figures and instruments to the Rector Magnificus and Faculty of the University of Denmark (the Royal University of Copenhagen), a body of scientists thoroughly familiar with polar exploration.

I know I am right and I am confident their verdict will sustain the accuracy of my observations.

I decline to be held responsible for the varying stories of my interview with the correspondents at Copenhagen and am sure that if the interview was telegraphed as given it will be found to agree with and sustain in every detail my story of the discovery of the North Pole, as cabled to the Herald from Lerwick, Shetland Islands.

While retaining the highest respect for the courageous explorers who are unconvinced, I decline to engage in a controversy with them, their friends or members of their families. FREDERICK A. COOK.

The University of Denmark (the Royal University of Copenhagen was created in the seventeenth century by royal patent during the reign of absolutism in Denmark. But after the introduction of Protestantism from Germany through the preacher, Hans Tausen, the president of the university is termed rector magnificus, and with the appointed professors, holds a high rank in Court circles.

Danish students in the mediaeval ages used to go to Paris and Oxford to study, but with the creation of the Copenhagen University ship emigration of youth ceased. There are generally some three hundred to four hundred students admitted yearly to the university, the rules and examinations of which are very strict.

Only on extremely rare occasions does the faculty of the university confer honorary degrees, and the degree of Doctor of Philosophy is highly treasured—almost rare.

The well known lover of art and brewer, C. Facobsen, is one of the few Danes

(CONTINUED ON PAGE FIVE.)

Mr. E. H. Harriman Suffers Setback from Indigestion

Physician Announces That There Is Nothing Alarming in the Condition of the Financier—Nurse Is Called from New York to Care for Him.

[SPECIAL DESPATCH TO THE HERALD.]

ARDEN, N. Y., Monday.—Edward H. Harriman has suffered a relapse and is thought to be in a serious condition to-night. Dr. William G. Lyle, the family physician admits that there has been a change in the financier's condition, but insists that there is no cause for alarm.

"Mr. Harriman suffered a sharp attack of indigestion yesterday, but he is resting comfortably to-night," Dr. Lyle said to a reporter for the HERALD.

Dr. Lyle early to-day sent a message to Miss Taylor, superintendent of St. Luke's Hospital Central Registry, at No. 214 West 108th street, New York, requesting that a professional nurse be sent on the first fast train. The nurse reached Arden at eleven o'clock this morning and was taken to the Harriman house in an automobile. She said that she understood that Mr. Harriman was critically ill and required the attention of a nurse both day and night.

While no authentic information other than Dr. Lyle's brief statement has come from the Harriman house, the impression prevails both here and in Turner that Mr. Harriman is dangerously ill. The entire family is at the house and Judge Robert S. Lovett, general counsel for the Union and Southern Pacific railroads, was summoned here last night.

The old rumors to the effect that Mr. Harriman is to undergo a serious surgical operation have been revived, but the reports are not based upon any information coming from Dr. Lyle or members of the Harriman household. Two of the physicians who were in consultation with Dr. George W. Crile, the Cleveland surgeon, at the Harriman home a few days after the financier's return from Europe are said to be at his bedside to-night. They are Dr. Walter B. James, of No. 17 West Fifty-fourth street, and Dr. George E. Brewer, of No. 61 West Forty-eighth street.

Erie Railroad employes are authority for the statement that the two New York physicians reached here late yesterday, but no verification of the report is obtainable at the Harriman house.

A Wall street news agency sent out a bulletin to-day bearing a Turner date, which read:—

"That E. H. Harriman has suffered a serious relapse and that his condition is alarming is the report current to-day here and at Arden, but no information of any character will be given out at the Harriman house on top of Tower Hill."

Following the issuance of this bulletin ten or twelve reporters reached here to-night and have again established headquarters in a freight shed at the Turner station.

The New York newspapers withdrew their reporters last Sunday after Mr. Harriman issued a statement in response to a "round robin" sent to him by six newspaper men. At that time assurance was given the reporters that should there be a change in Mr. Harriman's condition bulletins would be given out at the Union Pacific offices at No. 120 Broadway. No announcement was made by Dr. Lyle, however, regarding his patient's relapse until he was questioned by a HERALD reporter to-day.

NO LONGER DEPENDENT ON MR. ROCKEFELLER

University of Chicago's Register Says Institution Can Get Along Without Further Gifts from Him.

CHICAGO, Monday.—The day of gifts from Mr. John D. Rockefeller, founder of the University of Chicago, except for specified purposes, is over, according to Dr. Thomas W. Goodspeed, Register of the University, who returned yesterday from his two months' vacation.

"The University is now self-supporting," said he. "It is no longer presenting a deficit each year, as it formerly did. Consequently the millions Mr. Rockefeller has given for general endowment will not have to be supplemented by more."

This does not mean, Dr. Goodspeed hastened to add, that the benefactor of the school is to be deprived of the opportunity of opening the strings of his purse for donors for projects of the future, if he so desires, but that as a debt payer his work is done.

Census Examinations October 23.

WASHINGTON, D. C., Monday.—Approximately three thousand temporary clerks will be appointed in the Census Bureau for the thirteenth decennial United States census, and the date of the first examination will be October 23 throughout the United States, at various cities, according to a circular announcement relative to the examinations and appointments, which will be issued jointly by the Department of Commerce and Labor and the United States Civil Service Commission.

MISS STEWART IS MADE A PRINCESS

Rank Conferred by Emperor Francis Joseph on New York Girl.

FIANCEE OF PRINCE MIGUEL

Their Wedding Is Announced to Take Place on the Fifteenth of the Present Month.

VIENNA, Monday.—Emperor Francis Joseph has conferred upon Miss Anita Stewart, daughter of Mrs. James Henry Smith, of New York, whose marriage to

MISS ANITA STEWART

Prince Miguel of Braganza will take place September 15, the rank of princess in her own right.

First Announcement of Royal Wedding in Scotland Since Reformation.

DINGWALL, Scotland, Monday.—The proclamation of the banns at Dingwall of the marriage, September 15, at Tulloch Castle, of Prince Miguel of Braganza and Miss Anita Stewart constitutes the first announcement of a royal marriage in Scotland since the Reformation.

Prince Miguel is the son of the Pretender to the Portuguese throne. Miss Stewart is the only daughter of Mrs. James Henry Smith, of New York.

You can see Europe on $90 if you know how. See the story that tells about the feat that appears in the next SUNDAY HERALD.

United States Attorney Resigns.

GUTHRIE, Okla., Monday.—John Embry, United States Attorney for the Western District of Oklahoma, to-day tendered his resignation.

Attains Highest Point on April 6, 1909, Year After Dr. Cook's Discovery

Sends First News of His Achievement from Indian Harbor via Cape Ray, on Newfoundland Coast.

FILES MESSAGES OF SUCCESS, THEN SPEEDS AWAY FOR HOME COUNTRY

Dr. Cook, Being Feted in Copenhagen, Is Among the First to Despatch Word of Congratulation to His Rival.

SAYS THERE IS HONOR ENOUGH FOR TWO

Declares His Pride That All the Victory Is American, That Two Records Are Better Than One and Will Add to Epoch Making Contributions to Exploration.

Indian Harbor, via Cape Ray, Newfoundland, September 6,
George A. Carmack, Secretary, New York Yacht Club.
Steam yacht Roosevelt, flying club burgee, has enabled me to add North Pole to club's other trophies.
(Signed) PEARY.

Indian Harbor, via Cape Ray, N. F., 6.
To Associated Press, New York.
Stars and Stripes nailed to North Pole.
(Signed) PEARY.

Indian Harbor, via Cape Ray, N. F., 6.
Herbert L. Bridgman, Brooklyn, N. Y.
Pole reached. Roosevelt safe.
(Signed) PEARY.

Indian Harbor, via Cape Ray, Sept. 6, 1909.
Mrs. R. E. Peary, South Harpswell, Me.
Have made good at last. I have the old pole. Am well. Love. Will wire again from Chateau.
(Signed) BERT.

South Harpswell, Me., Sept. 6, 1909.
To R. E. Peary, steamer Roosevelt, Chateau Bay.
All well. Best love. God bless you. Hurry home.
(Signed) JO.

Indian Harbor, Sept. 6, 1909.
Mrs. W. C. Fogg, Freeport, Me.
Arrived safe. Pole on board. Best year of my life.
(Signed) BEN

Tidings flashed from the bleak coast of Labrador by Robert E. Peary that on April 6, 1909, he had reached the North Pole, electrified the civilized world yesterday as kings of Europe were lionizing Dr. Frederick A. Cook, another American, who a year before the date had won in the same battle with the inhospitable Arctic realm.

The Roosevelt is now bound for Chateau Bay, Labrador, northwest of Castle and Henley Islands, and should reach there to-day.

Names of two intrepid explorers who reached the goal of a thousand years and planted at the axis of the world the Stars and Stripes are proclaimed by the trump of fate within a few days and all the earth is ringing with their praises and with congratulations to the land of their birth.

News from Mr. Peary was so sudden that when it first began to come through the channels of communication those who received it were scarcely able to realize its meaning. From Indian Harbor, in the exuberance of his joy in again coming in touch with his fellow countrymen, Mr. Peary telegraphed the news of his success to the Associated Press, to his wife at South Harpswell, Me.; to Herbert L. Bridgman, secretary of the Peary Arctic Club, and to the New York Yacht Club, whose burgee his vessel, the Roosevelt, was even then flying at her masthead. A member of his expedition, H. B. McMillan, of Worcester, Mass., also sent some messages.

The intelligence girdled the earth, and Dr. Frederick A. Cook, feted in far Copenhagen, was one of the first to send a congratulatory message, for he

from his experience in 1906. His northernmost land base was to be at Cape Columbia, the nearest point to the pole. The various sledge parties would keep close together; two main bases would be established on the ice, one as far north as possible, the other south of the 'big lead'–the wide stretch of open water that seemed to be a frequent obstacle around 84° North.

On his way north Peary received the usual happy welcome from the Eskimos. 'You are like the sun,' they said. 'You always come back.' He also came across Frederick Cook's base in Greenland, and learned that Cook was definitely trying for the pole. As Cook was alone with just two Eskimos, Peary did not take this challenge very seriously.

In September 1908 the *Roosevelt* found her old winter quarters at Cape Sheridan, and Peary set about shifting supplies westward to Cape Columbia.

The main journey began on 28 February 1909. The leading party was commanded by Bob Bartlett, who was to break a trail for those coming behind. The second group, under George Borup, left a few hours later. He was to cache supplies three days out and then return for a second load. The remaining parties left next day, with Henson leading and Peary in the rear. There was a strong east wind blowing, something Peary had not experienced before in that region. They advanced about ten miles and camped where Bartlett's advance party had built two igloos. They had 400 miles to go.

The most assiduous planning cannot cover all contingencies, and Peary was soon faced with a serious problem–a fuel shortage. The rough ice encountered north of the coast had badly jolted the sledges, breaking several, and some of the fuel cans had been pierced. It was essential that Peary should intercept Borup on his way back from dumping supplies and get him to bring more fuel on his second trip from Cape Columbia.

Towards the end of the second day, the main party was halted by a large lead. Bartlett had got across and was still ahead, making daily camps for the use of the main party. The lead closed during the night, but on the other side several anxious hours passed before one of the Eskimos found Bartlett's track. To Peary's consternation, there was also a track leading south; this meant that Borup had already passed him on his way back to base. Peary hastily detached a party led by Ross Marvin to make a fast journey back to Cape Columbia with instructions for Borup about the additional fuel. Marvin succeeded in his mission, reaching land as Borup was stocking up. But now Borup, accompanied by Marvin, had to overtake Peary, who was assumed to be advancing northward by about ten miles a day. The trail might be obliterated and, to make matters worse, a large lead had opened up near the coast which forced Marvin and Borup, biting their nails, to wait for five days before starting on their vital relief trip.

In fact, Peary was not advancing. The weather had changed, becoming much warmer, which while more comfortable in one way, made travelling more difficult and increased the likelihood of open water. Peary was held up by a lead stretching for miles to the east and west, and although it soon closed, he dared not cross it until Borup came up with the vital fuel. Some of the Eskimos, who naturally did not share Peary's obsession with the pole, were becoming restless and anxious to return to their families. Peary allowed two men to go back, and this turned out to be fortunate because the Eskimos met Borup and Marvin not far out from land and were able to put them on to Peary's track north of the coastal lead.

On 11 March Peary decided to push on and risk missing the extra fuel. The weather soon turned colder, improving the flat surfaces though not making the ridges any easier to negotiate. To Peary's relief, Marvin and Borup appeared in the distance three days later, 'smoking like a battleship squadron', as Peary said. (The first sign of approaching dogs in the polar regions is a moving white cloud of condensation.)

On the same day Peary's first support party turned back for land. Another followed on 15 March and five days later Borup retired from his first Arctic journey at 85°23′ North, a good record for a tyro. Ross Marvin departed at 86°30′, but he never reached Cape Columbia. Crossing thin ice over a lead he fell through and was drowned.

Peary was now making good progress, fifteen or sixteen miles a day. Soon he was following closely behind Bartlett, arriving at his camp just as the *Roosevelt*'s skipper was setting out from it. Thus the main party, now consisting of Peary and Henson each with two Eskimos and sledges, was saved the exertions of making camp.

On 28 March they were all camping together when the floe they were on began to break up during the night. Peary and Henson hastily got their teams across a widening gap to safety, but Bartlett was left stranded on another, smaller floe. Fortunately it drifted gradually near the edge where Peary and Henson were waiting and as the two floes came together for a few seconds Bartlett's team scrambled across.

At the end of March they were just short of 88° North. Here Bartlett turned back. This had been Peary's plan, and although Bartlett, having come so far with striking success, naturally wanted to go on, Peary insisted on continuing alone. His opponents say that Peary wanted to be the only white man at the North Pole; perhaps he did, but to have taken Bartlett with him would have increased food and fuel consumption by 50 per cent and, as Peary had the pick of the remaining dogs for his final dash, would probably have retarded progress.

Peary and Henson, with four Eskimos, five sledges and forty of the best dogs, pressed on rapidly. The weather was fine and the going extremely good. On 5 April they passed the 89th parallel; next day they were at the pole.

'The Pole at last!!! The prize of three centuries, my dream and ambition for twenty-three years. *Mine* at last. I cannot bring myself to realize it. It all seems so simple and commonplace. . . .'

It is of course almost impossible to determine the position of the pole to the nearest square foot. Wally Herbert, in his account of the British Trans-Arctic Expedition, reports amusingly how in 1969 he sent a message to the Queen that he had reached the pole, only to discover on making further observations that he was several miles short. There followed some hasty to-ing and fro-ing, backing and crossing, to make sure that by the time Her Majesty received the message it would be true, even then Wally Herbert found that while he could be certain of having passed over the pole in any direction, he could never get a precise reading of 90°.

Peary established that his final camp was within two miles of the pole and then advanced north until another observation showed him that he was going *south*. In all he took 'thirteen single, or six and one-half double, altitudes of the sun, at two different stations in three different directions at four different times'. He could say with confidence that 'I had passed over or very near the point where north and south and east and west blend into one.'

The return to land was accomplished with a speed that Peary's opponents found incredible. He left the pole on 7 April and on 23 April he was back at his base, having averaged about twenty-six miles a day as the crow flies – over the ground probably more than thirty.

On his way south, Peary met in Greenland the two Eskimos who had accompanied Dr Cook on his travels. They told him how Cook had instructed them to say they had travelled far over the sea ice although they had really never been out of sight of land. Peary still seemed comparatively untroubled, and before continuing south he went on his usual walrus hunt to provide the Eskimos with meat for the winter. At a little port in Labrador he sent off his famous message, 'Stars and Stripes Nailed to the Pole!'

Five days earlier, Dr Cook had telegraphed from the Shetland Islands that he had reached the North Pole in April 1908 a year before Peary. Americans were already celebrating the conquest of the North Pole, but their hero was not Peary but Cook.

Peary then committed an error in public rela-

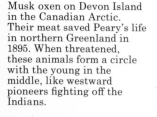

Musk oxen on Devon Island in the Canadian Arctic. Their meat saved Peary's life in northern Greenland in 1895. When threatened, these animals form a circle with the young in the middle, like westward pioneers fighting off the Indians.

tions, never his strong suit. He fired off a number of exceedingly angry telegrams to the Press denouncing Cook as a fraud and a liar. In the massive controversy that ensued the public was overwhelmingly on the side of Cook, a pleasant fellow full of congratulations for Peary – who by contrast seemed crassly selfish and overweening. A newspaper poll in Pittsburgh revealed that 73,238 people regarded Cook as conqueror of the North Pole, compared with 2,814 for Peary. Moreover, the vast majority of Cook's supporters did not believe that Peary had reached the pole at all.

Josephine Peary believed that the scandal shortened her husband's life. It was certainly a shattering irony for the man who had sought fame and glory with such dedication, and for a long time Peary could not tolerate even a joke about Frederick Cook.

Outside the United States, Peary's claim was generally accepted. A committee set up by the University of Copenhagen came to the conclusion that Cook's supposed proofs were unacceptable; the Royal Geographical Society in London tacitly agreed.

Meanwhile, Peary was subjected to extraordinary insults. He had to appear before a Congressional commission to answer hostile questions from legislators of mind-boggling stupidity. American public opinion remained for a long time anti-Peary, and the controversy is not over yet although Cook somewhat spoiled his image a few years later by getting sentenced to fourteen years in jail for an oil-shares fraud. Many modern Arctic experts, including Wally Herbert, still seem to have doubts about Peary.

Part of the trouble was of Peary's own making. His personality was not congenial, while Cook's was. The whole matter as summed up by Peter Freuchen in a memorable epigram: 'Cook was a liar and a gentleman; Peary was neither.'

In his last years Peary was an honoured if still in some circles a controversial figure. He preferred to live a quiet life with his family on the little island in Maine that he had bought as a young man. His advocacy of air power (before the First World War) was another example of his practical foresight. Perhaps also he enjoyed irritating the navy. Late in 1917 he became unwell and pernicious anaemia, for which there was then no cure, was diagnosed. Characteristically, Peary kept a cool, scientific record of his symptoms. He died in February 1920, and was buried in Arlington National Cemetery with full military honours.

Dr Frederick Cook explains to a sceptical audience in Copenhagen how he reached the North Pole.

The South Pole

Scott's last expedition almost failed to reach Antarctica when the *Terra Nova* was caught in a terrific storm on her way south.

In the south, there was no dispute about who reached the pole: Amundsen's and Scott's results confirmed each other. But there was great rivalry among those who hoped to get their first.

In their published writings, Scott, Shackleton and Amundsen were all fairly complimentary about each other, though less so in private. Arguments concerning their respective merits still continue, but on the whole such arguments seem futile. As Apsley Cherry-Garrard, one of Scott's men, wrote in 1923: 'What is the use of A running down Scott because he served with Shackleton, or B going for Amundsen because he served with Scott? They have all done good work; within their limits, the best work to date. There are jobs for which, if I had to do them, I would like to serve under Scott, Amundsen, Shackleton and Wilson–each to his part. For a joint scientific and geographical piece of organization, give me Scott; for a Winter Journey, Wilson; for a dash to the Pole and nothing else, Amundsen: and if I am in the devil of a hole and want to get out of it, give me Shackleton every time.'

Scott is the one polar explorer whose name everybody knows, but the reason is not so much his achievement as the heroic story of his death – a saga of which he is the chief author. Yet Scott remains a somewhat elusive figure, on the one hand a near-legendary British hero, on the other an over-analysed psychological case-study. Scott's streak of pessimism, his occasional brooding on the significance of life and the malign influence of fate, seems hardly enough to make him the Sophoclean hero he is sometimes made to appear. His rather sharp temper and highly sensitive nature, qualities that might be thought unsuitable in a commander, did not disqualify him as an effective leader nor damage his normally good judgement in any significant degree. His loyalty to his subordinates, often cited as the reason for what seems his unsound decision to add a fifth man to the party bound for the pole–though there may have been other reasons–can hardly be called a fault: it called forth a corresponding loyalty from his colleagues without which the progress of the expedition would have been poorer. Like many other famous men, Scott drew additional strength, mental and physical, from conquering what might be fairly regarded as weaknesses in his character: '. . . notwithstanding the immense fits of depression which attacked him, Scott was the strongest combination of a strong mind in a strong body that I have ever known', wrote Cherry-Garrard.

As an explorer, Scott certainly made mistakes. His prejudice against using dogs, which resulted partly from his horror of cruelty, is usually regarded as his chief error. Amundsen, who said he was 'startled' to read of Scott's preference for ponies, proved beyond doubt that dogs were the best transport in the Antarctic as in the Arctic. Scott's experience with dogs, apart from the wretched business of driving them to death, had not been happy, yet in several letters he remarked that Amundsen would make faster progress towards the pole–because he had dogs. Scott's feelings were clearly contradictory.

His ponies and motor sledges did not fulfil Scott's hopes–which is not the same as saying they did not fulfil his expectations. The ponies were not seriously expected to ascend the Beardmore Glacier, and the motor sledges, though they failed rather early, did enough to suggest that improved versions might be the answer for future Antarctic travellers, as proved to be the case. Ultimately, Scott pinned his faith on man-haulage. He felt that man *ought* to reach the pole on his own two feet.

Other points of criticism, such as insufficient food and (as the result of some unexplained mishap) fuel, the extra man in the polar party, etc.– all these were probably significant in the final event, but no plans are perfect: if Scott had reached the pole before Amundsen and had returned safely nothing much would have been heard of these criticisms. And that could have happened. Without decrying Amundsen's extraordinary achievement, it must be said that he enjoyed more than an ordinary share of good luck; Scott had more than a fair share of bad.

Scott knew nothing of Amundsen's intentions when the *Terra Nova* left England in August 1910. Nor did anyone else. Amundsen had borrowed the *Fram* for a scientific voyage in the

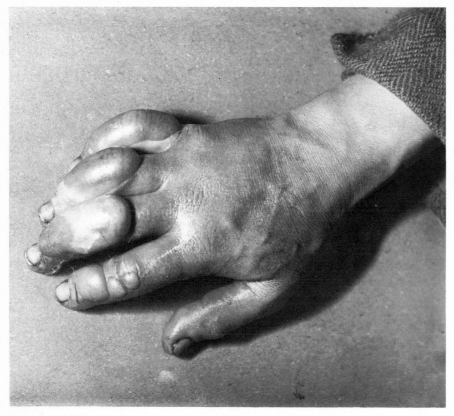

above
His Master's Voice? Such a scene would not have helped Scott to conquer his aversion to the ruthless use and slaughter of dogs.

top
The effects of frostbite. The hand belongs to Dr Edward Atkinson, a member of Scott's last expedition.

opposite
The *Terra Nova* icebound. Herbert G. Ponting's classic photograph.

land. For some hours it looked as though she were doomed. 'It's a bad business,' Scott observed although, up to his waist in water, his calm presence suggested that 'he might have been at Cowes'. Raymond Priestley noted that 'if Dante had seen our ship as she was at her worst, I fancy he would have got a good idea for another Circle of Hell'. Sacks of coal had to be flung overboard; two ponies and two dogs were lost. It was the suffering of the animals that worried Scott most.

The storm blew itself out but, a week later, another setback occurred when the *Terra Nova* encountered the pack ice much farther north than expected. The pack was no longer the invincible Antarctic defencework it had been until the time of Ross, but it was still a dangerous and time-wasting obstacle. Scott threaded his way through slowly, sometimes making only a mile or two in twelve hours. He had hoped to reach McMurdo Sound by Christmas, but the landing at Cape Evans, Ross Island, did not take place until 5 January. Scott had been understandably gloomy on the voyage, but once a camp site had been established under the magnificent slopes of Mount Erebus, he cheered up, and turning on his rare but irresistible charm he went among his men, assisting, advising and complimenting them as they prepared, and went about their various tasks.

Because they were so far behind schedule, haste was needed in order to lay depots for next summer's journey. Scott led the depot-laying party. The going was soft and there were heavier snowfalls than expected. In these conditions the ponies did not perform well, and the final depot was laid at 79°29′, not as far south as Scott had hoped.

Meanwhile, the *Terra Nova* had taken another party westward along the Ross Ice Shelf. In the Bay of Whales they found – to their astonishment – a ship. It was the *Fram*, and Amundsen with his amiable but uncommunicative band of hardy Norwegians was encamped on the ice.

In his private diary, Scott wrote that he was 'disgusted' by what he called Amundsen's 'secret and deliberate' act, but he vowed, first, never to be drawn into public expression of his feelings and, second, to make no alterations in his own plans – an intention that he did not quite stick to. Scott had assumed that Amundsen would approach Antarctica via the Weddell Sea on the opposite side of the continent, perhaps because it was a convenient assumption that allowed him to put Amundsen out of his mind after receiving the disturbing cable at Melbourne. Scott's admirers still feel that Amundsen's action was not cricket. Inasmuch as the great Norwegian's expressed intention was to get to the pole before Scott his action was, perhaps, a trifle crude. But there was no reasonable cause to complain of Amundsen's decision to approach from the Bay of Whales. No previous expedition, British or otherwise, had pioneered that route and it did

Arctic, but on hearing the news that Peary had reached the North Pole, switched to the Antarctic. His telegram 'Am going south' reached Scott in Melbourne and caused him as much consternation as the news of Peary's success had caused Amundsen.

Amundsen wrote: 'The British expedition was designed entirely for scientific research. The Pole was only a side-issue, whereas in my extended plan it was the main object.' This was not entirely true. Although Scott's expedition included many scientists (a superior group, in Scott's opinion, to those on the *Discovery*) and carried out ambitious scientific programmes, the pole was not – for Scott – a 'side-issue', it was his primary aim.

The heavily loaded *Terra Nova* was caught in a severe storm two days after leaving New Zea-

Roald Amundsen, with Norwegian skis and Eskimo furs, equipped for the South Pole.

The main party left for the southward journey on 1 November 1911, travelling by night and sleeping by day. An advance party with motor-drawn sledges had gone ahead, but the motors only covered fifty miles before they were abandoned. The main party, of ten men, had ten ponies and twenty-three dogs.

Amundsen, after an abortive start in September, had set out on 19 October: five men with four sledges and fifty-two dogs, which he planned to kill and use as food on the way. On his first day he covered seventeen miles, and by the time Scott started he was south of 80° latitude. He had a shorter distance to travel from his base, and he had laid down supplies 200 miles farther than Scott's southernmost depot, One Ton Depot. Though neither party knew it, the race was—barring accidents—already over.

Scott's progress across the ice shelf was unspectacular. The first two men returned on 24 November at 81°15', two-thirds of the way across the ice shelf. By that time Amundsen was approaching the central polar plateau after ascending the hitherto unknown Axel Heiberg Glacier. He ate five dog cutlets for dinner.

The first week of December brought blizzards, holding Scott stationary for four days. Falling snow and rising temperatures slowed down progress further. Scott confessed in his diary that he was finding it hard to fight off a feeling of hopelessness. On the same day the Norwegians encountered a heavy snowfall: 'nevertheless, we made splendid progress'.

The last of Scott's ponies had to be shot on 9 December. Five days later the dog teams returned, having deposited their supplies as planned near the foot of the Beardmore Glacier. Scott wrote a note to his wife: 'Things are not so rosy as they might be, but we keep our spirits up and say the luck must turn.' On the same day Amundsen reached the pole: 'The goal was reached, the journey ended. . . . I had better be honest and admit straight out that I have never known any man to be placed in such a diametrically opposite position to the goal of his desires as I was at that moment. The regions around the North Pole—well, yes, the North Pole itself—had attracted me from childhood, and here I was at the South Pole. Can anything more topsy-turvy be imagined?'

Amundsen made a twelve-mile circle around his camp to make sure he had actually encompassed the pole. Then, 'five weather-beaten frost-bitten fists . . . grasped the [flag] pole, raised the waving flag in the air, and planted it as the first at the geographical South Pole'. Amundsen wrote a letter to King Haakon of Norway and a note for Scott asking him to deliver it, presumably in case the Norwegians failed to get back. Having moved his camp about five miles nearer to the actual pole, Amundsen set off on the return journey on 17 December. 'The going was splendid and all were in good spirits, so we went along at a great pace.'

not impinge at any point on Scott's scene of operations. Moreover, it is sometimes forgotten that Amundsen had been in the Antarctic before Scott, as a member of the crew of the *Belgica*.

At the end of June, Dr Wilson led a party of three to Cape Crozier, on the opposite side of Ross Island, for the purpose of collecting the eggs of the Emperor penguin. It was the first journey ever attempted during the depths of the Antarctic winter, and as Scott had half feared it was a rash journey. Although the distance there and back was only about 125 miles, the conditions endured by Wilson and his two companions, Lieutenant H. R. Bowers and Apsley Cherry-Garrard were probably worse than any polar explorers had encountered before. The light was dim, temperatures averaged less than −60 °F for days at a time, and blizzards of almost supernatural violence assaulted them, preventing thought, never mind movement. This was the eponymous journey of Cherry-Garrard's well-known book, *The Worst Journey in the World*, perhaps the best of the many books about Scott's last expedition: his account of the search for the Emperor penguin's eggs is the most vivid description of polar exploration at its very worst.

On the same day Scott established his Mid-Glacier depot at 84°33' South, 3,500 feet above sea-level on the Beardmore Glacier. At first the going was incredibly hard through soft snow, hauling sledges that weighed nearly half a ton each. The harnesses seemed to cut right through them. Four days later the first returning party was named. 'Nothing could be more heart-rending' than telling those he had decided must turn back. Scott struggled on, feeling anxious about the weather but reckoning that, on the whole, everything so far was going to plan. The plateau was reached at the head of the glacier by the end of the year and, looking back at the maze of ugly ridges and sinister crevasses through which he had skilfully picked his route, Scott metaphorically doffed his hat to Shackleton who had made the ascent before him.

Advancing across the plateau, Scott's spirits rose. All along he had been doubtful of reaching the pole. Now it looked more likely. There were two sledges left, each drawn by four men. On 3 January Scott decided that it was time for the last support party, led by Lieutenant 'Teddy' Evans, to turn back. Scott's party, consisting of himself, Dr 'Bill' Wilson, Captain Oates of the army and Petty Officer Edgar Evans, would continue to the pole. But before separating, Scott detached an extra man, 'Birdie' Bowers, from Lieutenant Evans' party for the march on the pole. Small and tough, Bowers had impressed Scott by his mental stability and physical endurance.

At forty-six, Scott was past the physical prime of life, a fact he was highly sensitive about; but he had already shown that he was as strong as anyone on the expedition and he and Bowers were, it seems, the toughest of the party. Wilson at thirty-nine was next oldest, but in spite of a history of ill-health as a youth, he had already proved his endurance on the *Discovery* expedition and with Bowers and Cherry-Garrard on the dreadful winter journey. Oates, the expert on ponies, was a little surprised to be picked as he had not considered himself 100 per cent fit. Petty Officer Evans, a powerful man, was picked partly for his physical strength and partly as a result of Scott's affection for a stalwart British tar with whom he had shared a sleeping-bag on the very demanding journey across the mountains of Victoria Land in 1903. Evans was suffering from a cut hand which would not heal in the low temperature.

Shackleton's 'farthest south' was passed on 9 January. The constant labour of hauling their heavy sledge through soft snow and across ridges was beginning to tell. Their rations were carefully calculated and they could not afford any delay not forced upon them by the weather. Still, they were not far behind schedule, and the pole was steadily drawing nearer. Scott reckoned to reach it on 17 January.

Bowers saw it first – a tiny black speck in the distance. Soon they came across dog tracks, leading north and south. The speck became a black flag, the flag of Norway. Amundsen had beaten them.

Characteristically, Scott's first thought was for his men: 'I am very sorry for my loyal companions.' He appeared, if not indifferent, then

A blizzard approaching a camp on the Ross Ice Shelf. It is virtually impossible to take a meaningful photograph *in* a blizzard, and that is why photographs of the Antarctic tend to give a misleading impression of frequent fine weather.

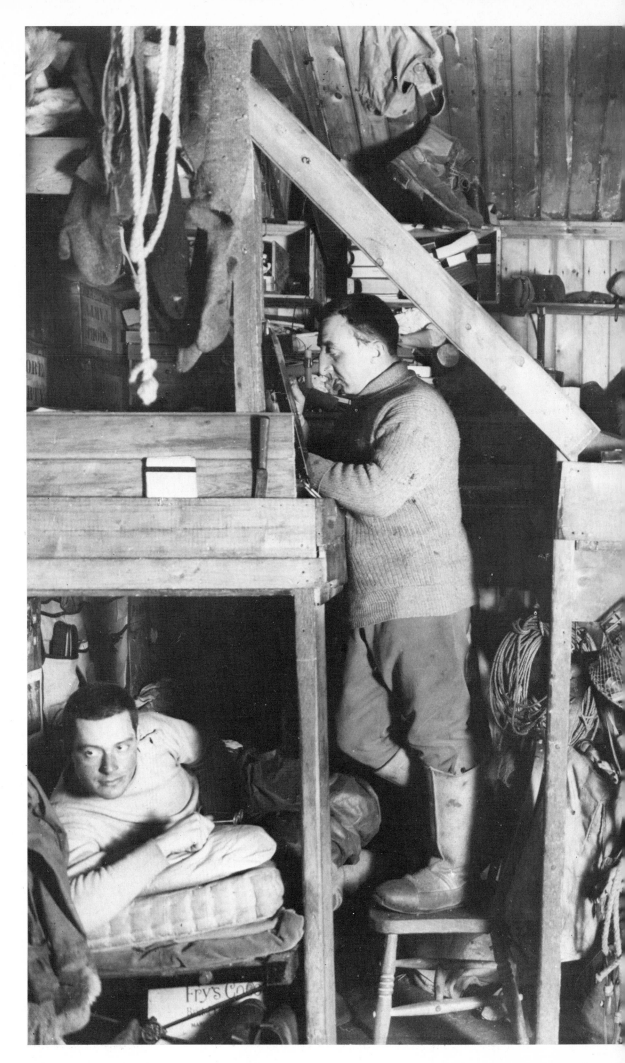

Scott's expedition in winter quarters – spartan surroundings very different from those enjoyed by the residents of America's McMurdo Base today. Left to right: Cherry-Garrard, Bowers, Oates, Meares and, below, Atkinson.

merely rather sorry; but undoubtedly the blow was devastating. In the famous photograph of the five men at the pole it is perhaps not too fanciful to see defeat in the weatherworn face of the expedition's leader as he looks, not at the camera (manipulated by Bowers by remote control), but inward, across some great ice-cap of the soul.

They began the long journey back, 800 miles to base through the thin air of the polar plateau, down the great glacier and across the vast expanse of the ice shelf. Already, Oates and Evans were showing signs of distress.

On 24 January the weather suddenly worsened. The wind gathered the dry snow from the ground and pelted them with savage force. Evans had frozen fingers and nose, Oates a frozen foot, Wilson was suffering agonies with snow-blindness.

The next day, Amundsen ended his journey: 'On January 25, at 4 a.m., we reached our good little house again, with two sledges and eleven dogs; men and animals all hale and hearty.'

Evans' hands grew worse. Scott noted that he seemed to be 'losing heart over it'. Wilson was limping badly with a leg injured in a fall. Scott had also fallen, and damaged his shoulder. It was soon clear that Evans was cracking. His mind seemed to be fogging up; he forgot to take simple precautions; he seemed bewildered and slow. At Three Degree Depot (87° South) the supplies were fewer than expected. But they were making fairly good progress, about fifteen miles a day, and the weather for once was fine. Scott and Bowers were still strong and Wilson's leg was improving: 'we should pull through all right, D.V. We are by no means worn out.'

At the top of the glacier they stopped to collect geological specimens at Wilson's special request. The weather was almost warm, and the wind had dropped. Their cracked faces began to heal.

On 11 February, beginning the descent of the glacier, they got into 'the worst ice mess I have ever seen'. They wandered about for hours before they found a way out. Evans was finding it difficult to keep up and could no longer help in pitching camp. Wilson and Bowers both suffered from snow-blindness. The toes on Oates' frozen foot had turned black. All were hungry, since Scott had been forced to cut down rations further: 'We are not going strong.'

The weather was good again on 17 February and they had hopes of covering a fair distance. Evans found his skis kept coming off and after several stops the others decided to press on to the next depot, leaving him to fix the recalcitrant things and follow on. When he did not turn up at lunch-time they went back to look for him and found him lying in the snow, unable to stand on his feet, his hands badly frozen. They fetched the sledge to bring him to their camp, where he passed into a coma and died within a few hours. He had possibly suffered brain damage when he fell.

They had made slow progress down the glacier, but having reached the depot at the bottom they were able to go on full rations again (though it is clear from later experience that even their full rations were not enough for men hauling a sledge all day in temperatures far below zero).

174

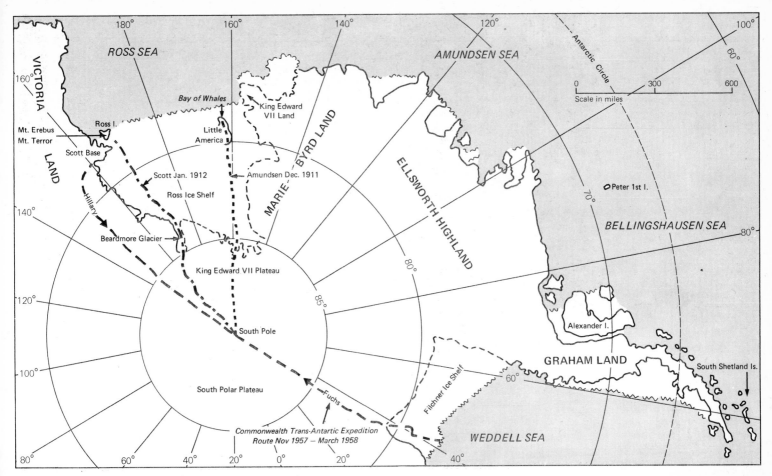

They still had about 400 miles to go, 250 to One Ton Depot. Although the journey across the ice shelf was relatively straightforward, a sudden severe drop in temperature and a bad hauling surface gave cause for anxiety. Everything really depended on the weather and so far the weather had not been kind.

Another problem had arisen: the fuel left at the depots was much less than it should have been. Without fuel they could not have hot meals and drinks. The weather was overcast and menacing. Oates' feet were much worse. Scott complained of terrible surfaces, perhaps not so bad in fact as the weakness of the men made them seem.

'March 4: Things look *very* black indeed. All the morning we had to pull with all our strength, and in 4½ hours we covered 3½ miles. We are about 42 miles from the next depot and have a week's food, but only about 3 to 4 days' fuel. . . . We are in a very tight place indeed, but none of us is despondent *yet.* . . .

'March 7: A little worse, I fear. One of Oates's feet *very* bad this morning. He is wonderfully brave. We still talk of what we will do together at home.

'March 10: Things steadily downhill. Oates's foot worse. He has rare pluck and must know that he can never get through. . . . The weather conditions are awful, and our gear gets steadily more icy and difficult to manage. . . .' They reached a depot that day and again found 'shortage on our allowance all round'.

'March 14: . . . everything going wrong for us . . . Bowers and I practically made camp, and

when we got into the tent at last we were all deadly cold'. The temperature was in the −40s. 'No idea there could be temperatures like this at this time of the year with such winds. Truly awful outside the tent. Must fight it out to the last biscuit, but can't reduce rations.'

'Friday, March 16, or Saturday, 17. Lost track of dates, but think the last correct. Tragedy all along the line. At lunch, the day before yesterday, poor Titus Oates said he couldn't go on; he proposed we should leave him in his sleeping bag. That we could not do . . . he struggled on and we made a few miles. At night he was worse and we knew the end had come. . . . He slept through the night before last, hoping not to wake; but he woke in the morning–yesterday. It was blowing a blizzard. He said, "I am just going outside and may be some time." He went out into the blizzard and we have not seen him since.'

Oates' companions did not go much farther. They struggled to within eleven miles of One Ton Depot, the farthest south of the depots laid in the previous year, containing plenty of food and fuel. Cherry-Garrard had gone there from Cape Evans, hoping to meet Scott on his way back from the pole. He stayed a week before diminishing supplies compelled his return on 10 March.

'Wednesday, March 21: . . . had to lay up all yesterday in severe blizzard. Today forlorn hope, Wilson and Bowers going to depot for fuel.

'22 and 23: Blizzard bad as ever–Wilson and Bowers unable to start–tomorrow last chance– no fuel and only one or two [days] of food left– must be near the end.

'Thursday, March 29: Since the 21st we have had a continuous gale. . . . We had fuel to make two cups of tea apiece and bare food for two days on the 20th. Every day we have been ready to start for our depôt *11 miles away*, but outside the door of the tent it remains a scene of whirling drift. I do not think we can hope for better things now. We shall stick it out to the end, but we are getting weaker, of course, and the end cannot be far.

It seems a pity, but I do not think I can write more.

R. Scott

Scott's party find the Norwegian tent at the pole. It is perhaps not too fantastic to see the morale-shattering effect of this discovery reflected in the random positioning of the figures in this photograph, taken by Bowers and found the following spring at Scott's last camp with the bodies of Scott, Wilson and Bowers. Left to right: Scott, Oates, Wilson, Evans.

The famous photograph of Scott's party at the South Pole, the mark of defeat apparent on the face of their leader (centre). The photograph was taken by Bowers (seated left) pulling a string attached to the camera's shutter.

opposite, top
Figures on a white ground: a photograph of members of the Scott expedition on the ice shelf, taken by Scott himself. It gives an indication of the disorientating effect of an all-white environment.

opposite, bottom
Captain Scott on his return from the depot-laying expedition across the ice shelf in preparation for the attempt to reach the pole. His attitude at this time seems to have been a mixture of doubt and determination.

177

opposite, top
The final paragraph of Scott's heroic message to the public. His courage and resolution, in the most terrible circumstances, can be discerned in every firm downward stroke of his pen.

opposite, bottom
Antarctic landscape – an aerial photograph of the type of terrain that Scott covered on the polar journey – though seldom in such fine weather.

Last entry. For God's sake, look after our people.'

In those last days in the Antarctic blizzard, Scott wrote letters to Wilson's wife, Bowers's mother, his friend Sir James Barrie, his wife (addressed 'To my widow'), and many others. He also left a 'Message to the Public' in which he summed up the cause of the disaster and ended with indomitable spirit:

'. . . for my own sake I do not regret this journey, which has shown that Englishmen can endure hardships, help one another, and meet death with as great a fortitude as ever in the past. We took risks, we knew we took them; things have come out against us, and therefore we have no cause for complaint but bow to the will of Providence. . . .

'Had we lived, I should have had a tale to tell of the hardihood, endurance, and courage of my companions which would have stirred the heart of every Englishman. These rough notes and our dead bodies must tell the tale. . . .'

A search party led by Lieutenant Atkinson found Scott's last camp the following November. The three men lay peacefully in their tent almost buried by snow. Scott in the middle, with one arm lying across the body of his friend Wilson. The sledge was still loaded with 35 lb of geological specimens. No trace of Oates could be found. Atkinson and his men, moving as if in a terrible nightmare, let down the tent over the bodies where they lay, and built a cairn over them. American scientists at McMurdo Sound have calculated that the grave is now fifty feet under the surface snow and fifteen miles nearer the edge of the ice shelf. In the distant future, the bodies will be carried by an iceberg out into the Antarctic seas. The memory of Scott's Last Expedition will last far longer.

We shall stick it out
to the end but we
are getting weaker of
course and the end
cannot be far.
It seems a pity but
I do not think I can
write more —
R. Scott
Last Entry —
For Gods sake look
after our people

The last entry in Scott's journal.

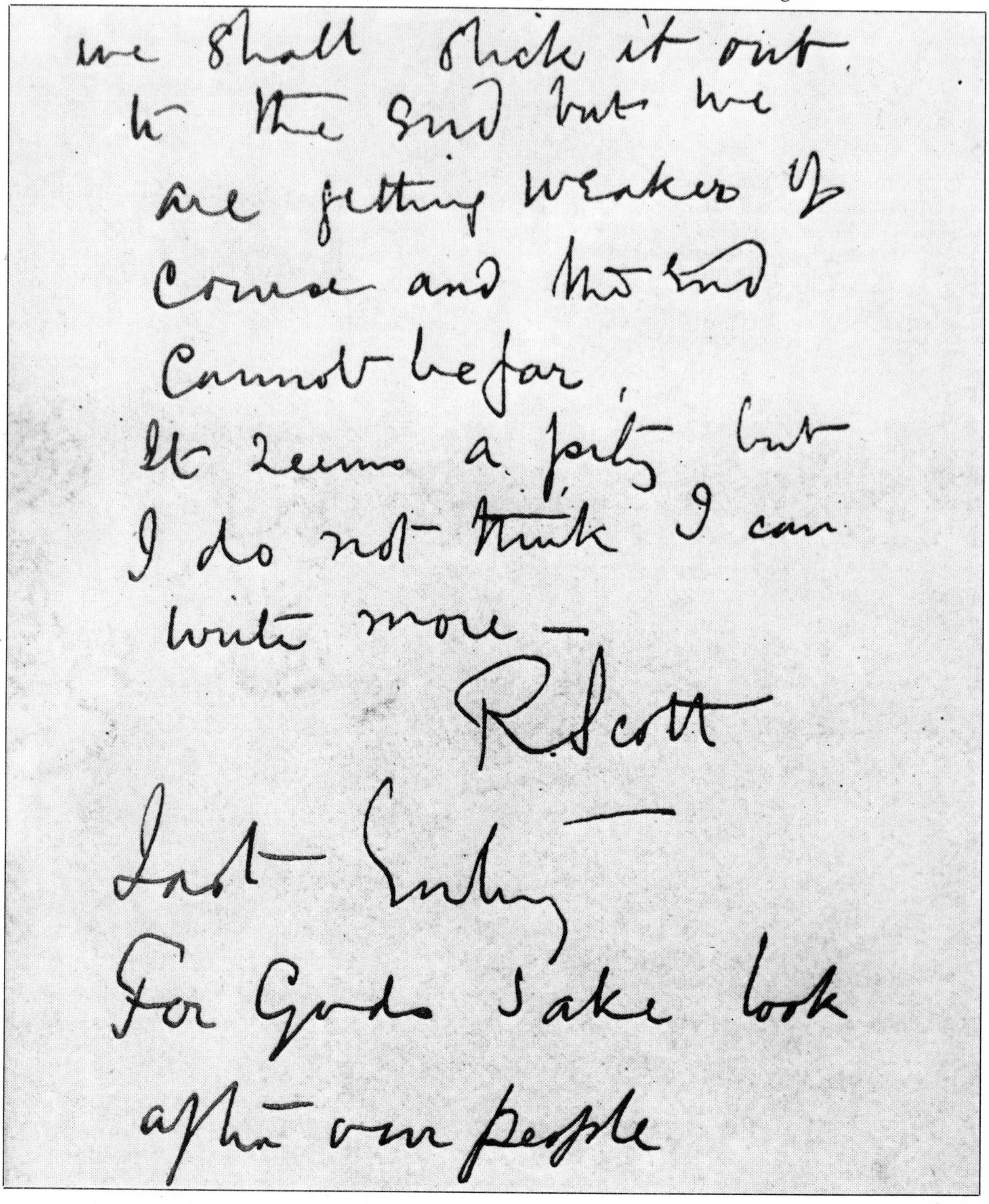

Had we lived I should have had a tale to tell of the hardihood, endurance & courage of my companions which would have stirred the heart of every Englishman. These rough notes & our dead bodies must tell the tale but surely surely a great rich country like ours will see that those who are dependent on us are properly provided for R Scott

The Antarctic after Scott

The conquest of the poles signalled the end of the heroic age of polar exploration. Those great professionals, Peary and Amundsen, had reached the points that, however indirectly, had attracted nearly all previous polar explorers and by reaching them had neutralized their attractive force. The portents of the new age were already apparent: Shackleton with his automobile, Charcot with his power launch, Scott with his motor sledges–the age of the machine was dawning in the Antarctic. Douglas Mawson in 1911 was equipped with radio, though Shackleton, fearing interference from London, successfully resisted pressure to instal a receiver on the *Endurance*. That Shackleton's fears were not groundless has been confirmed by subsequent events, notably the disputes that heated the radio transmitters on the Fuchs-Hillary expedition of 1957–58 and the Herbert expedition of 1968–69.

Not that geographical exploration was finished: Antarctica indeed remained largely an unknown continent. Except between the Ross Sea and the pole the interior was unexplored; many miles of coast had never been seen. During the 1920s and 1930s practically the entire coastline, and a large part of the interior, was to be surveyed, much of it from the air.

But the advent of the machine, in particular the aeroplane and the snow tractor, did not put an end to expeditions of a traditional kind. The dog sledge remained the best means of transport for some years and in certain circumstances is hard to beat today. Physical ordeals and individual endurance were not over either, as both Mawson and Shackleton, leaders of the chief expeditions in the post-Scott era, discovered.

Mawson was a scientist who ever since his travels on Shackleton's first expedition had been trying to organize an Antarctic expedition of his own. There had been talk of Scott transporting him to his destined area of King George V Land (so named by Mawson), east of the Ross Sea. This region turned out to be subject to the most ferocious gales that even Antarctica could generate. Mawson's name for it, Home of the Blizzard, was not idly chosen.

Mawson's expedition (1911–13) did great work, both in geographical exploration and scientific

research. It discovered some enormous penguin rookeries and brought back many interesting fossils–more evidence that Antarctica had not always been an ice-entombed continent. But Mawson is chiefly remembered for his remarkable solitary journey in 1911–12.

With two others, he set out across the Mertz and Ninnis glaciers, named after his companions, through country as inhospitable as any on earth. Amid a stultifying maze of ridges, cliffs and crevasses, Ninnis suddenly disappeared. With his team of dogs and heavily loaded sledge he had vanished into the depths of a sheer-sided crevasse that Mertz and Mawson, ahead of him, had crossed without mishap. Peering into the blue depths, Mawson could see an injured dog lying on a shelf 150 feet down. Of the rest there was no trace.

Ninnis' sledge had carried most of the food, all the dog food, and the tent. Mawson and Mertz were left in a desperate plight. They were some 300 miles from base, with wickedly rough country in between. They had to make a dash for it before they starved or froze to death, ignoring the normal safety precautions for travelling in

The USS *Atka* halted in McMurdo Sound amid 'the stark and sullen solitudes that sentinel the pole'. The modern icebreaker has solved many of the difficulties of navigating in polar waters, but even they can 'be beset for the simple reason that in very dense pack-ice there is simply nowhere for the ice to go when pushed aside or broken by ramming' (Frank Debenham, 1959).

184

rifted ice. They used the remaining dogs as food.

Mertz, an expert mountaineer and skier, weakened first. The dogs had all died or been killed, and Mawson had to add his helpless companion to the load on the sledge. When Mertz died, while lying in the same sleeping-bag next to Mawson, there were still 100 miles to go. Mawson cut the sledge in half and set off, hauling his few supplies on the half-sledge. Once he fell into a crevasse, but the sledge fortunately did not follow him and he managed to scramble out. Nearing base, he found cairns with food left by search parties, which probably saved his life. When he finally staggered back to his little hut he saw the ship which had been due to pick him up two weeks earlier disappearing into the distance.

Captain John King Davis on the *Aurora* had already waited dangerously late in the season. After Mawson he had to pick up another party, under Frank Wild, farther up the coast, and he knew that Wild's men were not equipped for wintering.

Five men had volunteered to wait at Mawson's hut, and they were able to signal the arrival of the expedition's leader to the *Aurora*. But already it was too late for the ship to get back, and Mawson, ill and exhausted, had to spend a second winter–close to a year in fact–in the Home of the Blizzard. He finally arrived in Australia in February 1914.

A current theory about Antarctica that had yet to be tested was that the two indentations of the Ross and Weddell seas were joined by a channel, dividing the continent into two large islands. This problem could only be solved by a journey across the continent via, or near, the pole. Since the pole had been reached moreover, the transcontinental journey seemed to be the next objective for adventurous Antarctic explorers.

Among these was the German Wilhelm Filchner, who left Hamburg in the *Deutschland* in 1911. To his disappointment, Filchner had not been able to raise enough funds for an expedition of the size that was needed for a transcontinental journey, but he decided to make a start on the problem by opening up a route south from the little-known Weddell Sea.

Having passed through the pack, the *Deutschland* sailed south along Coats Land and discovered Luitpold Coast. Filchner made some short sledge journeys across the ice shelf, but when he tried to withdraw northward the *Deutschland* was caught in the ice. During the next nine months she drifted gradually north towards South Georgia. She finally escaped, unharmed, in November 1912.

A similar plan was entertained by that pioneer of the Weddell Sea, William S. Bruce, who first proposed it in 1910. With Bruce's support, the plan was taken over by Sir Ernest Shackleton, who organized the British Trans-Antarctic Expedition in 1914.

On the outbreak of war Shackleton offered to turn over his expedition lock, stock and barrel to the government, but he was told to go ahead. The *Endurance* sailed from Plymouth three days after war began in August 1914.

The *Endurance* was to take the transcontinental party to the Weddell Sea, while the *Aurora* (purchased from Mawson) sailed to the Ross Sea with a party who would lay down depots across the ice shelf for Shackleton coming over the pole.

It is curious that the world is often more impressed by spectacular failure than success. Scott's last expedition, which ended in disaster, is far better known than Amundsen's successful

opposite, top
The *Manhattan*, a vast modern tanker that pounded her way through the Northwest Passage in both directions in the hope of opening a new route for Alaskan oil in 1969. It seems that even so vast a project as the trans-Alaska pipeline will prove a more economical proposition than the Northwest Passage in the future.

opposite, bottom left
Killer whales have a bad reputation – and it is not undeserved. They will emerge from the water to scan the surrounding floes for food and, if rewarded, buck the ice with astonishing power to tumble their prey into the water. Boats have been known to receive the same treatment, but experiments have shown that when not hungry the killer whale is apparently a highly intelligent and amiable creature.

opposite, bottom right
The British Trans-Arctic expedition of 1969 enjoyed the benefits of all the knowledge painfully learned by its predecessors. But the basic method of travel has not been improved upon.

left
A reconstruction of the ghastly scene in King George V Land in December 1912 as Mawson looks into the crevasse that had swallowed up his companion, Lieutenant Ninnis, and the bulk of their supplies.

below
Towing his sawn-off sledge the indomitable Mawson arrives at his base just in time to see his ship disappearing in the distance.

right
Sir Ernest Shackleton
(1875–1922) whose intense
ambition never swamped
his natural charm. He
inspired in his men an
affection equal to, though
different from, that of Scott's
subordinates and, like Scott
again, his failures were
somehow more impressive
than his successes.

dash to the South Pole. Similarly, the main interest of Shackleton's Trans-Antarctic Expedition is not its discoveries, which were minor, but its setbacks, which were major. Another reason may be Shackleton's account of the expedition, entitled, with up-to-date brevity, *South*. It is one of the most exciting books ever written by a polar explorer.

The year 1914–15 was a particularly bad one for ice in the Weddell Sea. As she pushed her way south trying to reach Vahsel Bay, where Filchner had moored, the *Endurance* was caught in the merciless grip of the ice. Unlike the *Deutschland*, which had been frozen in somewhat later in the year, the *Endurance* was not to escape. By the following October she had drifted far to the west and north, beyond the 70th parallel. The Antarctic ice then began its final assault: 'The pressure ridges, massive and threatening, testified to the overwhelming nature of the forces that were at work. Huge blocks of ice weighing many tons were lifted into the air and tossed aside as other masses rose beneath them. We were helpless intruders in a strange world, our lives dependent upon the play of

The *Endurance* in her death throes, October 1915.

grim, elementary forces that made a mock of our puny efforts. [Next day] we could see from the bridge that the ship was bending like a bow under titanic pressure. . . . Millions of tons of ice pressed inexorably upon the little ship that had dared the challenge of the Antarctic. . . . It was a sickening sensation to feel the decks breaking up under one's feet, the great beams bending and then snapping with a noise like heavy gun-fire. . . . I cannot describe the impression of relentless destruction that was forced upon me as I looked down and around. The floes, with the force of millions of tons of moving ice beneath them, were simply annihilating the ship.'

Slowly, she disappeared. Shackleton and his men, encamped on the ice, continued to drift until, nearing the edge of the pack, they were able to launch their boats in April 1916. Rowing by day and camping on a floe by night, they eventually reached Elephant Island, between the South Orkneys and the South Shetlands.

Shackleton decided that they could not risk wintering there. 'Privation and exposure had left their mark on the party, and the health and mental condition of several men were causing me serious anxiety.' He decided to sail in one of the ship's boats to South Georgia, and seek help from the whalers there. This was one of the most remarkable voyages of polar history, comparable, as L. P. Kirwan says, 'only with the wonderful open-boat journey of Barents' men in the Arctic in the 16th century'.

For 800 miles, through one of the most notoriously treacherous stretches of sea anywhere on the globe, Shackleton and five companions sailed in their twenty-foot whaleboat, over which they had rigged a flimsy canvas deck. On reaching South Georgia, Shackleton and two others had to cross the island, over sheer cliffs and crags, to reach the whaling port on the other side. What followed explains the comment of Apsley Cherry-Garrard when comparing the merits of Antarctic explorers: 'if I am in the devil of a hole and want to get out of it, give me Shackleton every time'.

Taking an English whaler (without the owner's permission) with a volunteer crew of Norwegians, Shackleton at once set out for Elephant Island. He was stopped by ice about seventy miles short, and after making several attempts to get through he was forced to withdraw; the ship carried only

Shackleton and his men on Elephant Island enjoying a welcome drink of hot tea after their voyage in open boats while 'the Boss' contemplates his next move – to South Georgia to seek help.

ten days' coal and she was not built for ice-breaking. He made for the Falkland Islands, where for the first time he was able to communicate with the world.

It was wartime and the British Admiralty was not in a position to mount rapid rescue expeditions to the Antarctic. However, Shackleton managed to get hold of a Uruguayan trawler. In June he was within sight of Elephant Island, but could not get through and, with only three days' coal left, had to turn back to the Falklands whence he hitched a lift on a British mailboat to Punta Arenas, on Magellan's Strait.

There he chartered a forty-year-old schooner, but his third effort to relieve the twenty-two men on Elephant Island was again unsuccessful; in August he was back in the Falklands. His fourth attempt was made in a tug lent by the government of Chile, and this time Shackleton had the luck he surely deserved. The tug was steel-built and highly vulnerable to ice, but miraculously Shackleton found a clear passage to Elephant Island. After eighteen weeks sheltering under their upturned boats, the crew of the *Endurance* were hastily embarked before the ice relented.

After brief celebrations and congratulations in Chile and Uruguay, the members of the expedition returned to Europe to take their places in the trenches of Flanders. But Shackleton's rescue operations were not over.

The *Aurora* party had begun well, laying their depots across the ice to the Beardmore Glacier, but in May 1914 a blizzard tore the *Aurora* from her moorings. Badly damaged, she drifted in the Ross Sea, leaving ten men stranded at Cape Evans. Eventually she escaped to New Zealand, where Shackleton met her in December 1916. In a remarkably short time she was refitted and set out once again, with Shackleton on board, to rescue the stranded men on Ross Island.

The transcontinental journey had always been a highly ambitious project. Not until 1957–58 was Antarctica crossed–by the Fuchs-Hillary expedition with their Snocats, radar and other marvels of modern technology. Shackleton himself, one of the most attractive of all polar explorers, died at South Georgia in 1922 on the way to begin his third exploration of Antarctica. He was forty-eight.

Sir Douglas Mawson had planned to take a small aeroplane to the Antarctic in 1911. It never got there, and Mawson's attempt to turn it into

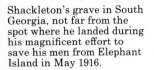

Shackleton's grave in South Georgia, not far from the spot where he landed during his magnificent effort to save his men from Elephant Island in May 1916.

a propeller-driven sledge was not a success. Nevertheless, the future of Antarctic exploration clearly belonged to the aeroplane: the disasters suffered by all the chief expeditions between 1911 and 1916 emphasized the frightful difficulties of exploring by land.

The first Antarctic flight was not made until 1928, by the Australian Hubert Wilkins, an Arctic veteran. He covered only the Antarctic Peninsula before being forced back by bad weather.

Another veteran of Arctic flights, Richard E. Byrd, succeeded in flying to the South Pole in 1929, in the course of the first American Antarctic expedition since Wilkes. The frail aircraft of Byrd and his companions could not gain sufficient altitude to top the 10,000-foot mountains guarding the Antarctic plateau until Byrd made the bold decision to jettison all the food supplies. If they had been forced to land before reaching their base on the Ross Ice Shelf the three men would certainly have died.

Byrd, the scion of a famous Virginia family, was chiefly responsible for the unparalleled interest of the United States in the Antarctic in recent times. He began his second expedition to Little America, his base near the Bay of Whales, in 1934. Exploratory sledge trips were made into unmapped regions and aerial surveys carried out. He also planned to establish a small base farther south to make meteorological observations throughout the Antarctic winter.

He had hoped to build his Advance Base at the foot of the mountains, but it was eventually built about 120 miles south of Little America. Byrd felt that in the close confinement and isolation of so small a place, two or three men would quickly get on each other's nerves. He therefore decided to spend the winter there alone.

His four months' sojourn is grippingly described in his book *Alone*. The hut was sunk into the ice and when the chimney froze up ventilation ceased. Fumes from his radio generator and a faulty oil stove began gradually to poison him. He became increasingly ill and weak. He was in daily contact with Little America, but as he did not want his men to attempt a risky rescue effort 120 miles over the ice in the dark, he said nothing about his worsening physical state. Eventually, suspicion was aroused by his peculiar radio messages, and a tractor party set out for the Advance Base. The journey took a month, and Byrd was so ill that he was not able to make the return journey to Little America for two months after his rescuers arrived.

Byrd's friend and disciple, Paul Siple, asked him if it had been worth while. 'Yes,' he replied, earnestly, 'I learned much, but I never want to go through that experience again.'

Byrd's third expedition (1939–41) was backed by the United States government, and strategic motives lay behind it. It was notable for the appearance in Antarctica of a science-fiction machine named the Snow Cruiser. This gargan-

tuan steel monster was fifty-five feet long and was equipped with wheels ten feet in diameter weighing three tons each. It was diesel-powered and carried a small aeroplane perched on top. Inside were living quarters, a laboratory, a machine shop, even a dark-room: it was in fact a movable camp. High hopes were entertained of its reaching the South Pole, its aircraft scouting the route ahead. But this amazing product of American capital and ingenuity had just one drawback: it would not go in snow. Ascending a level slope it was fine. But a six-inch ridge of snow in front of its wheels stopped it dead. Its total progress towards the pole was three miles. Nevertheless, during Byrd's third expedition, considerable new areas were added to Antarctic geography. Altogether, Byrd directly or indirectly was probably responsible for adding a larger region to the map than any other Antarctic explorer.

In the years that Byrd was active in Marie Byrd Land (named after his wife), Walgreen Coast and Graham Land, the Norwegians were also continuing their Antarctic exploits. By air and land they surveyed the long stretch of coast along Queen Maud Land. One major section remained undiscovered: from Enderby Land to Kaiser Wilhelm II Land. This coast was largely explored by the combined Britain-Australia-New Zealand expedition led by Sir Douglas Mawson in 1929–31. Some of the last gaps in that region were filled in by Norwegian air surveys in 1933–34.

The following year the first transcontinental

Richard E. Byrd cooking himself a meal on his faulty stove as he prepares for his four-month solitary sojourn over 100 miles south of his main base of Little America during the Antarctic winter of 1933.

flight was made by Lincoln Ellsworth. He did not fly over the pole, and landed several times, discovering the great highlands named after him in the course of his flight.

The Antarctic was gradually being drawn into world history. During the Second World War German submarines found a safe haven in Antarctic waters; the British set up observation bases on Deception Island and the Antarctic Peninsula to keep an eye on the German raiders.

Various countries had already laid claim to sections of Antarctica, dividing up the continent in slices like a cake. There seemed to be every likelihood of serious international dispute over these territorial claims, especially as some of

them conflicted: Britain, Argentina and Chile all claimed the Antarctic Peninsula. These claims still exist but are held in abeyance according to an agreement of 1959. Both the United States and the Soviet Union refuse to recognize the rights of other countries in Antarctica, while making no claims of their own; but with a big-power propensity to have one's cake and eat it they reserve the right to enforce such claims in the undefined future. Still, the situation at present seems fairly hopeful for the future of international co-operation in Antarctica. What would happen were some means suddenly found to tap the enormous mineral wealth of the continent is a matter for speculation.

The Arctic after Peary

In Antarctica the coming of the mechanical age, coinciding with the ordeals of Mawson, Shackleton and others, emphasized the difficulties of traditional methods of exploration. In the Arctic, however, the first use of aircraft and radio communications coincided with the perfection of traditional techniques of travel and survival.

The man who put the finishing touches to the century-long development of Arctic techniques was Vilhjalmur Stefansson, born in Canada of Icelandic parents. He demonstrated – at least to his own satisfaction – that providing a man approached it in the right way, the Arctic was not at all an inhospitable region. As proof, he lived for years at a time among the Eskimos, whose way of life he adopted as his own. Indeed, Stefansson went further, showing that it was possible to live in areas which the Eskimos themselves regarded as uninhabitable.

Stefansson could build an igloo as fast as any Eskimo. He could make clothes from the animals he shot, and he could find food in places that appeared to the inexperienced eye utterly barren. There was no food, the Eskimos told him, to be found on the Beaufort Sea, but during his expedition of 1914–17 Stefansson spent three months on the ice of that virtually unpenetrated desert, living entirely by gun and spear. In the course of his travels in 1914–17, in which he covered altogether something like 100,000 square miles of largely unknown territory, he also discovered Borden and Brock islands, the last major unknown lands north of the Arctic Circle.

Stefansson originated the idea of setting up a camp on floating ice, on which one of his colleagues made regular meteorological and oceanographical observations during a drift of 400 miles. This technique was to be more fully exploited in the Russian expedition of 1937, commanded by Ivan Papanin. The Russians built their observatory on an ice floe near the pole, landing all the personnel and equipment by aeroplane. During the following nine months, Papanin's observatory drifted southward towards Greenland. He was eventually picked up by Russian ships off the east coast of Greenland in 71° South.

After the Second World War, this hazardous but effective method of observing ocean currents,

Vilhjalmur Stefansson, born on the Canadian prairies of Icelandic parents, scholar-explorer and uncrowned king of the Canadian Arctic until his death in 1962 at the age of eighty-three.

ice behaviour, and weather conditions, was employed on a large scale by both the Russians and the Americans.

At about the same time as Stefansson was demonstrating that the Arctic was 'friendly' after all, a group of Danish explorers was completing the outlines of Greenland. Knud Rasmussen crossed the ice-cap from Kane Basin with Peter Freuchen in 1912, and in 1913 J. P. Koch crossed it in the opposite direction, investigating the strangely ice-free area in the north-east which had been previously discovered by his companion on this journey, the German Alfred Wegener. Koch's crossing was at a much wider point than any attempted previously – no less than 700 miles – and interestingly enough Koch used ponies, not dogs, as draught animals.

Rasmussen, perhaps the outstanding man among the Danish Greenland explorers, was half-Eskimo and passionately concerned with

Stefansson in Eskimo gear. He made the Arctic his home and destroyed the image of the Arctic as an utterly remote and inhospitable region.

until 5 May. It was in many ways a tougher, as well as longer, isolation than that of Byrd in Antarctica some years later, though the latter exploit is better known. Courtauld's shelter was a double-sided tent on a wooden frame, partly submerged in the snow. It had been intended to relieve the station at frequent intervals, but the weather on the ice-cap turned out to be a great deal worse than the cheerful forecast of the Air Ministry had led Watkins to suppose. Courtauld had no radio, and with his somewhat cavalier attitude towards rationing ('I prefer to eat my cake than have it') he ran out of fuel and tobacco before he was relieved.

Meanwhile man had acquired the ability, when travel on the surface of the earth proved difficult, of going above it or below it. It is of course questionable whether flights over the Arctic and Antarctic can be called polar exploration at all. In a letter to Jeannette Mirsky in 1934, Robert Marshall described this new method of exploration contemptuously as 'chiefly a matter of getting machinery to run a little further than normal from the factory'. It is not essentially more difficult to fly over the North Pole than to fly over Middlesex or Connecticut. But as a method of mapping new country, it is obviously superior to slogging along on foot or even ploughing one's way on a snow tractor. There were, moreover, one or two Arctic flights of unusual interest.

The first Arctic flights were made by the Russians as early as 1914, along the Siberian coast. In the West some preliminary flights were made in 1924–25 by the Englishman George Binney and the American Byrd, and in the latter year Roald Amundsen and Lincoln Ellsworth, a young American millionaire-sportsman, attempted to reach the North Pole in two flying-boats. They got to within almost 100 miles of the pole before landing in a lead, where one of the planes was wrecked. It was nearly four weeks later that the second seaplane, with everyone on board, managed to get into the air and back to Spitsbergen, and then it was forced down short of the land and had to chase an unobservant sealing ship along the sea to get a tow back to safety.

Next year, Byrd succeeded in reaching the North Pole from Spitsbergen. A few days later Amundsen and Ellsworth, operating from the same base at King's Bay, made a crossing from Spitsbergen to Alaska in the *Norge*, an airship designed and piloted by an Italian officer, Umberto Nobile. The great whale, as some Eskimos supposed the giant ship to be, cruised over the pole in beautiful weather but ran into storm and bad visibility as she approached the Alaskan coast. Warnings of a cyclone in the area were heard before the radio packed up, but after a tense hour or two this remarkable and never-repeated flight was successfully concluded at a settlement not far from Nome. In seventy-two hours the *Norge* had travelled well over 3,000

Eskimo culture. He was largely responsible for the protection of the north-west Greenland Eskimos by the Danish government from the exploitation of American whalers. Rasmussen's most famous journey (1923–24), across the North American continent from Upnarvik to the Bering Strait, followed the Northwest Passage for much of the way; it was mainly ethnological in purpose.

Other nations were also involved in scientific research in Greenland. Wegener, leading a German expedition, established a station in the middle of the ice-cap over 9,000 feet above sea-level in 1930. He moved there overland more than 100 tons of equipment. Wegener himself, who was fifty-one, died on this expedition.

The British were also established in Greenland in 1930–31, under the leadership of twenty-three-year-old Gino Watkins. The purpose of the expedition was to make meteorological observations with a view to opening a northern air route between England and Canada, but its most remarkable feat was the solitary sojourn of Augustin Courtauld, who inhabited his ice-cap observatory entirely alone from 6 December

miles across the Arctic Ocean.

The first aeroplane to make a successful crossing flew in the opposite direction – from Alaska to Spitsbergen – two years later. It was piloted by Hubert Wilkins and Carl Eielson, both veterans of many shorter polar flights, who were to clock up 500 hours flying together before Eielson's death in 1929. On their first major flight over the Arctic Ocean in 1928 they had been forced to land short of the coast by shortage of fuel. But the Australian Wilkins was an old associate of Stefansson, equally at home on the ice or above it, and he and Eielson, travelling light, made the seventy-mile journey to land without mishap.

The most famous – or notorious – of all Arctic flights was that of the Italian airship *Italia* in 1928. Personal relations between Amundsen and Nobile on the *Norge* during her successful trans-Arctic flight in 1926 had been frosty. Amundsen had subsequently criticized Nobile both for his personal conduct and technical capacity, perhaps unfairly as Amundsen knew nothing about airships and Nobile knew a great deal. It was partly Nobile's anxiety to prove himself and the viability of airships that led to the *Italia* expedition, backed by the government of Mussolini in its brash quest for world renown. The expedition was the greatest disaster in Arctic history since the Franklin débâcle, and is still the subject of doubt and argument.

Nobile's conduct has been fiercely criticized and although the defensive account he published as recently as 1961 does not ring true in a number of minor respects, there can be no doubt that he was harshly treated, nor that to some extent he was made a scapegoat by the Fascist government which, though eager for glorious national exploits, was intolerant of failures.

The *Italia* left Spitsbergen in May, and having carried out some surveys off the Russian coast, made rapid progress to the pole, averaging sixty-two miles an hour. In the early hours of 24 May she circled round the pole while Nobile tossed out a carved wooden cross given to him for the purpose by the Pope, who had remarked, 'Like all crosses, this one will be heavy to carry.'

The high winds that had speeded the *Italia* to the pole also impeded her return. Though her airspeed was about sixty miles an hour, her ground speed was hardly more than half that. She was under severe strain and icing up seriously. On the morning of 25 May her stern began to drop and Nobile found he was unable to correct the fault with all engines flat out. The rough pack below rushed terrifyingly towards them, and the *Italia* hit the ice hard.

The pilot cabin was broken on impact and ten men, including Nobile, were flung violently out upon the ice. The *Italia* was carried away by the wind and the six men left on board were never seen again. Nobile and one other man had broken limbs, but the rest were not seriously injured. On the face of things, it would seem that their situation was far from desperate, considering

An Eskimo couple photographed during Stefansson's 1913–18 expedition. He was on very close terms with the Eskimos and learned to live exactly like them, making his own clothes and hunting his own food.

the violent and unplanned nature of their arrival on the ice. A large supply of provisions had been spilled in the crash, together with spare clothing and even a tent – now firmly established in popular mythology as the 'Red Tent' though in fact it was not red. They were less than 180 miles from King's Bay, their headquarters in Spitsbergen where their support ship, the *Cittá di Milano*, was moored. Although they were moving rather swiftly with the drifting ice, they had a radio to signal their position.

However, for some curious reason the radio appeals for help broadcast from the Red Tent went unheard for many days. In his book General Nobile blames the Captain of the *Cittá di Milano* for not listening, and whatever the truth of this accusation, in the weeks following Nobile certainly did not get the support and co-operation he was entitled to expect from his own people. On the other hand the rest of the world, inspired by disaster as usual, was quick to lend assistance. The Swedes, the Russians, the French, the Finns, indirectly even the British, all joined in the hunt. On 2 June a Russian radio ham near Archangel picked up the trace of a message from the Red

Tent, which, though it did not lead to their immediate location, at least revealed that there were survivors of the so-far unexplained disaster.

Among those who joined in the international rescue efforts was the fifty-six-year-old Roald Amundsen, who had declared his retirement after the *Norge* expedition but naturally felt a certain responsibility towards the men on the *Italia*. The French government lent him a seaplane with a French crew to fly it. But somewhere over the Barents Sea something went wrong—exactly what will never be known. The aircraft simply disappeared; the great Amundsen and the French officers were never found.

According to the famous French explorer, Paul-Emile Victor, in his history of polar exploration, *Man and the Conquest of the Poles*, the French had only two modern seaplanes at this time. One had air-cooled engines, the other water-cooled. It was the water-cooled plane that was sent to the sub-zero Arctic, while the air-cooled plane went to the tropics, where it was grounded with mechanical failure.

On 24 June a Swedish pilot in a light aeroplane managed to land near the Red Tent. He could only carry one passenger and he had been told to bring out the commander, Nobile; this he did (he also carried Nobile's pet dog). The chief accusation that was subsequently levelled at Nobile was that he forsook his men and took the first chance of safety himself. But Nobile was injured (one other man was also) and it was reasonable to suppose that he would be more useful directing rescue operations than lying on the ice. What makes the accusation of cowardice seem

additionally unfair is that Nobile, when he left the Red Tent, had every reason to suppose that his companions would soon be joining him in safety. If a plane had taken one man off it could presumably in a very short time, take ten men off. But unfortunately, on his second flight the Swedish pilot wrecked his plane on the makeshift landing strip and for various reasons in the days following, which stretched—to Nobile's intense discomfort—into weeks, no other aircraft was able to land there.

The rescue was eventually made not by the intrepid Swedish pilots, nor by the Italian flying-boat that had been sent north by the government, but by the Russian ice-breaker *Krassin*, the most effective ice-breaker ever built up to that time, under the direction of the Soviet Arctic expert, Professor Rudolph Samoylovich.

A few days after the crash of the *Italia*, three members of Nobile's party had set off to reach land over the ice. Inexperience, the rough state of the pack and the contrary Arctic drift had defeated them. One of them, the young Swedish scientist Finn Malmgren, died; the other two, both Italians, were picked up by the *Krassin* on her way to rescue the men in the Red Tent on 12 July. One man was in a desperate state and died not long after. The third was fairly fit. His account of Malmgren's death was generally disbelieved, and although without proof it seems otiose to go on repeating the nasty stories that circulated at the time, this man was certainly guilty of abandoning Malmgren, if nothing worse.

On 26 July, Nobile left the *Cittá di Milano* after what he described as 'one of the worse

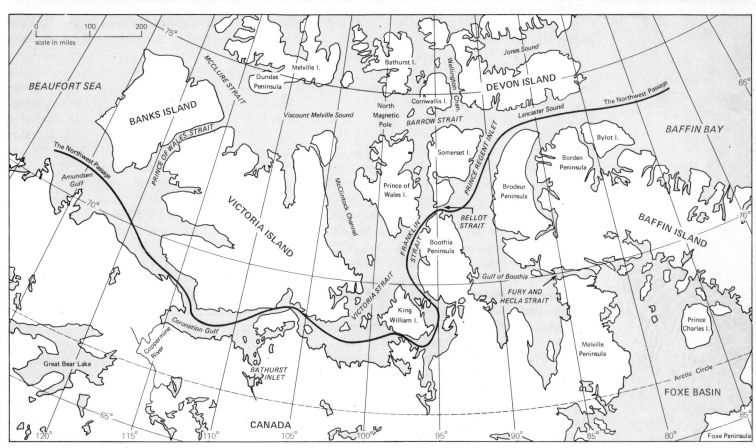

above
The *Italia* at King's Bay, Spitsbergen, in June 1928, preparing for the trial flight.

left
Umberto Nobile, before the flight of the *Italia*. The ensuing disaster provoked controversy compounded of what Nobile called 'contemptible trifles, base intrigues, passions of the moment' – and ruined a promising career.

periods of my life – 32 interminable days of indescribable torment', in which he had been kept virtually a prisoner and refused permission to join any of the rescue teams. He returned to Italy to official execration, demotion, and a period of exile in Russia, finally settling in Rome after the fall of Mussolini when his rank and to some extent his reputation were restored.

There were no more attempts to fly over the pole before the Second World War. But there was an attempt to sail under it. This plan was the brainchild of Sir Hubert Wilkins, the aeronautical pioneer, who in 1931 hired (for $5 a year) an old American submarine, renamed the *Nautilus*, and set out from Spitsbergen in the hope of sailing under the ice to the pole. In the event he sailed no farther than 82° North, partly because of unluckily rough weather and partly because the *Nautilus* was really too old and battered-about to undertake such a demanding mission. Like the flights of the first aeroplanes, the voyage of the *Nautilus* is chiefly interesting as a signpost to the future and as an example of men's eagerness to make use of new technology even before it has been sufficiently developed for the task they have in view.

The Polar Regions Since 1945

Unlike the First, the Second World War really was a *world* war, with submarine tracker posts in Antarctica and large convoys making use of Arctic sea routes. In the tense and chilly international atmosphere after 1945, it was strategic considerations that still largely dominated developments in the polar regions. In the north, where East and West confront each other across the Arctic Ocean like two giant crabs preparing to attack, a string of radar stations sprang up across the North American continent from Greenland to Alaska. No doubt similar constructions, equally obsolete, are strung along the Siberian tundra. A large American military base appeared at Thule in north-west Greenland, near Smith Sound. Soviet aircraft buzzed across the Arctic ice pack replenishing the multiplying stations located on drifting floes.

In the Antarctic, the Americans under Admiral Richard E. Byrd launched the largest polar expedition so far. Operation Highjump was largely a military-training exercise but had a number of important results notwithstanding, particularly in the aerial photography of nearly half a million square miles of the Antarctic continent.

With Operation Highjump we enter the era of staggering statistics: 4,000 men were involved, a fleet of no less than 13 ships including the famous icebreaker *Northwind* and a 35,000-ton aircraft carrier, 19 aeroplanes and 4 helicopters. This enormous expedition was designed for summer activities only and was evacuated before the onset of winter in 1947. Besides the areas mapped from the air and a second flight to the pole by Byrd, it was chiefly important for the experience in polar techniques gained by pilots and other service personnel who gained 'invaluable training for coming American bases in the Arctic' (Paul Siple).

Besides the United States, other nations that had not played a major role in polar history began

The last great polar journey? Wally Herbert and his three companions negotiating rough ice with their dog sledges during the British Trans-Arctic expedition of 1968–69.

above
A British meteorologist extends a greeting to a rorqual whale coming up for fresh air in a hole in the ice shelf.

above, right
Research workers wrestling with a seal as they seek to attach a depth recorder to its tail. Such work has revealed that seals may dive to the fantastic depth of 1400 feet, where the pressure is 700 pounds to the square inch.

to take an increasing interest in the polar regions. Chile and Argentina squabbled with Britain and between themselves over possession of the Antarctic Peninsula: ill-natured diplomatic notes were exchanged, the evidence of rival nations' occupations was obliterated, and on one occasion a few rifle shots were fired over the heads of a landing party. The Australian government declared its claim to a large segment of the southern continent, from the Ross Sea to Enderby Land, and established a permanent station at Mawson. The Australian territory was interrupted by the narrow French segment of Terre d'Adélie, which became the home of a series of expeditions by French scientists.

Under the leadership of Paul-Emile Victor, the French were also active in Greenland, the main scene of scientific research in the Arctic in this period.

A combined Norwegian-Swedish-British expedition went to Queen Maud Land in Antarctica in 1949. This was exclusively scientific in purpose, as was the American expedition to Graham Land in 1947–48 led by Finn Ronne, notable for the first Antarctic sojourn of women – one of them being Mrs Ronne. On some maps the names of Ronne and Filchner now share the ice shelf in the Weddell Sea.

Knowledge of the polar regions, and of the Antarctic in particular, took a giant stride in 1957–58 during the International Geophysical Year. Since 1882–83 the custom had grown up of holding an international polar year every half-century, but the rapid progress of science and technology made this interval seem inconveniently long. Following an American suggestion, the International Council of Scientific Societies approved the idea of an international geophysical year half-way between the polar years of 1932–33 and 1982–83.

Twelve countries were directly involved in setting up scientific bases and carrying out research. To summarize the many programmes of work carried out during the IGY would hardly be possible in a page or two but in any case the work was not, for the most part, concerned with exploration.

The American contribution to the IGY, Operation Deepfreeze, was by far the largest. It was really two operations, of which the second only was directly concerned with IGY programmes. The most remarkable accomplishment of Operation Deepfreeze, and perhaps of the IGY altogether, was the establishment of a fully equipped base at the South Pole, manned by seventeen men throughout the Antarctic winter. The entire base with all its equipment and personnel was transported to the pole by air. Until Admiral George Dufek, the commander of Operation Deepfreeze, landed for a preliminary inspection of the site, the South Pole had not been visited by man since Scott.

The Amundsen-Scott base, as it was named, contained all modern conveniences, and regular airdrops kept the men well supplied, even with luxuries. At Easter, the US Air Force parachuted down a crate of four dozen eggs. 'We hurriedly opened the crate,' reports Paul Siple, civilian commander of the base, 'expecting to find a mess of shattered shells and running yolks and whites. But only one of them was cracked and when Chet removed it, he found the following message scrawled on it: *This egg was cracked before we dropped it.* (*Signed*) US AIR FORCE.'

After the Americans, the Russians made the greatest efforts in Antarctica during the IGY. It had been a Russian offer to build a base at the South Pole that had forced the Americans, at that time only considering the possibility, to go ahead with the Amundsen-Scott base. Deprived of this prestige booster, the Russians instead constructed a base, Sovietskaya, at the pole of relative inaccessibility, over 11,000 feet above sea-level. Another Russian base, Vostok, was built on the polar plateau near the magnetic pole; it has been periodically occupied since and holds the record as the place that has recorded the lowest ground temperature on earth.

More closely related to traditional polar exploration, and more popular in the press—the British press, at any rate—was the British Trans-Antarctic Expedition of 1958 led by Vivian Fuchs and Sir Edmund Hillary, the New Zealander who had climbed Mount Everest. Following Shackleton's old plan, Hillary was established at Ross Island, from which he laid down depots across the ice shelf, while Fuchs, with Snocats and a couple of dog teams, made the much harder journey to the pole from the Weddell Sea. Despite severe difficulties in the crevasse-ridden terrain south of the Weddell Sea, the expedition was successful. Fuchs reached the South Pole almost to the hour he had planned, and after being briefly but royally entertained at the American base, completed the transcontinental trek, with Hillary, to the British Scott base, where he received a telegram informing him that he had joined his Commonwealth colleague in the order of knighthood.

Thus Shackleton's dream had at last come true. And in the same year, another remarkable journey, fulfilling another old ambition of polar explorers, was made in the far north. This was the cruise of the USS *Nautilus*, a nuclear-powered submarine launched in 1952. She sailed from Point Barrow, Alaska, proceeded under the ice to the North Pole and thence to the Greenland Sea. The journey, which had defeated Sir Hubert Wilkins in a very different *Nautilus*, was completed in ninety-six hours, and a few days later it was repeated by the *Skate*, a refined version of the *Nautilus*. In March 1959 the *Skate* made another crossing during which she actually surfaced at the pole, breaking through thin ice with her reinforced hull. In a sad yet satisfying ceremony the ashes of Sir Hubert Wilkins, who had died a few weeks earlier, were scattered at the pole.

The impetus delivered to polar research by the IGY has continued. In 1971 there were forty-three occupied stations in Antarctica run by ten nations, plus Norway and Belgium which had no stations of their own but co-operated with others in programmes of scientific research. Hardly a year goes by without some interesting minor discoveries. For example, in 1962 American scientists made a number of advances in scientific knowledge. They studied Weddell seals from a submarine observatory seven feet below the surface in McMurdo Sound and found that the animals communicated with each other under water by sound; they learned that Adélie penguins have a sense of time accurate enough to allow them to navigate by the sun; that microscopic animals exist only 300 miles from the pole; that the polar plateau under the ice in Queen Maud Land is not flat, as had been supposed, but

mountainous; that annual precipitation at the pole of relative inaccessibility is only one inch a year (three inches of snow).

In 1956 a hole was drilled through the ice-cap near the pole to a depth of 8,596 feet before the land was reached, nearly double the thickness of the Greenland ice-cap. Petrified tree-trunks were found in Queen Alexandra range in 1967, and in later years fossils 200 million years old of a variety of reptiles and amphibians, including the jaw bone of a giant salamander, have been unearthed, proving, if more proof were needed, that Antarctica was once part of the great proto-continent of Gondwanaland. In 1956, before the IGY, less than half of Antarctica was known. Ten years later there was hardly a single square mile that had not been mapped, both at ice-cap and actual ground-level.

There have been some notable journeys too. The first Americans to reach the South Pole

top
Fuchs (centre) and Hillary, despite disagreements, in cheerful mood at the American South Pole base in March 1958. Admiral Dufek is on the right.

above
The Americans on the move. A scene on the Ross Ice Shelf during the International Geophysical Year.

199

A British base on an island
off the Antarctic Peninsula,
with modern icebreakers in
the distance.

overland, eleven men with three snow tractors, completed the trip from Byrd Station in January 1961. Others have also reached the pole overland, including the Argentinians in 1965 and the Japanese, in the course of a 3,200-mile traverse, in 1969.

The French built a plant for distilling sea water at Dumont d'Urville base in 1968. The first Antarctic highway, a gravel-surfaced road, was constructed in the same year. The IGY had seen the first tourist trips organized to Antarctica. Ten years later there were rumours that the New Zealanders planned to build a luxury hotel on the Ross Ice Shelf, although this no doubt inevitable development has not so far materialized.

New Zealand is the country which, in total, is nearest Antarctica, and in recent years the New Zealanders have displayed a great and increasing interest in Antarctic research. They also encouraged another notable New Zealand tradition in putting on the first rugby match in the Antarctic in 1969. It was apparently played in whiteout conditions, and the final score is disputed. (The Americans at Byrd Station had been playing their own brand of football, at which the US Navy excels, some years earlier.)

Man's increasing activity in the Antarctic, though still confined mainly to the fringes of the continent, has already had some rather ominous effects. In 1965 it was thought necessary to run a series of tests for atmospheric pollution to determine how far the pure air of Antarctica had been corrupted by the growing presence of oil-burning vehicles. The problem of refuse at the American base on McMurdo Sound had become so acute by 1971 that waste material had to be airlifted out.

Conservationists are more keenly distressed by the effect of whaling in the Antarctic. In 1960–61 there were no less than twenty-one factory ships and 268 attendant catchers at work in Antarctic waters. The chief whaling nations then were Norway, Japan, the Soviet Union, Britain and the Netherlands (in that order). Since then, all but the Japanese and the Russians have run down their whaling operations. There were 5,773 sperm whales caught in the 1962–63 season, more than half by Japan and a quarter by Russia. The following year the International Whaling Commission imposed restrictions to conserve stocks. Three thousand sperm whales, and the same number of fin whales, were 'harvested' (the official word for it) in 1969–70. Two years later the United States outlawed whaling, though the International Whaling Commission, after debate, feebly postponed action on further restrictions.

The mark of man upon the Arctic is of course far heavier. For some time now parts of it have looked like a tatty industrial area. Ethnographers are hastening their investigations into Eskimo culture before all traces of it are obliterated in the liquor shops of Barrow and other settlements. Man's never-ending search for new mineral resources has drastically reduced the animal population, and there is some doubt whether restrictions can preserve certain species from extinction. In 1965, for example, a headcount of the caribou revealed that their number had declined by one-third since 1949. In that same year the polar bear was removed from the official list of big-game animals, and the use of aeroplanes for hunting was forbidden (shooting bears from aircraft is an activity that calls for little skill, or courage—just money). However it continues outside the territorial three-mile limit; at an international conference in Switzerland in 1970 it was stated that the polar bear was no longer capable of maintaining itself.

In the Arctic as elsewhere it seems that commerce will conquer conservation. In the bitter words of the polar zoologist Bernard Stonehouse, 'Civilized man has shot and bulldozed his way into [the Arctic], and is destroying it piecemeal for one empty reason after another. There will soon be no part of it untouched by his greed and pollution.'

Several interesting journeys in the old tradition of polar exploration have taken place in the Arctic far from the excrescences of civilization. A Minnesota businessman, Ralph S. Plaisted, attempted to reach the North Pole over the ice pack in 1967. He was using motor sledges, and the break-up of the pack in high winds thwarted his efforts. However, he succeeded in the following year, becoming the first man to reach the pole over the ice since Peary. What was surely the last of the great polar journeys began in the same year. Peary had reached the North Pole, Amundsen had reached the South Pole, Fuchs had crossed Antarctica: it remained to cross the Arctic Ocean, via the pole, over the ice. This was the task successfully completed in sixteen months, 1968–69, by the four-man British expedition with dog sledges led by Wally Herbert. Two years later an Italian expedition also reached the North Pole with dogs.

The year 1969 perhaps marks the high point of contemporary Arctic history. The vast oil pipeline in western Siberia was completed, though a similar line proposed in Alaska remained the subject of dispute. Production of oil and natural gas from the fields off Alaska has not so far lived up to the rosy forecasts of the entrepreneurs, though expectations are still considerable. In connection with its proliferating meteorological stations in the Arctic, the Soviet Union launched the largest Arctic expedition ever in 1969. This was the year, too, in which the *Manhattan* humped her way through the Northwest Passage.

Finally, it was the year that saw a change of policy in the Royal Canadian Mounted Police, those red-jacketed heroes of many a northern romance. The Mounties finished their last patrols through the wilderness of the Canadian North behind their yapping teams of huskies. In future, it was announced, dog sledges would be abandoned. The Mounties were going over to motors.

opposite, top
As the Arctic regions become more familiar to man—the despoiler—the future of its wild life becomes more uncertain. One of the species threatened with extinction is the magnificent polar bear.

opposite, bottom
Coal seams in the Theron Mountains beyond the Weddell Sea.

203

Appendix

Major Arctic Expeditions 1845–1911

1845–48	Franklin (British)	Northwest Passage
1848–49	James Ross, with McClintock, Richardson (British) and Rae Kellett	Search for Franklin
1850–51	De Haven (US)	Search for Franklin
1850–51	Austin, with McClintock, Vesey Hamilton and Mecham (British)	Search for Franklin
1850–54	Collinson and McClure (British)	Search for Franklin
1851–54	Rae (British-Canadian)	Search for Franklin
1851–52	Kennedy, with Bellot (British)	Search for Franklin
1852	Inglefield (British)	Search for Franklin and Greenland
1853–55	Kane (US)	Search for Franklin
1857–58	McClintock (British)	Spitsbergen (five expeditions)
1858 ff.	Nordenskjold (Sweden)	North-west Greenland
1860–61	Hayes (US)	Frobisher Bay
1860–63	Hall (US)	Search for Franklin
1864–69	Hall (US)	East Greenland
1869–71	Koldewey (Germany)	Greenland
1870	Nordenskjold (Sweden)	Smith Sound– Lincoln Sea
1871–73	Hall (US)	Franz Josef Land
1872–74	Weyprecht and Payer (Austria)	Northwest Passage
1875–76	Young (British)	Lincoln Sea
1875–77	Nares (British)	Northeast Passage
1878–79	Nordenskjold (Sweden)	East Siberian Sea
1879–82	De Long (US)	Ellesmere Island
1881–84	Greely (US)	Across Greenland
1888	Nansen, with Sverdrup (Norway)	North Greenland
1891–92	Peary (US)	North Greenland
1893–95	Peary (US)	Ocean drift
1893–96	Nansen, with Sverdrup (Norway)	North from Spitsbergen
1897	Andrée (Sweden)	Ellesmere Island, Greenland
1898–1902	Peary (US)	Sverdrup Islands
1898–1902	Sverdrup, with Isachsen (Norway)	North from Franz Josef Land
1899–1900	Duke of the Abruzzi, with Cagni (Italy)	Northwest Passage
1903–05	Amundsen (Norway)	North Greenland
1905–06	Peary (US)	North Pole
1908–09	Peary (US)	

Bibliography

Amundsen, Roald *The North-West Passage* 1908; *The South Pole* 1912

Andrée, Salomon *Diaries* 1931

Armstrong, T. E. *The Northern Sea Routes* 1952; *The Russians in the Arctic* 1958

Back, George *The Arctic Land Expedition to the Mouth of the Great Fish River, 1833–5* 1836

Barrow, John *History of Voyages into the Arctic Region* 1818

Borchgrevink, C. E. *First on the Antarctic Continent* 1901

Brosses, Charles de *Histoire des Navigations aux Terres Australes* 1751

Byrd, Richard E. *Alone* 1938; *Little America* 1930; *Antarctic Discovery* 1935

Cary, M. and Warmington, E. H. *The Ancient Explorers* 1929

Charcot, J. B. *Le Français au Pôle Sud* 1906; *Expedition de Pourquoi-Pas?* 1911

Cherry-Garrard, Apsley *The Worst Journey in the World* 1922

Cook, Frederick A. *My Attainment of the Pole* 1911

Cook, Captain James *A voyage Towards the South Pole and Round the World in 1772–5* 1777

Dalrymple, Alexander *Voyages and Discoveries in the South Pacific Ocean* 1771

Debenham, Frank *Antarctica: The Story of a Continent* 1959; (Ed.) *The Voyage of Captain Bellingshausen to the Antarctic Seas* 1945

Dodge, Ernest S. *The Polar Rosses* 1973

Dufek, George J. *Operation Deepfreeze* 1957

Dumont d'Urville, J. C. S. *Voyage au Pôle Sud* 1846

Ellsworth, Lincoln *Air Pioneering in the Arctic* 1929

Fisher, James and Margery *Shackleton* 1957

Franklin, John *Narrative of a Journey to the Shores of the Polar Sea* 1823; *Narrative of a Second Expedition to the Polar Sea* 1828

Freuchen, Peter *The Book of the Eskimos* 1961

Fuchs, Vivian and Hillary, Edmund *The Crossing of Antarctica* 1958

Greeley, Adolphus *Three Years of Arctic Service* 1886

Gerlache, Adrien de *Voyage de la* Belgica 1902

Golder, F. A. *Russian Expansion in the Pacific, 1641–1850* 1914; *Bering's Voyages* 1922

Hakluyt, Richard *Principall Navigations, Voiages, and Discoveries of the English Nation* 1598–1600

Hall, Charles F. *Arctic Researches* 1864; *Life with the Esquimaux* 1864; *Narrative of the North Polar Expedition* 1876

Herbert, Wally *A World of Men: Exploration in Antarctica* 1969; *Across the Top of the World* 1969

Kane, Elisha Kent *Arctic Explorations* 1856

King, H. G. *The Antarctic* 1969

Kirwan, L. P. *The White Road* 1959

Long, Emma de *The Voyage of the* Jeanette *1883*

Loomis, C. Chauncy *Weird and Tragic Shores* 1972

Markham Clements *The Lands of Silence* 1921; *Life of J. Davis, 1550–1605* 1889

Mawson, Douglas *Home of the Blizzard* 1915

McClintock, Leopold *The Voyage of the* Fox: *Discovery of the fate of Franklin* 1859

Acknowledgments

Mill, Hugh Robert *Siege of the South Pole* 1905

Mirsky, Jeanette *To the Arctic* 1949

Nansen, Fridtjof *The First Crossing of Greenland* 1890;
Farthest North 1897; *In Northern Mists* 1911

Nanton, Paul *Arctic Breakthrough: Franklin's Expeditions,
1819–47* 1971

Nares, George *Voyage to the Polar Sea, 1875–6, in HMS
Alert and Discovery* 1878

Newton, A. P. (Ed.) *The Great Age of Discovery* 1932

Nobile, Umberto *My Polar Flights* 1961

Nordenskjold, A. E. *The Voyage of the Vega* 1881

Nordenskjold, Otto *Antarctica* 1905

Payer, Julius von *New Lands Within the Arctic Circle* 1876

Peary, Robert E. *Northwest over the Great Ice* 1898; *Nearest
the Pole* 1907; *The North Pole* 1910

Pound, Reginald *Scott of the Antarctic* 1967

Powys, L. *Henry Hudson* 1927

Parry, Anne *Parry of the Arctic* 1963

Parry, W. E. *Journal of a Voyage for the Discovery of a
Northwest Passage, 1819–20* 1821; *Journal of a Second
Voyage for the Discovery of a Northwest Passage, 1821–3,
in HMS Fury and Hecla* 1824; *Journal of a Third Voyage
for the Discovery of a Northwest Passage, 1824–5, in HMS
Fury and Hecla* 1826; *Narrative of an Attempt to Reach the
North Pole, 1827* 1828

Rae, John *Expedition to the Shores of the Arctic Sea, 1846–7*
1850

Rasmussen, Knud *Greenland by the Polar Sea* 1921; *Across
Arctic America* 1927

Ross, James Clarke *Voyage in the Southern and Antarctic
Regions, 1839–43* 1847

Ross, John *A Voyage of Discovery in HMS Alexander and
Isabella* 1819; *Narrative of a Second Expedition* 1835

Scoresby, William *Account of the Arctic Regions* 1820

Scott, Robert F. *Voyage of the Discovery* 1905; *Scott's Last
Expedition* (Ed. Huxley) 1913

Shackleton, E. H. *The Heart of the Antarctic* 1911; *South*
1919

Simpson, Thomas *Narrative of Discoveries on the North
Coast of America* 1843

Siple, Paul *90° South* 1959

Skelton, R. A. *Explorers' Maps* 1958

Stefansson, Vilhjalmur *The Friendly Arctic* 1921; *Three
Voyages of Martin Frobisher* 1938; *Unsolved Mysteries of
the Arctic* 1939; *Greenland* 1942

Victor, Paul-Émile *Man and the Conquest of the Poles* 1964

Weddell, James *A Voyage towards the South Pole* 1825

Weems, John E. *Peary: The Explorer and the Man* 1967

Wilkes, Charles *Narrative of the U.S. Exploring Expedition*
1845

Wilkins, Hubert *Flying in the Arctic* 1928

Williamson, J. A. *Voyages of the Cabots* 1929

Arctic Bibliography, Vol. 14, 1969. Published by The Arctic
Institute of North America, Montreal

Annual publications of The Hakluyt Society

Polar Record. Annual publication of The Scott Polar
Research Institute, Cambridge

Polar Times. The American Polar Society

Black and White Photographs:
Aldus Archives, London 48–49, 123; American Geographical
Society, New York 67; H. Aschenhoug and Company, Oslo
128; Douglas Botting, London 51, 55, 56, 164–165; British
Antarctic Survey 188; British Museum, London 16, 61, 162;
Fred Bruemmer, Montreal 38, 39, 44–45, 73 right, 106–107
bottom, 126; Camera Press, London 42–43, 68, 198, 204; Mary
Evans Picture Library, London 33, 101 top; Hamlyn Group
Picture Library 27 top, 58 right, 79, 80 top, 84–85, 90–91, 93;
Hamlyn Group Picture Library–Hawkley Studio Associates
Limited 82 right; Mansell Collection, London 7 top, 22–23,
78, 96–97, 98, 99, 100, 105 bottom, 106–107 top, 112–115, 118–
119, 120 bottom, 134 top, 155, 165, 185; Mitchell Library,
Sydney, photograph Brian Bird 62, 63; National Archives
and Records Service, Washington 191; National Maritime
Museum, Greenwich 59 right; National Portrait Gallery,
London 102, 103, 105 top left; Paul Popper Limited, London
Title-page, 7 bottom, 8–9, 10, 11 bottom, 12–13, 89, 90 top left,
94, 142–143, 167, 168, 169, 171, 172, 174–175, 176, 177, 178, 179;
Public Archives of Canada, Ottawa 192; Radio Times Hulton
Picture Library, London 9 bottom, 13, 15, 19, 20–21, 25, 27
bottom, 28, 29, 31, 32, 34, 41 top, 47, 48 left, 50, 58 left, 59 left,
64, 73 left, 74, 74–75, 77, 80 bottom, 82 left, 84 top, 101 bottom,
104, 105 top right, 106 top left, 106 bottom left, 109 left, 112
top, 116, 118, 120 top, 121, 122, 130 top, 131, 132, 133, 134
bottom, 135, 137 bottom, 138 bottom, 141 top, 141 bottom,
144 left, 149, 150, 151, 156, 157, 158, 159, 160, 173 bottom, 189,
193, 195, 196; Royal Danish Ministry for Foreign Affairs,
Copenhagen 87; Royal Geographical Society, London 186
bottom, 187; Royal Norwegian Embassy, London 170;
Scott Polar Research Institute, Cambridge 22, 41 bottom, 42
left, 66, 83, 90 bottom, 109 right, 124, 125, 137 top, 138 top,
144 right, 161, 180, 186 top, 194; Topix, London 197; Trans-
antarctic Expedition 14, 199 top, 200–201; United States
Information Service 199 bottom; United States Navy 202
bottom; H. Roger-Viollet, Paris 88, 152, 153, 154;

Colour Photographs:
Aldus Archives, London 145 top, 60; American Heritage
Picture Collection, New York 72 top; Douglas Botting,
London 36; Fred Bruemmer, Montreal, 18, 35, 53 top, 145
bottom left, 148 top, 181 bottom; Culver Pictures, New York
148 bottom; Giraudon, Paris 17; Hamlyn Group Picture
Library–Hawkley Studio Associates Limited 53 bottom, 54
bottom, 71; Michael Holford, London 54 top, 72 bottom;
Parker Gallery, London 146–147; Dr Hugh Simpson, Glasgow
184 bottom right; Charles Swithinbank, Cambridge 145
bottom right, 182–183, 184 top; Transantarctic Expedition
181 top, 184 bottom left.

Index

Figures in italics refer to illustrations

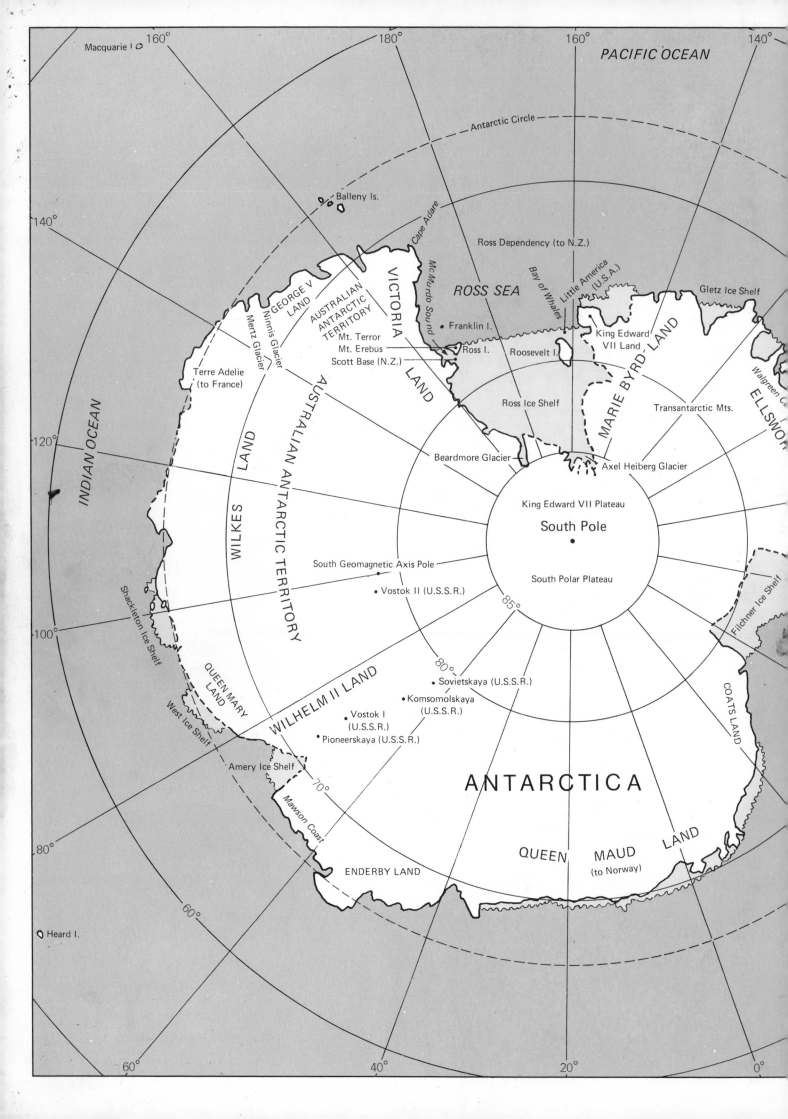